I CAN-CER VIVE

Live Free, Be Happy

Monya Williams

ARCHWAY
PUBLISHING

Scripture taken from the King James Version of the Bible.

Archway Publishing books may be ordered through booksellers or by contacting:

Archway Publishing
1663 Liberty Drive
Bloomington, IN 47403
www.archwaypublishing.com
1 (888) 242-5904

ISBN: 978-1-4808-4003-4 (sc)
ISBN: 978-1-4808-4004-1 (hc)
ISBN: 978-1-4808-4005-8 (e)

Library of Congress Control Number: 2016919496

Print information available on the last page.

Archway Publishing rev. date: 1/26/2017

I have become my own version of an optimist. If I can't make it through one door, I'll go find another door—or I'll make a new door. Something fantastic and happy will come no matter how dark the present may seem.

—Rabindranath Tagore (revised by Monya Williams)

Dedication

First, and most importantly, to my husband, children, and grandchildren: Your love and zest for life is what has kept me alive. I love you all so much.

To all the children and adults who have felt the anguish of abandonment, abuse, depression, and loneliness: You are not alone. You are strong, you are brave, and you are beautiful. Hope is on your side. Don't give up.

A special dedication to my dear friend Sheldon Cook: I miss you. You kicked cancer's butt and won. Now you are in a happy, glorious place where cancer will never exist.

To my hero, Viola Williams: Thank you for visiting me on long, dreary, painful days and nights. Because of you, I know heaven is real. I know God has a plan for me. I'll see you later!

To my cancer buddies: I love you for your strength on earth and beyond the grave. You've inspired me to say, "I CAN-CER VIVE every storm that comes my way with dignity and grace."

Contents

Note's To Consider

Some of the names in this book have been changed in order to protect the dignity and privacy of their lives. If proper names have been included it is with verbal or written consent from the individuals.

Most of contents in this book are taken directly from the hand written journal's and blog of the author. The perspectives are from the author's point of view not only as a child but now as an adult. Please keep in mind while reading there are dates given at the top of some entries. Those dates represent what was happening on that particular day.

Introduction

I've seen better days, but I've also seen worse. I certainly don't have everything I want, but I do have all I need. I woke up with some aches and pain, but I woke up. My life may not be perfect, but I am continually blessed.

—Monya Williams

I was diagnosed with breast cancer in 2009 at age forty-six while training for a marathon. I'm also a survivor of physical, mental, and sexual abuse. I believe cancer lies dormant in all of us. However, it may not manifest itself with a doctor saying, "You have cancer." There are many variables to consider other than the typical risk factors that can actually activate those cancer cells. My instinct tells me trauma and stress throughout my life were major factors in my breast cancer diagnosis.

The story in this book started long before I was given a diagnosis of breast cancer. The title of I CAN-CER VIVE came to me one night when I was desperate for answers. I wanted to know why my life had taken such a 360-degree turn in what I thought was rapid speed. I began journaling my feelings, and the words "I can survive" kept coming to mind. I took out a piece of paper and simply wrote it out.

A few months after I began writing the manuscript, I was cleaning out some boxes of old childhood memories. To my surprise, a picture I had drawn in second grade brought me to tears. It is the inspiration for the cover of this book. The teacher asked us to draw a picture of anything we wanted. The only rule she gave us was the drawing needed to represent a feeling we were experiencing.

As the other children stood and presented their drawings, I discovered how different my life was compared to theirs. Several of the children drew happy faces or stick figures of families holding hands. What a complete contrast to my reality. I was suffering from hearing loss due to my birth father slapping me across the head in an intoxicated, drug-induced rage, and my stepfather was ridiculing me verbally and physically. Later, he would add sexual abuse to his list of defilements.

I felt like an outcast. I was quiet and withdrawn and no longer wrapped in the warmth and comfort a child should feel at home. A dead tree represented exactly how I was feeling. I was in a drought and in desperate need of attention and unconditional love. Leaving one green leaf on the tree gave me hope for a better future. I think I held on to that picture for all those years because I will never forget the teacher giving me such praise for my artwork. Even at such a young age, I recognized the importance of being kind.

Watching my fifteen-year-old brother die and not being able to do a thing about it added another dimension to my stress and lack of confidence. I promised him I would never leave him alone to live in that toxic environment. Keeping my promise to him gave me strength to move out after he passed away. I tried to start over in life, but I soon found out that secrets fester and grow into cancerous tumors if they are not addressed. When they finally came to the surface, it allowed me to live free and be truly happy in any circumstances.

In the midst of a life full of turmoil and feelings of helplessness, I found a way of coping. I prayed to God even when I wasn't sure he was listening or if he was real. My continual faith in a heavenly presence helped me grasp an endless amount of heartache and pain.

The faith I had as a child turned into an anchor as an adult, especially after my cancer diagnosis. There are so many unknowns and myths surrounding the capacity to fight cancer. For example, I always believed a cancer diagnosis meant death and was primarily linked to the genetic makeup of our ancestors. This is not always the case.

Through my own research I discovered all of our bodies are continually producing deficient cells. This is how tumors are born. However, our bodies are so perfectly equipped with many mechanisms that are able to keep those defective cells at bay. This is why not every body is diagnosed with cancer-some die from other causes.

I chose the medicinal path and soon found out for myself there are no smooth answers. While I was busy receiving chemotherapy and radiation I had friends who were taking the cutting edge alternative approach with hyperthermia, sono-photo dynamic therapy, virotherapy, biological vaccines and energy therapy. Some did very well and are living full happy lives, while other's have passed on. I believe whether you choose medicinal or natural path there is no simplicity to this terrible disease. For some people the decision is easy for many other's it's a struggle to decide. I also think that medicinal and a natural path approaches can work together.

Most of us were born with perfect bodies and minds, but somewhere along the way, we were exposed to the environment and stresses of life. We need to take responsibility for what we put into our bodies, let go of negativity, and be intentional with the foods and drinks we intake. These can have a lasting effect when addressing a cancer diagnosis. Being proactive with diet and exercise can potentially eliminate ever hearing the C-word from your doctor.

A 517-page report published by the World Cancer Research Fund in 2007 proved that even a small amount of exercise during chemo and radiation will help keep depression minimal and increase a person's energy, which makes enduring treatments easier. The report showed that 40 percent of cancers could be prevented by simple changes in nutritional intake and physical activity. Another report by the French National Cancer Institute released in 2009 came to the same conclusion. I think it is important to understand there is a direct connection between the body and mind. Both work together in harmony, and it's crucial for proper development of mind, body, and spirit.

As a child, I believed I was worthless. I felt constant belittlement from my stepfather. I believe the feelings of helplessness and the stress of abandonment at a young age by my birth father (and later in life by my mother) helped promote my cancer. With my brain being constantly bombarded with negative input and the absence of a loving home, I withdrew from a "normal" state of being. I hid in the shadows of my own body. By the time I realized the abuse and how I dealt with it were not my fault, I had already been diagnosed with breast cancer. During the course of my treatments, I began to fully understand and appreciate my body and the brain's incredible power. This helped me overcome a lot of insecurities and gave me the determination to move forward.

In 2013, doctors discovered a tumor in my inner ear canal. I endured a long, hard surgery and recovery, but my inner ear became severely infected. To this day, it's inconclusive what started the infection. The skin in and around my ear became severely infected. This sent me back to surgery. My recovery seemed to be going well until it didn't. I awoke one morning with partial facial paralysis and was rushed to the hospital. I stayed in the ICU for three weeks to recover from three more surgeries—only to be told the paralysis was permanent. A nerve that controlled the right side of my face had died. It was a daunting and miserable time in my life.

Devastation beyond my belief set in once again and sabotaged years of working on becoming whole again. When a doctor said, "Your face will never be the same," it pierced my heart. I had to believe there was another doctor out there who would have answers for a full recovery.

After being released, we began searching for a surgeon. I was referred to a highly recommended surgeon in Cleveland, and I stayed there for seven weeks. Enduring the lengthy surgery and living through what I thought was a near-death experience shook me to the core and changed my perspective on life.

Just before the diagnosis of permanent facial paralysis, I joined a relationship-marketing company within the anti-aging world. I returned home from Cleveland with no resolution to the facial paralysis. I wondered how I could possibly represent a company in the beauty industry when I wasn't feeling beautiful myself. I was quite sure that task was not going to be on my to-do list.

Shortly after my return home, Renee Olson—the cofounder and chief leadership officer of Nerium International—asked me to speak at Nerium's semiannual convention at the SAP Center in San Jose. There were eighteen thousand people in attendance, and several thousands more streamed it live in their homes.

Renee went onto the stage and said, "Very rarely in life is everything perfect. This next story is to show you that, in life, there are never any excuses. After this story, whenever you see this next speaker, I want you to look her in the eye and say, 'You are so beautiful.'"

Renee, who has now become a dear friend, escorted me out onto the stage. I was lovingly welcomed by the people in attendance. I began by telling the story of how my face was disfigured and shared a bit about my cancer. I spoke of wanting desperately to be happy and feel beautiful.

A friend from the audience, Frank Filippone, yelled, "You are beautiful."

A lady in the upper balcony yelled, "You are so beautiful."

These people didn't know me—not the real me, not the little blonde girl who cried herself to sleep at night and wanted to be accepted and loved. Those words of affirmation were pleasing to hear. I told them how grateful I was to be surrounded by people who were so happy, generous, giving, and caring. I loved the values they represented: "making people better," "pursuing constant self-development," "creating a positive atmosphere for family and friends," and "living happy."

I talked to them about how I embraced the "live happy" attitude and began doing acts of kindness every day. I set a goal of sharing happiness for 365 days. A year later, I was able to say, "I successfully accomplished this goal."

Doing those "happy acts" changed me. I was finally able to get out of my world and help other people who needed it more than I did. I still do my happy acts. I've branded myself as the "happiness girl," and I see life through a different lens. I told them to never give up. No matter what the circumstances are in your life, you can choose to be happy or miserable. I shared my successes with Nerium. While I was in the hospital, I shared happiness and Nerium every day. I earned an iPad and a Lexus because I never gave up.

The overwhelming feeling of love and acceptance during and after that speech has helped me move forward in life. When I arrived home, I sat at my computer and was ready to pour my heart out on my blog. The house was quiet, sullen, and peaceful. The sounds of tweet messages coming through my computer started and didn't stop for several minutes. In my inbox on Facebook, I was stunned to see I had more than nine hundred private messages. I started to read them, and my eyes began tearing up. Could it be true? Had I touched this many people with my story?

I wanted to say that I loved your story. I watched you in San Jose; you left me speechless and inspired. It took a lot of courage to do what you did and fight like you have. I applaud you for your strength and wish you the very best. XOXO

—Living with Passion, Barbara Nakatomi

You are the one who is helping me take my trials from my head to my heart. Your wonderful strength, humor, brutal honesty, and beauty really touched my heart. Thank you from the bottom of my heart.

—Vicki Olson

Hello, beautiful amazing Monya! I feel so honored and blessed to have had the opportunity to listen to your story. As I was listening to you, I cried along with you the entire time. My motto is that my tears are simply the fear leaving my body. You truly are an amazing, beautiful, inspiring woman. The word that continued to come to my mind was courage. What courage it has taken you to fight your fight! I wish I knew the people who publish the dictionary because I would insist that the definition of courage be coupled with your picture. Thank you.

—Sara Ann

The most inspiring, heartfelt story I have ever heard! How does it feel to have touched thousands and thousands of hearts and inspire them to be better people? You are so beautiful.

—Amy Heim

You have moved me beyond more than you will ever know! I love you. You are a mentor, an inspiration, a fearless warrior, and a people connector! Thank you.

—Dawn Baker

What a beautiful inspiration you are. Thank you for sharing your story and your heart with all of us! You touched everyone in attendance and those watching the live stream. What an incredible, beautiful, brave, loving, caring sharing woman you are. Congratulations and cheers to great success as you inspire and change lives.

—Marilyn Creek

Your story is so incredibly inspiring. Thank you so much. You are beautiful and have changed my life today.

—Bev Aguirre

Nothing prepared me for a message I read from an individual who went to the conference with the intention of committing suicide. With nothing to live for, this person's emptiness was difficult to explain. The pressures of family life, divorce, and loneliness were obviously controlling the thoughts of this vulnerable individual. This person thanked me for sharing my story and for potentially saving a life. That story left an imprint on my heart.

We never know if what we say or do can ultimately save a life or inspire a person to move forward by taking baby steps to a better future. We all have trials and tribulations in life. Some are obvious, and others are hidden deep within our souls. I kept secrets for more than twenty years. Those secrets caused stress and anger to grow within me. I believed I was worthless and pitifully unattractive. Just like the person who contacted me, I wanted my life to end at times. Through years of self-development and learning how to love myself, I've discovered I'm not so bad after all!

I did not know that sharing my story so openly with such a large crowd of wonderful people would change me, but it did. I was so unsure of myself when I stepped out on that stage. I had no idea that anything I had to say would resonate with so many people. I only wanted to inspire one person to believe in himself or herself.

I believe anger, hate, envy, and an unforgiving heart can be cancerous. So many people live their entire life with bitter unforgiving hearts. Eventually, unresolved problems can cause cancerous tumors to grow within them. If not treated or dealt with, they become diseased. It eats them from the inside out. These people are hard to live with and difficult to love because they cannot forgive themselves or others.

I CAN-CER VIVE is my journey from sad to happy. In the wake of all the destruction in my life, I have learned to gain a new perspective on the disease. I now see life through the eyes of a warrior!

Chapter 1

Wake Up

Tuesday September 29, 2009

"Mrs. Williams? Mrs. Williams, it's time to wake up now."

Lifting one eyelid and then the other, out of haziness, I woke up from a surgery I never thought I'd encounter.

"Yes, yes. I'm awake. Where is Eric?"

"Is that your husband, sweetie?"

"Yes, he's my husband. How is he doing? Can I see him?"

The recovery nurse replied, "We need to make sure you're stable and ready to be seen first."

"Does he know I am out of surgery?"

"Oh, yes. The doctor is with him now. It won't be long. We will get him back here as soon as possible. Now, relax."

Relax? I wasn't quite sure how to do that. My mind was wandering in and out of consciousness. How did I get here? Two months ago, I was training for a marathon. I ran my first consecutive ten miles on the beach in Mexico. I was enjoying life with my youngest daughter in Hawaii before her senior year of high school. I'm the healthy one. I'm the one who arrogantly thought if I exercised and ate right, I would never have health issues.

"Hello, sweetheart. It's me. I love you so much."

I opened my eyes, and my tall, dark, handsome husband was smiling down at me. Eric is the ultimate enthusiast and optimist. In all the years I've known him, I've never heard him say an unkind word about anyone. Surprisingly, no vulgar words have ever been uttered from his mouth—at least not that I have ever heard. He has always been kind, and everyone loves him.

I looked at him and wondered how I got so lucky. Since that day, I've replaced the word lucky with blessed because I have learned nothing in life is by luck. I believe all things happen for a reason. I'm also convinced people work hard for their blessings.

"Thank you."

Eric gently wiped a tear from my cheek. No words were needed. I could see the fear of unknowing in his eyes.

"What did the doctor say?"

With a big smile, he announced, "Well, good news. She said you will probably not have to go through radiation. She took out some of your lymph nodes and had them sent to the lab. In her professional opinion, she thinks they are clear of cancer."

"That is great. She really said that?"

"Yes, I just got through speaking with her. She removed both breasts. The other surgeon, Dr. Kreymerman, placed the expanders and performed nipple sparing. Are you in any pain?"

"It hurts, but this is great news. When can I go home?"

The nurse came in and said, "You will be going back to your room soon. Right now, you need to rest."

Eric took me by the hand and said, "You look beautiful. The kids are all here. Your sisters have been here all day, and they are anxious to see you. We'll meet you in your room."

As I watched him walk away, I closed my eyes and began to think about my sisters and all we had gone through together.

Sonya, Kris, and I were the "three sisters from hell." That's how Uncle Fred had always referred to us because he couldn't understand how we could live in Phoenix during the summer. Sonya is two and a half years older than me, and Kris is two and a half years younger. As the middle child, I fit the description and stereotype well. I was always unsure of my self-worth and was constantly trying to please my parents. I stumbled over my words and was a self-induced outcast.

As the giver, Sonya was always doing things for everyone else. Kris was living in Louisiana with her family, and I considered her the studious child. She was studying to get a degree at a late age in life; she was destined for success. I have always had issues with my self -esteem and felt as though I had no talents. Sonya was a master on the sewing machine. I hated sewing, but I could at least sew on a button or two. Kris was a swimmer. She held the breaststroke record in Arizona in her age category for years. Because of ear problems, I was never able to go in the water or learn how to swim. I struggled desperately to fit in as a teenager, and I wanted so badly to have something of my own.

Mom and my birth father married young. He was in the Navy, and they lived in California where he was stationed. Mom was sixteen. She was not pregnant, but she was hopelessly in love with him—and his family. My birth father's sisters became her best friends, and she loved my paternal grandmother dearly. His family introduced her to the Church of Jesus Christ of Latter Day Saints, and she was baptized. My birth father was never active in the LDS church. After they divorced, Mom was inactive with the LDS church until we moved to Arizona. Then she did her best to take us to church. I chose to be baptized when I was ten.

I never heard Mom say anything critical about my birth father or his family. She was always positive. She never really talked about the divorce. When I was a teenager, I asked her about it. She said he was grueling to live with because he had a drinking and drug problem, but he was a good man otherwise. She said he loved his girls, and she knew he loved her too. She added that he was not the type of person to be physically abusive, especially with his girls or her. She rationalized his behavior by saying drugs and alcohol were the cause of his irrational demeanor. Eventually, his actions under the influence ended his marriage—and any hope of ever becoming a genuine father to his girls. He went to his deathbed regretting that.

Mom gave me her recollection of the night he landed his massive hand on my head. I was only three years old. Mom was a nurse and worked late-night shifts. She came home, and the ironing board was out. He was passed out on the sofa. I was holding my right ear and crying. She rushed me to the hospital. My eardrum was broken. With that blow to the ear, I began a lifetime of hearing loss and surgeries. Mom divorced my birth father. Hitting me was the final straw for her. He had never hit her or any of us before that night. When she questioned him about what happened, he told her he asked me to stop playing with the ironing board. When I didn't obey, he hit me. We never did get a clear understanding of exactly what happened.

I have no memory of that night or of having him as a daddy. My earliest memory of my birth father was around the age of six or seven. Mom allowed us to visit him at my paternal grandmother's home. He seemed huge. I remember his hands, they were strong yet comforting. I sat on his lap on a barstool. He stroked my hair and called me "sweetheart" and "honey." He said my hair was white like the inside of a bonbon, and I received the nickname "Bonbon," which is the name my grandchildren know me by.

I didn't see my birth father again until I was about eighteen or nineteen. My family told me he had been in prison for those years. He was gone during the most desperate time of my life. I needed a father figure. As a teenager, I began to hate the man with the huge hands and seemingly sweet, kind heart. I was confused and quietly furious with him. I held onto those feelings of abandonment and resentment for years.

Tuesday September 29, 2009

The nurse opened the curtain and said, "Mrs. Williams?"

I jumped a bit and said, "Yes."

He said, "I'm here to take you back to your room now."

Still heavily sedated, I remember being wheeled into the room. I was continually in and out of consciousness.

When they finally got me into the bed and hooked up with IVs and monitors, they allowed everyone to come in.

Sonya rubbed my leg, kissed my forehead, and said, "You look beautiful."

I was bound pretty tightly around my chest and attached to wires, which made it difficult for anyone to really hug me. Kris was in tears. She was smiling at me, but she had a hard time saying anything.

I must have looked dreadful. I looked at my girls, and I went into brave mode. I needed to be strong for them. I could see they had been crying. The surgery was extremely long, and it must have been exhausting as they waited for news from the doctors. I would open my eyes and then drift off again.

When they had all said their good-byes, Eric stayed with me all night. Later, I saw that he had given massive updates on Facebook from the time I entered the hospital until I woke up in the morning.

On the wall in front of my bed, there was a poster that brought me to tears: "Mom, You are my hero. You are strong, and I love you. Love, Blake." I missed him. I knew it would be a long, hard two years without him, but I felt so blessed that my son had made the decision to serve an LDS mission.

For people who are not members of the Church of Jesus Christ of Latter Day Saints, I'll explain exactly what a mission is so you can understand the emotion behind the significance of him returning with honor. When a young man chooses to serve a mission (usually at the age of nineteen), he has prepared for it his entire life. While these boys serve the Lord, they are given strict rules to show their obedience and focus. They are devoted to the work they are doing. They are given the opportunity to call their families on Christmas and Mother's Day. Other than those days, they do not speak to family or friends while they are gone. They are allowed to e-mail family once a week.

Just like anything in life, when we are able to devote our time or talents without the distractions of girlfriends, boyfriends, or life, we are able to accomplish so much more. These young men cannot have physical contact with females while they serve. The missionaries are scattered across the world; they do not choose where they will serve. They are sent by assignment from church leaders in Salt Lake City. Blake was called to serve in the Dominican Republic.

Ultimately the call to serve a mission is an honor. While they are serving, many learn a new language. Blake learned Spanish. They study scriptures in that language. They also study and teach from a book called Preach My Gospel, which basically tells of Christ's ministry. Missionaries learn to plan. They know before the day or week begins what they will be doing—and who they will be doing it with. Many times, those schedules are interrupted by people canceling. When this happens the missionaries go out and serve people in need. Each missionary is assigned a companion. They pray, study, eat, and teach together. During his two-year ministry, Blake walked hundreds of miles, knocked on hundreds of doors, and preached about Christ. Some accepted them into their homes, but most didn't.

Wednesday, September 30, 2009

Eric stepped up to the bed and said, "Good morning, sweetheart." He looked tired.

I asked, "Did you sleep at all last night?"

"No. I couldn't. I just watched you sleep. I love you so much."

"I love you too. Thank you for being here."

He was brushing his fingers through my hair and staring into my eyes.

I asked, "How are the girls doing?"

"Everyone is good. Your sisters stayed all day yesterday while you were in surgery. Do you remember seeing them and the girls last night?"

I nodded, but tears were running down my cheeks.

Eric asked, "What's wrong? What are you thinking about?"

"I'm just thinking how blessed we are to have each other and four beautiful children. We did the best we could as parents, right?"

Eric looked puzzled. "What are you talking about? The kids love you so much."

"I know and I love them so much too but I feel so guilty. I feel like this is my fault. I've spent too much time worrying about my mother and our relationship; now I realize she did the best she could with what she was taught."

Eric looked at me and said, "Monya, this is not your fault. Life happens—and you have been an amazing mother."

Mom remarried a Baptist minister who claimed he had received a degree in Christian philosophy. However, I have never seen a certificate or proof of that. He adopted the three of us, and he treated us as if we were his possessions. It was like he owned us. He was our stepfather, and we called him dad. He had three children from a previous marriage who came to live with us. Suddenly we had more siblings, and we loved them.

When I was around seven or eight, their mother snatched them from right in front of our eyes at the elementary school we attended. She told the front office she was their mother, and they had dentist appointments to go to. We never saw them again.

The night they were taken, I remember a conversation between Mom and the stepdad.

Mom asked, "Is there anything you can do?"

He said, "No. She'll just come and take them again. We'll just let it go." Hearing this really bothered me. Seriously? "Just let it go?" What kind of answer was that?

I always thought it was strange, and I wondered why fathers didn't fight to keep their children. First my birth father—and then the stepdad. Is this the way it is supposed to be? Did all fathers abandon their children to pursue other lives?

Now having my own four children, I realize their mother knew more than I did. She removed them from a toxic environment. I would fight to the death for my children. I see her as a heroine in that situation.

My maternal grandmother lived on a farm. Mom and the step dad parked our trailer there. Those years were fun. As a little girl, I'd gather eggs from the chicken coop and drink fresh goat's milk. Chasing turkeys and roosters was an adventure. My grandmother had huge trees we could climb. She also had another tree she took branches from to whip our legs with if we acted up. The grass at her house was clover with tiny flowers. In the summer, we ran around barefoot. It was not unusual for us to get bee stings on our feet as we ran through the clover. Sonya, Kris, and I had fun living on the farm.

A few years later, we moved to a home close by. My brother was born there. When Mom brought Lance home from the hospital, Sonya, Kris, and I decorated the front yard with toilet paper, signs of welcoming, and cheers of joy. We were so excited to have a baby in the house.

When mom and the step dad drove up the driveway in our station wagon I was a little nervous, thinking maybe the stepdad would yell at us for the mess, but he didn't. He just asked us to clean it up, and we did. Lance was pigeon-toed. In those days, the doctors put little white pediatric shoes on babies with a red metal bar attached between the shoes to stretch their legs so they would grow correctly.

I'd hear him cry at night, and I thought it was so mean. I asked, "Mom, why do you let him cry at night?"

"This is what the doctor says will help him."

When Lance started to walk, it was awkward. With his legs spread, he waddled his way through. Eventually, they took the bar off and he was no longer pigeon-toed.

Mom loved her only son dearly. He was the only child she and the stepdad had together. He was my brother, and I loved him. We all adored him.

Wednesday, September 30, 2009

The Mayo Clinic took excellent care of me. The nurses and staff were kind and attentive to my needs. Two days and nights after my surgery, I wanted to go home. The narcotics in my body were so foreign, and I didn't like how I felt. I asked them to take off the nerve block and stop all intravenous narcotics.

I was still in pain, but I felt I could better control it with my mind. I could not believe what a difference it made once the meds wore off. My head was clear, and I could actually remember my thoughts. However, I started dealing with an emotional ache.

When Eric left, I was finally able to move the sheets back and look down at my chest. It was covered in wrapping and bandages, but there was no doubt my breasts were gone. I was constantly saying little prayers and hoping I could adjust to the new me.

Eric was always positive and didn't make reference to anything but my comfort level. The thought of him seeing my mutilated breasts sickened me. How could we ever get back to a "normal" intimate relationship?

Thursday October 1, 2009

Thursday started off much better. I was on less invasive drugs to control the pain, and I felt like a new person. I was able to walk around with the help of Eric, and I had my appetite back.

They started to take out the needles one at a time, freeing me from the wires and tubes.

My surgeon came in with another doctor, which was normal for the Mayo Clinic. Since they are a teaching hospital, residents usually follow the doctors around.

She asked, "Can I sit next to you?"

I began to worry. I looked at Eric, and we knew something was going to come out of her mouth that neither of us wanted to hear.

She pulled up a chair, and the resident put his hand on my shoulder.

I turned my head to look at her.

Eric stood at the foot of the bed and held my feet.

She took my hand and said, "I am so sorry. Your cancer has spread. We'll need to do another surgery." She told us the chemotherapy would be more aggressive than they had anticipated and that radiation was no longer an elective choice—I would be receiving it.

Eric asked, "Didn't you tell me after surgery it all looked good?"

She explained, "Yes, and in my experience, her lymph nodes looked good. The lab came back with a positive diagnosis though. I was only telling you this from …"

As she continued, I began to cry. I didn't want to hear anything else she had to say. My heart was shattered. What about my children? Blake was so far away, Kaitlyn was getting married in two months, and Kayla was having our first grand baby in three months. Haleigh was the only one at home, and she was beginning her senior year of high school. How would she deal with it?

The doctor said, "Yes, she will have radiation."

I popped back into the conversation. "It's Friday. Are you going to do the surgery tomorrow?"

She explained that she would be going out of town and could not do the surgery until Monday.

I said, "I want to go home then. I want to be with my family for the weekend."

To my surprise, she agreed.

When she left, Eric took me by the hand and said, "It's all okay. You can do this."

With tears in our eyes, we said, "We need to let Blake know."

Eric began making calls and communicating with church leaders, friends, and family. We needed all the prayers we could muster. We were able to get a message to Blake since he was already in the Mission Training Center in Provo, Utah. The significance of letting him know was important. We wanted him to hear it from us since word travels fast in our LDS community. He needed to hear it from his Mom—not spectators who didn't know the entire story. Eric and I wanted to play it down. We didn't want him to worry since there was nothing he could do.

I would return for more surgery on Monday. The lymph nodes needed to be removed, and a port would be put in the right side of my chest so chemo would be easier for me.

Later that day, Dr. Kreymerman came to visit me. He sat in the same chair to my left, took my hand, and told me how sorry he was to hear the news. His sincerity was unmatched by any doctor I had ever come across. He will never understand what that moment meant to me. I will never forget his compassion and authentic emotions. He told me the surgery he did with the expanders and nipple sparing might not work with radiation. He wanted to examine my breasts. Anxiety rushed through my body. I asked Eric to please leave the room. I knew it would be hurtful to him, but I hadn't seen myself—and I certainly didn't want him there until I had time to process it.

Eric said, "We've been married for over twenty-five years. I've seen your breasts."

I didn't need to say anything.

Dr. Kreymerman said, "I know this is hard, but if she doesn't want you here for this, we are required to ask you to leave. Don't worry. It will only be a few minutes."

When Eric walked out, it made my stomach sick. I had hurt him. I wasn't prepared or ready to face the inevitable yet. I put my head back, closed my eyes, and let the doctor do his job. Even with my eyes closed, tears ran down my cheeks.

Dr. Kreymerman finished binding me back up and said, "Everything looks great. I just don't have any promises for the nipple sparing. I will have to see you after radiation."

I opened my eyes and said, "Thank you."

As he was walking out the door, he turned and said, "You'll be okay, kiddo."

When Eric came back into the room, he was with Sonya and Kris. They were making small talk as I wandered off in my own world, again thinking about years past.

Sonya and I walked to school every morning as children. She had a big, red, furry coat in the winter. When she accidentally sliced her hand open with a butcher knife, she had to have it stitched and wrapped in gauze. I felt so bad for her when we walked to school that winter. Her fingers were blue since she couldn't fit them in her pocket with all the gauze wrapped around the wound.

We always walked to and from school. It seemed like a long walk. Recently, I drove by to see how long it was. In today's school districts, it would be too long to have first and third graders walking alone, but back in those days, there was no such thing as buses in our school district. Every child walked, rode a bike, or had parents who dropped them off.

In first grade, my teacher was Ms. Davis. She was beautiful, had long, sandy brown hair, and spoke softly. She sat me in the back of the room because I was taller than everyone else. I began daydreaming, looking out the windows, and not paying attention. I never grasped anything being taught.

The school did a yearly lice, scoliosis, and hearing test—and I would fail the hearing test every year. The nurse would call Mom and tell her I had problems hearing in my right ear.

Every year, Mom said, "Yes, I know. She is partially deaf in that ear."

We laughed about it year after year because it was the same nurse calling to give the update. Mom was always flabbergasted. "How many children at that school are partially deaf? Why can't she remember or write it in your records?"

In second grade, Mrs. Byrd wrote in my report card: "Monya seems to be distracted. She is having a hard time staying focused in class."

I needed friends. I was the weird girl who couldn't hear. I was the girl who daydreamed and stared out windows. If they only knew, maybe things would have been different. I couldn't hear or comprehend anything being taught. I dreamed of a better day— almost every day. I was too young to ask why it was happening to me. I had no idea my life was not normal. When I felt worthless, less talented, and unconfident, I should have been able to grasp onto family to help my roots to grow. This never happened. In my mind, I was damaged and unusually awkward.

During Christmas break that year, I had a surgery on my ear. It was the first of many. Dr. Borland was my ENT. Mom seemed to really like him, and since my grandmother was an RN at the hospital, he was highly recommended.

Dr. Borland loved Grandma and often spoke of her in admiration. After she passed away, he said, "Your grandma is in the medical history journals for having the largest, fastest growing melanoma they have ever witnessed."

When I came back from Christmas break, my ear was still wrapped up in white gauze. A huge lump of cotton covered my ear. During recess, a boy ran by, hit me in the head, and knocked me to the ground. It broke my eardrum again.

Dr. Borland took me back to surgery to repair the damage, but little could be done. He had to schedule another surgery for later in the summer. Mom didn't want me to miss school. Surprisingly enough, the one accomplishment I had in school was perfect attendance from first grade through my sophomore year of high school.

That next summer, I went back to the hospital for another surgery. I was always in the same room at that hospital. The pediatric room had eight or nine children in one room. I endured this surgery, and he was able to repair what needed to be corrected.

When I finally came home from the hospital, Mom let me go outside for some fresh air. The Solice boys lived across the street, and they were throwing a football back and forth to Sonya and Kris. The ball had been run over by a car, and the inner tube was bursting through the seams. We didn't care because it was fun. I was still not feeling well, and I sat and watched.

One of the boys yelled, "Monya, catch it."

Just as I stood up to catch the ball, it exploded in my arms. I screamed in pain. Mom rushed me back to the hospital. This time, the eardrum was beyond repair. I left surgery with no hearing in my right ear. Mom was told I was never to put my ear underwater. I had to learn to wash my hair without getting any water in it. Mom washed it when I was little. I needed to learn on my own, and I did.

Mom never complained or mentioned anything about my birth father. In fact, it was as if she had forgotten all about him and what he had done to me. I have always been grateful to Mom for her grace in how she handled what was obviously a delicate situation. Because of how she controlled her emotions toward my birth father, I never felt that I needed to forgive him for anything. Not being able to hear was normal to me.

My elementary years were difficult. I was always stuck on the back row, unable to hear clearly. My report cards were riddled with notes: "Monya is distracted." "She isn't learning multiple time tables." "She should be considered for holding back in school."

One teacher suggested that I watch The Electric Company to help with my educational needs. Mom told the stepdad that he would have to give up watching TV at six o'clock. He was furious because he always watched TV during dinnertime. We sat at the table with Mom while he sat in the living room with a TV table for his food. She always made his plate for him. He only gave up his TV for one night so I could watch what the teacher had suggested. He had no problem pronouncing to the family how I had ruined his night and how stupid I was. He laughed and said, "She has to watch a baby show. She's too dumb to learn in class."

I remember going to bed and feeling invisible. When Mom gave up on me, I gave up on me. My teachers gave up on me, and the little blonde-headed girl was the one who suffered in the end.

For fifth and sixth grade, we moved to another home. Mom was active with her church assignments and seemed to enjoy being a part of something important. One year, she and Sonya went to church camp for girls. I was so jealous. I didn't want to be left with the stepdad while Mom was gone. I knew things would only get worse, and I was right. The first night, he came into our bedroom and told Kris and me that one of us would have to sleep in his bed with him. Since Mom was gone, he needed a warm body in his bed. If we didn't, he wouldn't be able to get "a good night's sleep." He gave us such a guilt trip. If he couldn't get a good night's sleep, he would be too tired to work the next day—and then he wouldn't be able to bring home food or pay our electric bills. I agreed to be "the one." After all, I was older than Kris. It seemed right that I should at least take the first night.

Chapter 2

Beyond Fearful

The night that never ended. The night that defined my life for years. I sheepishly walked down the long, dark hallway into his room. He pulled the covers back on the side where Mom usually slept. I crawled my little body under the covers, hovering by the edge of the bed.

He said, "You need to sleep closer to me so I can touch you. I need a warm body next to mine."

What is he talking about? What is he going to do to me? I was petrified of this man. It was above and beyond what any child should have to suffer through.

He pulled me close to him, and he was naked. I could feel his body next to my backside. His arm was around me, holding my body next to his. Scared to death, my young mind was not certain what to do. I tried to slip out of the bed and go back to my own room, but he always woke up, grabbed me, and pulled me back.

When he slipped his hand down my panties and onto my private parts, I cried. I pushed his hand away. He rolled over the other way, and I quickly jumped out of the bed. I ran into the family room, found a blanket, put it over my head, and tried to camouflage my body next to the sofa. I stayed in that position all night long. When the sun came up, I heard him getting ready for work in the kitchen. He was whistling as if nothing had happened. I remained frozen and still until he left.

The next night, we were expected again to choose which one of us would sleep with him. I didn't want Kris to experience what I had, but I didn't want to either. How could I suffer through that again? He pretended nothing had ever happened. Did he suddenly have amnesia? I'm not sure how it was decided, but I went down that long dark hallway and into his bed again.

He leaned in and said, "What are you afraid of? Why did you get up and leave last night? I was so tired at work. I can't do that again tomorrow. You need to stay in here all night."

I gave no reaction, but I was sick to my stomach. My eyes didn't shut for hours. I listened to him snoring in my ear. Then, there it was. His hand slipped into my panties again.

Whimpering, I quietly bolted out of the bed and went to my hiding place from the night before. This is not happening. How do I handle this? Do I tell Mom? My head was spinning out of control as I thought about all the scenarios. If I told Mom, she would leave him and be sad. Another divorce? No way—it would be my fault. Her being alone was not an option. There was no way I would ever talk about it to her or anyone else. I refused to ever get back into that bed with him. I decided to run away.

If I told Dottie Hulshoff, she might help me figure out what to do. I'd heard her talk about feelings with her own children. Dottie was easy to talk to. She often chatted about thoughts and feelings with my sisters and me. Yes, that is what I will do. I'll go over to her house tomorrow and talk to her.

It seemed reasonable to me. Dottie was our neighbor, and her children were the same ages as my sisters and me. We played kick the can and hide-and-seek in the summer, and we spent a lot of time in their home.

After he left for work in the morning, I crawled back into my own bed and waited for Kris to wake up. The only thing I could think of was how it would hurt Mom if I talked. Dottie was a strong-willed woman. There was no way she would keep it a secret. She would definitely tell Mom or the police. I made the decision to let it go. Mom would be home soon, and I would never have to do it again. I was sorely wrong. The abuse continued well into my twenties.

Friday, October 2, 2009

Being released from the Mayo hospital was both happy and sad. I was happy to be going home, but I was sad that it was only going to be for two days. On the way home, I stared out the window and watched life pass by.

Eric was not saying much, and I wondered what he was thinking about. Every once in a while, he would grab my hand and ask, "How are you doing?"

I'd say, "I'm tired. I just want to get in my own bed."

At home, Eric helped me out of the car and upstairs to my bed. He had strict rules about no visitors except for family. I was so blessed to have a wonderful husband who loved me so much. When I was comfortable in my bed, I asked for my journal. I wrote until I fell asleep. "Tomorrow will be a new day. The sun will come up. All my children will come and surround me with their love."

Sunday October 4, 2009

On Sunday night, I asked Eric if he would give a special prayer or blessing over me. I said, "Just say what is in your heart."

All of my children were there as he placed his hands on my head to pray. I can't tell you exactly what was said, but the room was filled with a spirit I won't forget.

Kayla and Jeremy were expecting their first child. Jeremy had tears running down his face. Eric and I were blessed with a great son-in-law, and another would join the family in a month. I still had wedding plans to get done.

Kaitlyn and Brian were getting married on November 14, 2009. Planning their wedding was a great distraction during the surgeries and chemo. I went to bed that night with a heavy heart not wanting to return to the hospital.

Monday October 5, 2009

We woke up early, and the drive was cloudy and overcast. I was going back into surgery for the lymph node removal and to place the port in my chest. Eric tried to convince me I was strong, still the tears fell from my eyes. I wasn't sure what was ahead of me, but I tried to mentally prepare for it. In hindsight, I can see this type of surgery is not one a person can prepare for.

We registered and entered the waiting area. I was afraid I would have panic attack, but they took me back quickly. My anxiety was soon relieved. I kissed Eric as they rolled me into surgery. I had to believe the journey I was embarking on was going to help me understand and be more compassionate as I encountered others who were suffering. I wondered, how different my life may have been if someone would have been brave enough to ask me in elementary school, "Is everything okay at home?" Those were the last words I was thinking of as I drifted off.

Junior high was even more difficult. I never really learned how to multiply or divide. I'm not sure how I got through elementary school. I had friends, but no one I could call a "best friend." I was hiding a secret that did not come out until I was married and had three children. I was being humiliated at home by the stepdad. We all were. He constantly told me I was too skinny and too dumb for college. One of the words he used to describe me was "boob-less." For some reason, he found humor in that one. He was continuously belligerent. He enforced his authority with intimidating rage. I never saw him act controlling with Mom. How could he? She was the "perfect wife." He treated her with respect. To this day, I'm still not sure why he had so much hostility toward us. He put terror in me that I will never forget.

I don't want to go into a lot of details about the sexual abuse. It is private. I have discussed it with Eric, two doctors, and a therapist. It has taken many years to get over. I choose to move forward, but I think it is important to understand his character and the demons I faced daily.

I was punished for even the smallest of mistakes—mistakes most children are naturally going to make. He would take me to my room and have me take off my pants or shorts—and my panties—while he watched. It was humiliating. That part was worse than the actual beating he would give me as I bent over the bed with a bare bottom. Leaning over the bed, the sound of him taking off his belt was like waiting for a ticking bomb to go off any minute. I always jumped when he slapped the leather together. It was like a warning for what was about to shatter my backside. With every strike, I would cry out in pain. One time, he hit my bottom with the buckle and brought blood to the surface. The welts took weeks to go away, yet it always seemed validated by Mom. Did she think this was okay? Was she becoming immune to his perversions?

One of his mandates was we had to take showers with the door open. At the time, I thought his reasoning made sense. He told us the steam would build up on the walls and cause mold. However, he never asked us if he could stand in the doorway and watch as we showered. It was demeaning and uncomfortable. I went into and out of the shower fully dressed, hoping it would give me some dignity, which I desperately needed.

One hot, sweaty day, I arrived home from school and was excited that no one was home. Maybe I could take my first shower with the door shut. I knew I needed to hurry in case he came home. I was not quick enough. With the door shut, he entered the bathroom, slid the shower door open, and waved a butcher knife inside. He entered the shower and said, "Now that you're getting older, let me show you how a girl should clean herself." He lifted my leg up to the side of the bathtub, took a bar of soap and a washcloth, and proceeded to show me. I was terrified. My entire body trembled. I was only thirteen. I was embarrassed about my body, and I was scared to death of him. What was the knife for? It was an intimidation, a control, a warning to never say anything or he would "kill someone you care about." I didn't take another shower with the door shut until I was married.

The same rule applied for bedroom doors. Many times I dressed in my closet. Sonya, Kris, and I never talked about whether or not he was molesting them. I thought he was taking all his rage out on me. I knew he inspected the bathroom garbage so he would know when we were on our menstrual cycles—and he kept track. I overheard him talking with Mom about it. She didn't seem to be bothered by it either. I always felt as if I was being watched. Being paranoid is an unnatural emotion, but for me, it came suddenly and at regular intervals.

One Saturday, the stepdad came into my bedroom and sat on the side of my bed. Just doing that was enough to startle me. When I turned over, he was completely naked and holding a needle full of insulin. With force, he stuck the needle in his thigh. He looked me right in the eyes, laughed, and walked away. If he was trying to put the fear of death in me, he succeeded. I wanted to die. I wanted to roll over, close my eyes, and not wake up. I hated him. I hated my birth father for leaving me in those prison walls that we were supposed to call a home.

I began to wonder if my birth father was ever coming back. During my teen years, I don't remember having much communication with my birth father's family. I always thought about cousins, uncles, aunts, and my grandmother. Did they care? Did they know how to get in touch? Is the stepdad keeping them from us? The confusion was so overwhelming at times that I literally thought I would go crazy. Would I ever know what love was? As an adult, I understand that he was trying to plant fear into me. He made regular installments and was buying insurance, hoping the fear he deposited would be enough for me never to talk.

There were circumstances within the walls of our home that were commanded. He would lie on his stomach in front of the television with all of his clothes off for "back rub time." Each one of us was assigned fifteen minutes to give him a back and leg rub. He would always ask us to rub lower, eventually touching his private parts. I hated this time of night. Mom usually was sitting on the sofa, but she never suggested it might be wrong. Because she didn't acknowledge the behavior as odd, I always did exactly what he demanded. Inside, I was slowly beginning to understand the sickness of his behavior. In fact, I wondered what his childhood must have been like.

One time, a friend came to pick me up for a church activity. We hadn't gotten more than a mile away when a wave of anxiety overpowered me. I asked her to turn around.

"Did you forget something?" Linda inquired.

"Yes, I forgot to kiss my dad good-bye."

She said, "You have such a great dad. I wish I had that type of relationship with my dad."

It was an unforgettable moment. Little did Linda know that I was jealous of her incredible dad. If I did not kiss my stepdad on the lips good-bye or good night every night, there would be a consequence that was not worth the cost to pay.

He would play controlling mind games with me. As a teenager, I looked forward to going to the Saturday night dances at the church. I always had to ask "permission" to go. I'd make sure all my chores were done before asking. There was a particular way

I had to ask: "Dad, may I please go to the Saturday night dance tonight?" Easy enough, right? Nope, he pretended to not hear me until I walked away humiliated and sad, knowing I wouldn't get to be with my friends. Then, just about the time the dance would be starting, he'd walk into my room and say, very nonchalantly, "Oh, you're not going to the dance?" He strategically did this, knowing it was too late for me to get ready and find a ride.

For so many years, I thought the stepdad hated me. I must have been a burden to him. Ultimately, I was not his "real" daughter because he adopted me. I was assuming he did that for Mom; why else would a man marry a woman with three girls and agree to adopt them?

One Saturday, the front door slammed shut. He was roaring mad at Lance. I will never forget the panic in Lance's voice as he screamed, "Please stop." I dashed off my bed into the hallway to see the stepdad kicking Lance down the hall. He was yelling and shouting about something Lance had done wrong. He kicked and hit Lance all the way into his room and told him to stay there. He treated Lance like a dog.

I went into Lance's bedroom, hugged him, and said, "I love you, Lance. You'll be okay. Just do what he says—and you'll be okay." I went outside to where the stepdad was mowing the lawn, shoved his back, and asked him to turn off the mower.

He looked at me in shock.

I said, "Don't you ever lay a hand on Lance again. Take it out on me—but never ever touch him." I walked off, and he continued to mow.

The control and abuse continued through my high school years. Sonya moved to Utah soon after she graduated from high school. She married Greg at a young age. Kris followed in Sonya's path when she graduated and moved out.

Lance and I were still living in that house; worry and self-doubt were always on my mind. When I was allowed to go out, my curfew was midnight. I always came home at least fifteen minutes early to avoid being grounded for a month—or worse. In earlier years, he treated Sonya and Kris with total disrespect. His rules were all he cared about—not that they were home safely. Instant yelling, grounding, and violence overtook him. He always stuck to the discipline. No excuses were good enough—ever!

I was jealous. I couldn't believe the bravery of Sonya and Kris to get out, leave, and move forward. I wanted that for myself, but I had made a promise to Lance—and I was not going to leave him alone in that situation.

I always knew what was happening in our home was not "normal." Mom tried to take us to church every Sunday. Throughout my life, friends and people from the congregation said, "You are so lucky to have such a great father and mother." I always smiled and agreed. At church I made a prayer rock and painted the words "Don't forget to pray." I placed it on the floor next to my bed. I'd stumble on it before getting in or out of bed, and it helped me get into the habit of kneeling to pray every morning and night.

One night, I prayed, "Heavenly Father, please let me live through this nightmare. If you will help me endure this, I will follow you. I will serve and help others." I included this in my prayer morning and night. Even if I had no one to talk to on earth, it brought great comfort to know I could always tap into a heavenly presence.

Prayer became a beautiful tender mercy in my life. During my years of growing up, not much was advertised or talked about when it came to abuse in the home. A friend at work asked me if I had ever seen a talk show called Oprah. I had no idea what she was talking about. As far as I knew, the only talk show was Phil Donahue. I replied, "Nope. What's it about?"

"Well, Oprah is a black woman for one thing. Imagine that—a black woman going on national television and talking about sexual abuse and other issues that most people wouldn't and don't talk about. I'm sure her show won't last. I love watching because it is so real, but I don't think …"

My brain was in overdrive. What the heck was she saying? I was suddenly in a fog—somewhere between elated and unimaginable. Was it true? I could not comprehend that other people in the world had been abused like I was. Would they talk about it on television? If this was true, I had to see it for myself. Oprah came on at three o'clock. How was I going to be able to watch it? I worked at that time. I was obsessed. I had to know more about this woman. Who was she? How was she brave or arrogant enough to think she could get people to talk about such intimate things?

I was able to watch the show one day, and the guests on her show were talking openly about abuse and other subjects that had never been spoken about. I will never forget sobbing and wondering if the show was real. Were the people for real? Was a volcano about to erupt and spill the black tar of my life all over America?

I mentioned the show to Mom, and she told me not to watch it ever again. She and the stepdad were both racist. I thought it might be the reason for her not allowing me to watch it in our home. I loved Oprah, and I could not believe she was exposing real life. I did everything I could to find out what happened on the show. My friend would record it, and sometimes I could even watch it. At that moment, I knew the lies would eventually become truths. The facts would be revealed someday—just not today.

Chapter 3

Emotionally Hijacked

Sonya was married and living in Glendale, Arizona. She called and suggested I come for a visit. This was not unusual. I frequently swung by her home to play with my nephew.

When I walked into her home, a large man was standing in front of me. I instantly recognized him as my birth father. I was eighteen, and I hadn't seen him since I was seven. He was larger than I remembered; his body could easily block a doorway. The tattoos on his body were a quick indication of the life he had been living. He looked rough and tough. My immediate thought was to look at his hands. His hands were just like I remembered: colossal. This man was not a person anyone on the streets would mess with. So many thoughts ran wildly through my head. Where has he been? Why is he here? What does he want? Why the hell did Sonya shock me with no warning? I felt emotionally hijacked.

My birth father approached me with understandable hesitancy. He probably knew I would not welcome him with open arms. His smile was sincere and warmed my heart. His blue eyes were welcoming, and his enormous hands were surprisingly comforting.

"Hello, sweetheart. How are you?"

My heart melted. There it was—that familiar remembrance of a tenderhearted father who seemed to be reaching out. We embraced, and with tears in our eyes, we enjoyed the moment. However, I felt as if I had betrayed Mom and the stepdad. Gutwrenching guilt overwhelmed me. I would not—I could not—allow myself to feel any emotion toward my birth father. Sooner or later, he would disappoint me again. I would be left with a hollow, hard heart. I needed to be strong because, at the end of the day, I would not be calling him "Dad."

I don't really remember what the conversation sounded like or what we discussed. All I remember about that moment was feeling guilt, shame, and anger. I felt as if I was stranded on an island with no paddle to get me where I wanted to be. It was time to find away out of the darkness I was living in, but I thought it would go away if I hid it.

The shadows of that day followed me for years. Out of honor to the stepdad who terrified me, I didn't keep a relationship with my birth father. Although I now believe everything happens for a reason, I desperately wanted to run into my birth father's arms and never let go. Sonya and Kris kept in touch with him, but like a thief in the night, he wandered in and out of my life for years. Each time, he was carrying the burdens of his past.

The next time I spoke to him was after I was married. Out of the blue, we received a phone call from my birth father. He said he would be coming to town and wanted to meet Eric and my children, I invited him to dinner. We waited for hours, but he never called or showed up. I have to admit my heart was broken. I really thought a relationship could eliminate the deep divide we had built up.

Trusting in father figures soon became insignificant. Eric was an incredible father to my children. I was always able to get over the setback and pound my way through. I'd pick up the pieces of my heart that were scattered about like a puzzle. Some pieces fit, but others never completely fit back together. Each time he passed through my life uninvited, tears bubbled up and streaked my cheeks. He was not capable of fulfilling any obligations as a father figure.

Although I'd close the door on him, I always let him back in, hoping it would be different. Knowing he was my father, I hoped each time would be a new beginning. He'd enter my life like a storm with no warning—and no invitation—and then leave without knowing the collateral damage he was causing on my heart. Every time I had to dry my eyes, redefine who I was, and not allow him to settle in my heart as if it were a pit stop. My heart could not handle it anymore.

Years later, I clicked on my answering machine. A familiar voice said, "Hi, honey. It's your dad. I'd like to talk to you. Please call me."

The sudden contact confused me and altered my state of mind for a moment.

One of my children said, "Who was that?"

I replied, "That was my father."

Finishing up dinner, all I could think of was how to deal with it. I retired to my bedroom and dialed the numbers.

To my surprise, my birth father answered quickly. His deep voice said, "Hello, sweetheart. How are you?"

"Hi. I'm good. How are you?"

He sighed. He was thoughtful about his responses. "I'd just like to know more about your life … more about your children. I want to write down their birthdays so I can send them something." This pleased me, and I had him get a pen and paper.

I basically opened up my heart, forgetting and forgiving any prior transgressions of vacancy in my life.

Eric, listening to the conversation, was fearful. I could see it in his body language.

I ended our conversation with a desire in my heart to move forward with no expectations. Fortunately, I didn't invest much emotion in the conversation. I didn't hear from my birth father for years.

I've always been a journal writer. I have books and books of journals. When I read back through them, I can see the gaps and untruths. The secrets were hidden so deep. The first journal was a gift to me from Mom. On the inside cover, she wrote, "Only write the things that are positive." That explains a lot. She wanted our home life to seem perfect. I counteracted my low self-esteem with jokes, but I was far from being a happy teenager.

While I was still living with Mom and the stepdad, Sonya called me and said, "Monya, I need to ask you a question. Did anything inappropriate ever happen to you in our home growing up?"

I replied, "Yes." It was the first time the subject had come up between my sisters and me. I knew we had all lived through the stepdad's humiliations. His verbal and physical abuse were hard to hide, but I had no idea if they had been touched also.

Sonya called Mom and asked for a family meeting. Sonya, Kris, Lance, Mom, the stepdad all showed up.

Sonya stared at the stepdad and said, "Why did you abuse us?"

He turned and looked at me with warning eyes. "Did I ever do anything to you?"

Knowing he had abused me earlier that day, I looked at him and said, "No. I have no idea what Sonya is talking about."

The discussion was heated.

My mother said Sonya was a rebellious teenager who was always in trouble and was trying to take it out on them. She looked at us and said, "Now, this is done—never to be talked about again. What should we have for dinner?"

I knew I would be nursing my broken heart for many years to come. Denying the abuse was such a violation of trust and loyalty to my sister, but Lance and I were still living under Dad's roof. Our lives would become even worse if I admitted anything had happened. I never told Sonya I was sorry, and I continued to live in hell.

Sonya and Greg decided to not allow a relationship to continue with the stepdad. He was not welcomed in their home, and their relationship with Mom was strained too. From the outside looking in, our family was seemingly perfect—just the way Mom wanted it.

I always felt guilty for not admitting how this man had violated me. I began to have so much animosity toward him. It literally made me sick to be around him. I promised Lance to always be with him until he was ready to move out. That day never came; when Lance was fifteen, he died in our home.

I loved running. I ran throughout my school years for self-therapy, and it helped clear my mind and refreshed my soul. When I graduated from high school, I weighed ninety-seven pounds and was five foot nine. Mom put me on a diet to gain weight. It wasn't that I didn't like food. I just forgot to eat with so much on my mind.

After high school, I paid for myself to go to the SST Travel School in Scottsdale. I met Eric at a church dance on the night I graduated from travel school. I was wearing a white eyelet dress with red shoes and a red belt. My friend Brent Stapley introduced us. I thought Eric was very nice, and he seemed to be liked and known by many. A few days later, he called me and asked me out on our first date.

After working for American Express Travel for a couple years, I earned a trip to Switzerland. The night I got home, Eric picked me up from the airport and drove me to my parents' home where I was still living. It was Veteran's day weekend, mom and the stepdad went to Flagstaff to stay at a time-share. When I arrived home Lance was feeling sick, he was worried if he didn't do the dishes the stepdad would be very angry with him. I told him to go to bed, and I would do them in the morning.

Kris and John were married and expecting their first child. They were living with us at the time and staying in Lance's room. Kris and John were sleeping. Lance slept in the room with me; we had double beds.

Knowing I had to work in the morning, Eric said his good-byes and told Lance he loved him. I thought it was sweet for Eric to express his love to Lance. During the night, Lance got up several times and ran into my bed. I was so upset with him. I had jet lag, and I needed to be at work early in the morning. I said, "Please go and sleep in Mom and Dad's room. I need to work tomorrow."

He was going to the bathroom to throw up. I thought he had the flu. Lance had just gotten out of the hospital and had finally gone back to school. The doctor removed his spleen and found that his appendix had erupted at least eighteen months earlier. His bowels were blocked up to his chest; he was a walking miracle. He told me he had eaten some food his stomach was not quite ready for, and that was why he was throwing up.

When he went to Mom and the stepdad's bed, I heard him making gurgling noises. I jumped out of bed, ran into the room, and saw that he needed immediate attention. A white substance was running out of his nose, mouth, and ears.

He said, "Monya, please help me."

I called 911, woke up Kris and John, and waited for what seemed to be hours. Actually, it was only a few minutes. I called Sonya and Greg and then Eric.

The paramedics had me wait in the kitchen. They said, "We will take him to Maryvale Hospital. You can follow us."

What a relief! I assumed they were able to save him. I prayed the entire way to the hospital.

At the entrance, the coroner was waiting for me. "He's gone. He passed in your home. Can we get in touch with your parents?"

Shocked and paralyzed, I called the forest rangers in Flagstaff. Since it was Veterans Day, no one was answering at the time-share. I described their car, and the ranger found them.

"Mom, it's me."

"Oh, is Kris having her baby?"

I hesitated, knowing it was going to destroy her. In a few simple words, her life was going to change forever.

"Mom, no. It's not Kris. It's Lance. He died. He's gone … he …"

She threw the phone, and I could hear her wailing. "No, no—not Lance!"

Her words rang in my head.

That night, our home was filled with family and friends from church. The emotions were raw, and I was not in my right mind. Eric has always been a quiet man when it comes to death and emotions. I was appreciative of his strength when being put on the spot. He was a rock—unlike myself.

The guilt I felt for Lance's death took many years to get over. Why didn't I take him to the hospital earlier? He was so sick. Why didn't I see he needed further attention? There has never been a day since then that I have not thought about him. It took six weeks for the autopsy to return. He died from a blood clot in his lung, which was caused by all the peritonitis in his extremely infected body. I miss him dearly, and I look forward to our reunion in heaven.

Shortly after his death, I was kneeling in a tearful and solemn prayer. I did not know what to say, but I felt Lance's hand on mine. I kept my eyes closed and enjoyed this incredible blessing I was being given.

As clear as day, Lance said, "I'm okay. This is where I should be, and it's not your fault. Now it's time for you to move on." I can't say the pain immediately left, but that experience got me through the next few years of complete and utter pain.

Losing a child changed Mom and the stepdad. Their life would never be the same. Lance was the bond that they shared as husband and wife. He was Mom's only son. As dysfunctional as it was, they seemed quieter.

Many nights, I listened to Mom crying herself to sleep. The stepdad was less combative, and I didn't interact with him much. Watching their pain wreaked havoc on my heart, and I wasn't willing to be the fixer. It was time for me to leave and let my parents figure this one out on their own. I kept my promise to Lance. He was gone, and I couldn't do anything to bring him back. It was time to take responsibility for my own life. I moved into my own apartment when I was twenty-three.

Chapter 4
On the Wings of a Prayer

ric and I met in 1981. I had just turned eighteen, and he was twenty-three. I dated a bit before we met, but not much. I have only kissed five guys in my lifetime. I loved Eric and felt respect and affection from his family. He has two brothers. Doran is eighteen months younger than Eric, and Kurt is my age. His sister Raylani is the oldest and was already married. She and her husband Dean had three children and one on the way. The first time I met his mom, she hugged me like she had known me for years. Viola became Mom. She was the most beautiful woman I had ever met. I wanted to be like her.

Many nights, her doorbell would ring to a young adult not wanting to go home. They just wanted to talk to her about a mistake they had made or a girl problem they had. She never complained, and she sat for hours with them. She'd always convince them to go home and talk to their parents or church leader for guidance. She never prejudged anyone. Her testimony of Jesus Christ was stronger than any I had ever heard. Oh, how I loved her, the presence of respect and love in their home was nothing I had ever felt. This was what a real family was supposed to be. They were loving, compassionate, and fun.

I spent weekends at their home in Mesa. It was too far for me to drive to my own home in Phoenix. Since Raylani's room was empty, I slept there. I've never heard anyone say a bad thought or feeling about Vi. Everyone loved her. She was funny too. I never saw her without a smile. When I would do something silly, she always said, "Oh, you're a yahoo." I assumed it was her way of saying, "You're silly." To me, it will always be Vi's way of saying, "Thank you for being you." Her attitude toward me was such a contradiction to what I was used to feeling. At times, I thought I was imagining her affection. Her attentive love toward everyone she came in contact with was contagiously charming. I wanted to learn from her. She knew how to communicate with people, and she made sincere heart-to-heart connections.

Ray and Vi were the epitome of a perfect marriage. Many times, Eric and I came home to see them snuggling up on the sofa, watching a movie, and laughing like children. They loved deeply. They never missed their boys' softball games. I always looked forward to going to the games so I could watch them interact with each other. They were like schoolchildren in love. They held hands and cheered the team on to victory. Seeing them smile at one another was a gift. They were in a world I wanted to be a part of. Viola Williams was exactly the mother I always wanted, and she would be the example I'd look to for guidance in my own life.

One morning, I woke up and saw Vi in her silky nightgown. Her chest was flat on one side. I was confused and asked Eric what had happened. "She had breast cancer, but she's fine now."

Wow! We had dated for a few years, and I didn't know anything about her having breast cancer. How could that be? I inquired more about it, and what I found out was amazing. Vi was diagnosed with breast cancer in her forties. The night before her mastectomy, she asked Ray to say a prayer for her. She told him all she really wanted was to see her sons grow up and go on missions. She and Ray both served missions. Vi served in Hawaii, and Ray served in Canada. Heaven granted her that prayer, and she went into remission for many years.

When her youngest son returned from his mission in Tahiti, Eric and I were already dating. I could see right away that Kurt was special. He was—and is—the most like his mother. Since her own mission to Hawaii, Viola had a deep love for Polynesian culture. Kurt seemed lost after coming home from Tahiti. Because of the love they both shared for the Polynesian people his mom was able to comfort him in a way no one else could. I loved seeing them share the same passion.

When missionaries come home, they often suffer from depression. While serving their days are filled to the brim with appointments and service to others. They have to find a way to fit back into life when they return home. Most become very attached to the language and the culture where they serve.

Watching Vi interact with her Polynesian friends was magical. She loved them, laughed with them, and partied with them. We went to incredible luaus in their backyards. I started people watching at those backyard celebrations. Everyone was so happy. I desperately wanted that feeling. I began to call Vi "Mom," and I called Ray "Dad." It never felt weird. It felt like I was finally placed in a home where I was valued. I felt they deserved the titles of Mom and Dad. One night, I wrote in my journal after getting home from being with them:

> Tonight, was amazing. Vi, Ray, Eric, Kurt, and I went to Vai Sikahema's for a party-till-you-drop luau. Kurt wore his traditional Tahitian skirt from his mission. He looked so happy. Vi and Ray loved the music, the food, and the company. Eric was social with everyone … no big surprise. He also forced me to eat everything. Poi included. I thought I was going to throw up. I hated it, but he said if I didn't try it, the people would be offended. I love every minute I get to spend with Eric and his family.

Whether I am blessed to be a part of the Williams family or not, I will always remember to be passionate, to be honest, to be happy, and to laugh. I will teach my children to love freely and not judge by race or religion. I'll teach them they can achieve any dream.

I must not be the woman Eric is looking for. We've been dating for three years—and no word of marriage. Maybe it's time for me to move on. I enjoy dating, but I'm ready to be married. I talked to Vi about it. She told me not to give up on him. "He's a challenge, positive in all he does. He wants things to be perfect. Be patient with him." I will never forget that talk. We sat on their brown weaved sofa. I listened intently while she explained her oldest son to me. I remember asking myself, "How does she know these things about him? Mom and the stepdad knew nothing about me. They definitely don't know how I deal with things." That was one of the many moments that endeared my heart to Viola's. She knew her children—and what they needed and wanted in life. I want to be this type of mother to my future children.

For Christmas in 1985, Vi and Ray had their entire family together. All their boys had returned from honorable missions. Raylani and Dean's family was growing they had five children. I thought Eric would ask me to marry him. We opened gifts together—no engagement.

Vi looked at me with her big blue sad eyes, and said, "I'm sorry. I love you."

I cried. It was time to go visit my family. I was prepared to tell Eric it was over between us. It was killing me, mostly because I didn't want to give up Vi and Ray. I loved them and wondered if I loved them more than I loved Eric. Maybe this is why he doesn't want to marry me. Maybe he thinks I'm too attached to his parents.

We drove from Ray and Vi's home in Mesa to my parents home in Phoenix separately, and I cried the entire way. I was angry with Eric. It was sad and disappointing. It was not supposed to end like this. What happened to my happily ever after? Instead of ruining the day, I decided to wait until he was ready to leave that night before I told him.

When we arrived at my parents' house, Eric surprised me with a loose diamond he had picked out. He knew a lot about diamonds and explained the value to me. Are you kidding me? I didn't care if the ring came from a candy machine. I was so happy. I don't think he ever really officially asked, but he wanted me to pick out a setting.

We went with my parents to see Star Wars. We began a tradition of seeing movies on Christmas. We set a date to be married on April 28. Mom and the stepdad seemed to be happy for us. I couldn't wait to see Vi and Ray. She knew it was coming, but she was sworn to secrecy, another attribute I loved about her. She sat me down and said, "You are perfect for Eric. You will need to have patience. He always wants things to be on his time line for everything to be 'his' idea. He has passion and determination to be successful financially, and he will take care of you. Don't let him take that too far. You will be the one who can balance him out."

With her soft way of sharing her heart with me, she leaned in, hugged me tight, and whispered, "I love you—always have and always will. I'm thrilled you are the one he chose. Welcome to our family … finally."

With tears, we both smiled. Not only did she like me—she loved me. She wanted me for a daughter-in-law. April 28 could not come fast enough. I am going to bed with a happy heart. I am good enough.

The wedding planning started in January. We wanted it to be simple since we had dated for three years.

On a cold January morning, I woke up hearing Vi throwing up in the bathroom. It seemed to go on for a while. Most of the night, I couldn't sleep listening to her. I went into the kitchen to get some water.

She was standing with her back to me.

I asked, "Mom? Are you okay?"

She turned to look at me, and her stomach was bulging. It looked as if she was pregnant.

I asked, "What's going on?"

She gently took my hand. She seemed weak.

We walked into her living room, no one ever sat in this room. We spent most of our time in the kitchen or family room. She led me through the room and asked me to sit down. She sat across from me. I was getting a weird vibe. I was not sure where it was going.

She looked at me and said, "I'm going into the hospital this morning. I need you to be strong. I need you to let the boys know I will not be coming home this time. Raylani is strong. I don't want to bother her with this. She has her little children to take care of, and she needs to be there for them."

Shaking my head in disbelief, I said, "No. I can't do this. You are not doing this to me. You are going to come home. Everything will be fine. They will fix you, and you will come home."

With conviction, she looked into my tearful eyes and said, "Don't cry. It's my time to go. My life has been amazing. I am in love with Ray, but he has no idea how bad my cancer has spread. God answered my prayer all those years ago. He allowed me to see my boys go on missions. Now Kurt is home, and the cancer is back. I need you to be strong. Can you do that for me?"

I looked down at my bare toes and wondered if my feet could lead me where she wanted me to go. I didn't think I had the strength to do what Vi was asking me to do. I continue to shake my head back and forth saying "No, I can't do this."

She leaned into me, lifted my face, and said, "Chin up. You can do this. I love you, and I am so happy you are here. I am so glad you are going to marry my son."

"But—"

"No buts. This is it. Eric will be stubborn and hard to crack. He will not accept this. Kurt will be crushed, but Raylani and Doran will understand."

No words were needed. I looked up at the woman I had claimed as my hero. I didn't know what was going to happen to her or how I would explain this conversation to Eric. I nodded, she hugged me tight and she went to her room to get ready for the hospital. I said a quiet prayer. I was frozen inside. I can't do this. She doesn't know me. She doesn't know I'm weak. I'm fragile. Why did she ask me to do this? Why does she think I am the one to give this horrible news? I'm not saying a word until I know for sure.

She entered the Desert Samaritan Hospital in Mesa on January 31st. It was the hospital where all four of my children were born. Just a few days into her stay, Eric and I were sitting at the foot of her bed as she slept. She always slept with her eyes open. At the time, I thought it was creepy. Since then, I've seen Kayla sleep like that, and it's endearing. She sat straight up, looked at us, and said, "No matter what happens to me, I want you two to get married." She went back to sleep within seconds.

Eric and I looked at each other, shook our heads, and wondered if it had really just happened. Was she dreaming and just letting us know of her approval? To this day, I'm not sure what was going on with that. I knew it was getting close, and I needed to talk to Eric. My heart was in my throat.

I watched him greet every person who came to see her. It was like a parade of people all day and night. Everyone loved her.

The nurse said, "Who is she? Is she famous? She seems to be well liked."

I had no idea what to say. I looked at her and whispered, "Yeah, something like that."

The nurse didn't seem to really care. She was just making conversation.

It was time to speak with Eric. I looked at the nurse and said, "Get these people out of here. Can't you see she needs help? This is not a zoo. I feel like she is on display."

The Williams clan came running to see what was going on. Eric asked me to come out of the room. This was it after ten days in the hospital t was time to come clean with the information Vi had so reverently left me with. He said, "What are you doing? These people are here to see her. She knows they're here. They will help her wake up. She's just sleeping."

"Eric, I need to tell you something."

He looked at me with a strange look, he knew I was about to unload something he didn't want to here on him.

"Your mom is not coming home from the hospital this time—" as expected Eric was out of control angry with me

Quietly yet firmly in control he said "You need to leave. If you can't be positive I don't want you here."

"Eric, she wanted me to tell you—all of you. She asked me to do this the morning she came to the hospital."

"No. You keep your mouth shut. Don't say stuff like that. You are being negative, and you need to leave." He walked off, put on a smile, and started shaking hands with all the people who were there to visit. He reminded me of a politician—not wanting the truth to be known.

I felt like I was in a nightmare, and it was going to get worse before it got better. I went to the cafeteria, cried like a baby, dried my eyes, and walked back. I was gone for an hour. Fear attacked me as I walked toward her room. The people were gone. Oh no, is she gone? I didn't get to say good-bye.

When I ran around the corner, Eric and Kurt were talking.

I asked where everyone had gone.

Kurt said, "I asked them to leave. Mom needs her rest."

Eric turned to me and said, "Kurt and I are going in alone. We want to pray for her."

I knew it was best, and it was a moment I will never forget.

They walked into the room and shut the door while Ray and I waited outside.

Doran was driving from Utah. When he finally arrived, it was his time to have his private time. We all waited out side, when it was time we all entered the sullen quiet room the inevitable was going to happen and I wasn't sure I was prepared or could process having her gone.

In the room, Ray was holding Vi's hand, like they always did. He said, "I love you, sweetheart." Immediately, she squeezed his hand.

Like a little boy at Christmas, he said, "See? She can hear us. She's just sleeping. I'm sure she's probably tired from all the visitors. I'm going to go call her doctor and see what he can do. Maybe he will tell me when we can take her home."

Oh geez. He has no idea, and no one in the room is trying to stop him. I turned my back to them, trying not to make eye contact or cry.

In a few minutes, the door slowly opened.

Ray said, "The doctor said he can't help her anymore."

I was trying to imagine how that conversation went. He literally had no idea. How could that be? They were best friends. They told each other everything.

Ray was crying. "It's time for us to let her go."

As hard as it was to hear, I knew it was time. She was struggling to breathe. We all took a moment to whisper our good-byes. Since I didn't have that moment with my brother when he passed, I will always value those few moments. "I love you. Thank you for loving me," I whispered in her ear.

I don't remember exactly what time it was, but I remember how it felt. It was unimaginable and reassuring at the same time.

Ray prayed over her, told her it was okay to leave, and asked for her spirit to be with God. The second he said, "Amen," she took one last breath and was gone. On the wings of a prayer, heaven received an angel. On February 9th, 1985 she died in the hospital with all her loved ones surrounding her.

The immediate shock of losing her was overwhelming for everyone. My heart felt like it was going to beat out of my chest as we drove home. The sullen mood was inevitable. None of us knew what to say or do. There was no blueprint or book to help us grieve. Her children and grandchildren were confused, hurt, and quiet.

Ray was devastated. I heard him several times sobbing uncontrollably in his room not knowing how to comfort him weighed heavy on my mind. It was difficult to walk in the house and feel Vi's presence in every room.

The word of her death spread quickly. People swarmed the house with gifts, flowers, and food. There wasn't much time to really let it all sink in. We had a funeral to plan. The family gathered around and began the preparations. It was the largest funeral service I have ever attended. The chapel was full, the chairs overflowed into the hallways, and speakers were set up on the lawn. It was no secret Viola Williams was adored by every person she interacted with. She had a special way of making each person she ever came in contact with feel special, she wanted them to know she cared and she showed her sincerity with a smile and or a hug. Everyone felt they were her 'best friend.' This became apparent to me when nearly every person I spoke with after her death referred to Vi as their 'best friend.' Still today I meet people who knew Vi and immediately when they hear I am her daughter in law will say "Oh, I loved her. I've never met anyone quite like her."

The Polynesians wore traditional clothing and played their ukuleles. When they mourned Vi's passing, it was heart-wrenching to watch. They wailed, wept, and threw their bodies over her casket. She was loved deeply by so many people, but at the end of the day—when the storm passed and the quiet set in—I was struck with absolute despair I wasn't sure where I would turn for guidance and reassurance.

We all dealt with her death in different ways. None of them were right or wrong. Viola Williams taught me more in the four years I knew her than I had learned in my entire life. Knowing I spent those last few moments with her when she was conscious made me feel a sense of responsibility to help Ray. Vi did everything for him. He was lost without her. I helped him go through his bills and get them organized. When the time came, I helped him go through some of her personal belongings. He kept some and was able to give some to charity, knowing that was exactly what she would want him to do. The process literally took years.

Even after the death of Ray, signs of Viola were scattered throughout the house. Her shoes stayed neatly by the door for month's after she passed. Her brush on the vanity, her scriptures on the night stand, cookbooks and magazines she loved. Some things were so sacred to Ray we did not touch them. One of the memories I treasure was Vi's knowledge and conviction of the atonement of Christ. She bore testimony to me one night, repeating reverently what she had been taught. Quietly she explained the atonement as the single most significant gift ever given to man. What I would give to have her teach my children these priceless lessons.

I wish I could bottle up every lesson she taught me about forgiveness of others and myself. I was struggling with it, and it would take years to overcome some of the unnecessary guilt I felt. I understand now what she was trying so benevolently to relay to my heart. Because of her unwavering teachings and beliefs in the atonement, I have been able to move forward in faith and forgive fully. The legacy she left my children with will forever be a solemn and sacred thing to me.

One of my favorite Christian artists is Hilary Weeks, and she sings a song that always reminds me of Vi.

Hero

You probably won't be in the papers,
It won't be talked about in the morning news.
You and heaven might be the only ones who ever know
All the good you do.
You've never done it for the glory,
And you're not looking for fame
You and I both know it's never going to
Make you wealthy, but you give just the same.
At the end of the day, I can't help but wonder if you know.
You're a hero, quietly changing one life at a time,
You may never know what a difference you've made in mine
I hope someday you'll see you're a hero to me.
You give everything that you have.
Then you keep on giving, you always know what to say.
And you know when to make us laugh and when to let us cry
Your faith gives us faith to the soul that is lost,
To the weak and the weary, your heart is a home.
You're a hero, a friend to the lonely a light in the dark
You may never know what a blessing you are,
Maybe someday you'll see you're a hero to me.

Viola Williams is one of the elite angels in heaven. I've always thought of this song as a tribute to her. Wouldn't the world be a better place if all of us had someone we could describe as a hero? She lived every day happy. With little financially, she was completely at peace and overwhelmingly content.

Chapter 5

The Comparison Game

The death of Viola was a complete and utter interruption of our lives. Without her presence in a room, life was gloomy. I was not sure how the family would recover. I wasn't sure how I could get over it. She was the light I'd never seen in a mother, my confidante, my cheering section, and my hope. Growing up, I had never heard the words "I love you." For Vi, those words rolled off her tongue daily. I knew she really did love me. It felt good for the first time in my life to feel acknowledged. Now she was gone. Dealing with that reality was surreal and seemed so unfair.

Eric and I were supposed to be married on April 28, 1985, but we postponed it. Trying to help Ray adjust to losing the love of his life was hard we didn't want him to be lonely and we all tried our hardest to spend as much time with him as possible. Within a couple of months, he started to date. Ray was married to Betty in December of 1985—the same month Kurt married Amy.

Betty and Vi had been friends for years. She was divorced and had three adult children and some grandchildren. The marriage of Ray and Betty did not settle well with Eric or Kurt. They wanted Ray to take more time, and they even asked him to date more women. It wasn't that they didn't like Betty; they just wanted what was best for their dad. It was a difficult time. Now as we look back

Eric and I realize how much Ray needed companionship. I believe Betty kept him alive and spunky for years to come.

After seven years of dating, Eric and I were married in January of 1988. Doran was married to Shannon and they lived in Utah. Kurt and Amy live in Mesa. Raylani and Dean lived in Gilbert with their five children. I felt blessed to be a member of the Williams family; they loved me and cared about me, but it was not the same as when Vi was alive. The dream of my children having a grandmother who would play with them, teach them to love the scriptures like she did, and tell stories of her mission in Hawaii were forever gone. It would be my responsibility to let them know of her legacy. I hope I have done a good job describing her to my children. She had a contagious laugh, bright blue eyes, and her desire to serve others was incomparable to anyone I have ever met. With Vi's ability to make everyone she met feel like her best friend, I began to compare myself knowing I could never live up to that gift.

When Eric was twenty-nine and I was twenty-four, we moved into a small home in Chandler, Arizona. He worked as a Realtor, selling residential homes. I worked for American Express Travel until Blake was born. Being a full-time mom was exactly what I wanted to be. The memory of Vi telling me Eric would take care of me financially was true. He loved what he did for a living and worked hard in a competitive real estate market.

I will never forget the instant love I had for Kayla when she was born. It was enough to take my breath away. I couldn't get enough of her. I was a mom, and although it was tiresome and difficult at times, I wanted to be a good mom. When Kayla was only three months old I found out I was pregnant with another baby. Kayla was only a year old when Blake was born. People thought they were twins and often stopped to ask me how old they were.

I was raised in a home that was the opposite of Eric's home. The stepdad was controlling and overbearing, and we were expected to have our home in perfect order at all times. As a young wife and mother of two, I was trying to keep my home clean and incorporate motherhood in the same fashion Vi had done with her children. Balance was becoming more difficult.

We had a nightly routine. Everyone bathed, brushed their teeth, knelt for prayers, and was tucked in with a kiss and an "I love you." One night after our routine, I remembered I had left a fork in the sink. As I was ready to clean it, I remembered Vi telling me, "If Eric ever comes home from work and wants to take a drive—or if your children want you to read a book to them or play with them—leave the dishes. They will be there when you get home, but Eric or your children may not be there tomorrow." I dropped the fork in the sink, checked in on my sleeping babies, and crawled in bed next to my sweet, sleeping husband. I will never forget those words Vi shared with me, and I have kept them close to my heart. Sometimes I still have to remind myself about what really matters in life.

Having children and being pregnant was beautiful to me. I loved every second of it. I was never sick during pregnancy; maybe a little nauseated in the mornings but a saltine cracker would always take care of it. I had never been sick in my life. I'd never thrown up, had a fever, or experienced the common cold. That would explain why I had perfect attendance in school.

My children were everything to me. Their lives would be so different. The moment they were born, I adored them. My heart was full. As scary as it was to be a first-time mother, all I really cared about was doing the "mother thing" the right way.

I've made many mistakes, but I always made sure my children knew I loved them. Saying it out loud was important to me. It was so easy to say, it never felt uncomfortable or took any effort. Many times I questioned why my mom had never said those words, because she had never taught us to say "I love you" we never did. I've wondered many times if perhaps her mother had never told her.

One night, when I was talking to my mom on the phone, Eric started writing on a piece of paper. He pushed it my way: "Say I love you." Startled, I looked up at him with fear. Closing out the conversation, I said, "I love you, Mom."

She said, "Okay. Well, I'll talk to you later."

I knew right then that I was never going to hear those words from her, and that was okay.

In prayer, I thanked God for keeping His promise all those years ago. I would now keep my promise and follow Him. I would raise my children as a new generation to love and serve others. I will never forget the overwhelming feeling I had after that prayer. I knew He was listening. I'd done all I said I would do, and I would continue to be faithful to the end.

I took my children to church every Sunday. It was very important to me. I wanted them to know what I had learned. The atonement of Jesus Christ is for all of his children, I wanted them to learn how to forgive and love unconditionally. I knew this could not be taught all of a sudden when they were teenagers and struggling with identity. They needed to evolve into who they would become, and my best defense for fighting off what the world sees as acceptable was teaching them from a young age of their individual worth.

Our lives were surrounded with family and gospel beliefs. I was finally moving on. However, in the back of my mind, I could not completely close the door on some dysfunctional past experiences. I recognized all the signs of it at unexpected times, and I was always trying to shake it off. Like a furious storm, it would randomly enter my heart, take over, then abruptly exit. When it was passing through, I would be moody, depressed, tearful, and inconsolable. There were times I didn't think my heart could take much more, but then I'd recognize the wonderful miracle of being a mother. I knew I had a chance, the power within me to stop the cycle of abuse by teaching my children to love who they were and believe in themselves. That realization would always snap me back into the present moment and make me forget the past—until the next time.

Eric began to be busier and more successful in the real estate market. Business in Arizona was booming, and we were so blessed financially. I felt watched over, affording us financial and time freedom. We moved from Chandler into a custom home in Gilbert. We both had grown up meagerly with not much money. We loved our new home, and we continued to attend church. We were faithful members of the gospel at home and in our everyday lives.

I thought about Lance a lot. I missed him and struggled with blaming myself for his sudden death. That tragic night would forever leave a scar on my heart. I never let a day go by without thinking of Viola. I wondered what life would be like with her around. Eric didn't talk much about her. His love for her was undeniably deep. She was an amazing wife, mother and friend. Comparing myself to her would sometimes be overwhelming. I knew I was not anywhere near the caliber of woman she was and often wondered if Eric thought he got cheated in comparison to his mother. There were times I had a hard time believing he really did love me.

With no urging on his part, I would sometimes say, "I'm not your mom. I never will be able to fill those shoes."

I know it was frustrating and confusing to him, but he never expected me to be his mother. I had put her on such a pedestal that it was impossible for me to live up to what I thought Eric wanted and needed from his wife and mother of his children. I know there are very few women comparable to Viola Williams. In fact, I have yet to meet one. Still, I had my times of insecurities. I watched other mothers who seemed to have it all together.

I wasted so much time playing the comparison game. I'm not sure why so many of us waste time playing that game. The only purpose it served in my life at the time was damaging my already wounded soul. I watched intently as mothers in our playgroups seemingly had everything in life figured out. They were up at the crack of dawn to grind their wheat for homemade loaves of bread, gathered fruits and vegetables from their gardens, had immaculate homes, and were perfectly groomed. I, on the other hand, dragged myself out of bed, was lucky if I got the kids to the bus on time with a brown-bag lunch of store-bought bread for a sandwich, a Ding Dong or Twinkie, and a bag of chips. My home was picked up and clean, but it was far from immaculate. I spent most of my days wearing pajamas, wiping peanut butter and jelly off of walls and chairs, and wondering how I could keep up with my "perfect" friends.

With time and maturity, I learned motherhood is a precious calling—and not a competition.

Chapter 6

Breaking The Cycle

After the birth of Kaitlyn, my life was so busy. We had three children under the age of four, and it was not an easy job. Many times, I was overwhelmed, sleep-deprived, and moody.

When Eric came home from work, he was so happy to be home with his children. They always loved when he walked through the door. One night, after a long day I sat on the family room sofa and watched as all three children jumped on his back, wrestled, and played with him. The sight felt like a bomb detonating in my brain. The sudden memory of the stepdad making us rub his back came flooding back to me. I jumped up, grabbed my babies, and told Eric to get out. I was sure he was abusing our children. How could this happen? I tried so hard to protect them.

Eric did not know what was happening and immediately called our bishop to see if he could talk to me. Over the next year, I met with the bishop and explained my abuse as a child.

Every week, he would ask, "Are you ready to face your stepdad?"

And every week, I replied, "No, not yet. It will hurt my Mom too much."

When I was twenty-eight, my ear started to hurt again. After years of seemingly good functionality, why now? I made an appointment to see Dr. Borland right away. It had been many years since I had seen him. I was now a grown woman with children, but he still talked to me about my grandmother and how much he loved her. While he was examining me, he told me a tumor in my ear was affecting my equilibrium. He sent me to a specialized surgeon.

My appointment with him was on a Friday, and on Monday, I was in the hospital having surgery to take the tumor out. He also repaired my ear enough to allow me to go underwater this was exciting as I had never been able to swim growing up. During my recovery, Mom wanted to help me with the children while Eric worked.

One morning, I woke up and could hear the stepdad's voice downstairs. I said, "Eric, please help me downstairs. I don't want our children to be with him." I was uncomfortable and watched his every move. From the sofa, I watched Kayla and Blake playing on our back patio. They were having so much fun together with their water guns.

Kayla squirted Blake, and he did the same to her. It was playful and fun. Suddenly, the stepdad jumped up, opened the door, grabbed the squirt gun, and began squirting Blake in the eyes over and over again. "How does that feel?" His voice was controlling, loud and mean.

I grabbed Blake and held him tightly as he cried in fear. He had hurt Blake's eyes and feelings. I asked Blake and Kayla to go to their rooms to play for a little while.

When I got them settled down, I looked at the stepdad and said, "Don't ever touch my children again. That is not how we handle things in our home. We use time-outs and explain the consequences of making bad choices. I saw the entire thing. They were just playing—like siblings do."

The stepdad said, "Well, then you can expect Blake to grow up a sissy."

I was still in so much pain from the surgery, and I was in no mood to argue with him. Mom was watching from a distance, but she never said a word.

The next day, I told Mom I didn't need help. I lied and told her I was feeling much better. I was not about to tell her I refused to have the stepdad in my home with my children.

I decided to discuss bits and pieces of my abusive childhood with Eric. Knowing the hatred he had for Mom for letting it happen and the stepdad for being a coward, I decided more hatred on Eric's part was not going to help him move forward. He could not comprehend the amount of disrespect I grew up with. I knew it was not time for him to forgive yet. He needed distance. His heart was broken, and the tears fell as I explained some of the irrational behavior of the stepdad.

Eric took me in his arms and said how sorry he was. However his curiosity wanted to know "Why did you let it go on for so long?"

I replied, "Are you saying I let him do those things because I enjoyed it?"

"No. I'm not blaming you. I'm just trying to understand why and what you were thinking."

"Well, I was thinking that I wanted to get out of it alive and I never wanted to hurt my mother."

Within a few weeks, I was ready to dump years of agony on the shoulders of the man who needed to take responsibility: the stepdad. We decided he might be more likely to admit his guilt if Mom was not there. It was hard to do, but I phoned him and arranged for him to come to our home—without Mom. I asked a friend to watch our children, and I felt good about my decision.

I'm simple minded and naive I thought the stepdad would come over, face the facts, and ask for forgiveness. I was sure this was exactly how it would happen.

Eric, being the intelligent and sensible husband, said, "I don't want you to get your hopes up. I don't think this is going to happen how you think it is."

I was angry. How could he say that to me? After all, I had been praying for this for years. I knew it would be exactly as I had imagined it. I was ignorant enough to believe the simple truth would set the stepdad free. I was agonizingly wrong on so many levels.

When the doorbell rang, I opened the door. The stench of Old Spice took my sense of smell back to a gut-wrenching, disgusting place. The stepdad gave me a hug that was awkward yet reassuring. I wondered what Eric was thinking as he watched. He was careful not to say or do anything that would spark an emotion.

We went into the family room, and Eric and I sat on our burgundy leather sofa.

The stepdad sat on the love seat across from us. "Thank you for having me over. It's been hard being out of a job. I appreciate you helping me however you can."

In amazement and shock, I looked at Eric. How could I even start this conversation? He actually thought we were going to offer to help him financially?

Eric said nothing.

I looked the stepdad in the eyes with tears running down my cheeks. "Why? Why did you do those things to me?"

He looked at me and said, "What are you referring to?"

Having Eric with me was surprisingly empowering, and I was brave. "You know what I am talking about … the abuse."

"No. I don't know. Did I touch you?"

The words made my body quiver. I was going to be physically sick. Was he being serious? How could he not remember? Did he not remember?

Eric squeezed my hand as if to let me know it was ok, I was safe and could express anything and everything I ever wanted to; and I did.

I wiped my tears, looked at him, and said, "You either have a sickness or amnesia. I only moved out of your home six years ago. How could you have possibly forgotten how you violated me?"

There was silence from him not a peep as he glared at me.

I yelled, "All these years, I've thought I was not good enough or pretty enough. I had no self-worth or self-confidence—and now you are denying all of it? You've caused me to feel those horrible feelings of insignificance." The words that came from his mouth next rang in my ears for years. I will never forget them.

On the wall, there was a picture of Lance. I could see him looking at it. He said, "Now it makes me wonder if I ever did anything to Lance."

Something horrible was happening to me. I was trembling. I could feel the rage of hatred engulf every cell in my body. He could see this too, and in some sick way, I think he found pleasure in it. In a calm creepy way he said "What would you like me to do? I will do whatever you need me to do."

I stood up. I wasn't able to contain my anger. I looked at him, shook my head and said, "Go talk to Mom. You need to be the one to tell her."

Eric walked him to the door. "You are not welcome in our home. If you ever touch one of my children, I will kill you with my bare hands now get out." That was the last time he saw the stepdad, and those were the last words he uttered to him. It was not what I had expected to happen but Eric never said "I told you so." At the time I was so confused and thought maybe I didn't take enough time? Was I too hard on him? All I did for a week was kneel and pray to soften my heart. "Please forgive me for what I have done to this family." My prayers were being heard, and the answers came quickly and to the point. I was reassured this was not about me. I had done nothing wrong.

About a week later, the phone rang. Mom said in a matter of fact fashion, "Monya, your dad told me why you wanted to talk to him without me."

Inquisitively I asked "Oh really, Mom? What did he tell you?"

"Well, he said that you felt closer to him than me and wanted to let us know that we should have been better parents."

It was not a big surprise that he didn't tell her everything. "Mom, you need to go back to him and have him tell you the entire story."

Another week went by. It was killing me and interrupting my focus on being a good mother. Our schedules were completely off. I couldn't get out of bed. My children sat on the floor, watched Disney movies and listened to me cry.

Mom called again. "Before you say anything, I want you to know—unlike you—I have been praying about this for a week. I'm not sure why you are out to ruin our lives. You must have nothing else to do but sit over there in Gilbert with all your money, making up stories instead of helping us when we need it so badly."

I felt a mixture of anger, sadness, and guilt. "Mom, do you seriously think I have not prayed about this? It has taken me more than a year to confront Dad, knowing it was going to hurt you. I have been praying about this since I was eight years old."

She announced, "You're ruining our lives."

The conversation was getting heated. Voices were raised, and I couldn't contain myself. "Your life? Are you kidding me? My life has been a huge secret, trying to protect you."

She shouted, "Well, it's all a lie. I'm not going to listen to these lies." She hung up, and I didn't hear from her for months.

During the next few months, I was a mess. There are no words to explain the guilt I had. Again, I asked myself What have I done to this family? I wanted to crawl in a hole. I was in despair. I was never angry with God, but I did wonder if I was being heard. I relied on God to keep His promise to me. I made all my choices by praying and listening to the spirit. I began to question my own intentions. Was I doing this to get back at the stepdad? I thought he would say, "Oh, Monya. I'm so sorry." I thought he'd thank me for finally confronting him so he could repent and move forward. We'd get some counseling and be one big happy family again. After all, it was "only" physical. I could get over that.

I've since learned that the physical and sexual abuse were much easier to get over than the demeaning, harsh, criticizing words he used to scorn me with. And in fact we were never a big happy family.

Kris and I tried to talk to Mom alone one Saturday. I even offered to pay for some counseling.

She said, "You watch too much Oprah. All psychologists do is try to convince you that you were abused. They put those thoughts in your head so you'll pay them and continue to come back."

After months, I was exhausted. I begged her to listen to us. I wanted her to at least have a relationship with her daughters.

She said, "If you cannot have a relationship with your dad, I cannot have one with you."

As she got up to leave Kris's home, I tried to stop her. "Mom, please sit down and talk this out. If you leave, I can't do this anymore. You are walking away from your children and your grandchildren."

She left, and she never called me again. She told people we knew that I kept her grandchildren from her. Hearing that didn't hurt as much as knowing that was what she took from the conversation. My purpose was never to "take her grandchildren" from her. In fact, it was just the opposite. I wanted them to have a grandmother.

Over the next few years, she would send my children Christmas and birthday cards with a five-dollar bill. I always told them they could call her and thank her. They never wanted to; their loyalty was to me.

The guilt I felt was ruling my life. How could I claim to be a Christian and not be able to forgive? I needed to forgive the stepdad and Mom too. It was such a battle. It was not what I had taught my children to believe. I taught them to turn the other cheek. I knew I would have to forgive before I could move forward.

Eric was devastated to see me so beaten down. It was tearing our relationship apart. He would say, "Why do you care? They've hurt you so much. Just walk away from them."

I didn't see it that way. For me, I was the one giving up. It was not as easy as he thought. How could he know how this feels? He grew up in a perfectly respectful, normal home. The thought of abuse in his home was unheard of. For me, it was a reality. It may be something he would never understand. Eric had no problem walking away from them. In fact, he never saw them again. He never wanted them brought up in conversation, and quite frankly, he didn't care or have one bit of emotion toward them. Even with sure answers to prayer I beat myself up wondering if I was to blame. The feelings of guilt were textbook behavior.

Trying to move forward was one of the most difficult things I have ever done. Every once in a while, my phone would ring. I'd say hello, but the person on the other end would hang up. I've always wondered if it was them.

Unfortunately, over the next few years, I took it out on my husband and friends. I became isolated and depressed to the point of not wanting to get out of bed. When we found out we were having baby number four, my focus was once again on being a mother. Our three children were so excited, and Blake wanted a brother. Haleigh was born on April 14, 1993.

I came home from the hospital with a little postpartum blues. Maybe my mind was still on Mom knowing she would not be there to help me. I would never be able to call her for a recipe. What if I needed a shoulder to lean on when I had questions about motherhood? I was on my own.

In the shower one day, not long after Haleigh was born I remembered that awful experience with the butcher knife. Eric came home and found me huddled in a fetal position at the bottom of the shower. It took a lot for him to get me out and calmed down. Were these memories going to flood my mind and pop up to destroy my day or week at random times? The flashbacks seemed so unfair after all I had been through.

A few weeks later, I was rushing into the house with a baby in my arms and three children following behind. I could hear the phone ringing. I answered, and it was my my mom's sister. She said, "You have ruined your mother's life. You know you can't hide that you had a baby? Your Mom knows Haleigh was born. She knows how much she weighs and all the details."

I said, "Don't call here again. We are moving forward. I didn't keep this from Mom. I'm glad she knows. I hope she is happy. I really doubt she is since she chose to walked away from us."

Then the words that came out of her mouth shocked me "You must have wanted your dad to do what he did to you—or you would have stopped him. I was abused when I was younger, and I got over it—so get over it."

I hung the phone up and looked down at my precious baby. Haleigh had just come from heaven, and she was beautiful. She had tiny little fingers and toes, and the curve of her eyelashes were perfect. Her pouting lips were adorable and she fit perfectly in my arms.

Kayla and Blake were coloring at the kitchen table. They were quietly enjoying each other's company. Kayla looked so much like Eric. Her olive skin was flawless. She would be my artist, something inherited from me. Blake's eyes were the color of the Caribbean Sea. He inherited those from my birth father and Eric's mom. He had white hair and dark skin. The curve of his fingers as he grasped the crayon was tender and sweet. I knew those hands would someday be the hands that comforted and helped others as he served.

Kaitlyn was eating a banana. She was incredibly sweet and had no care in the world. She munched on the banana like it was all she had eaten in days. When she joined the coloring frenzy, she didn't exactly have as much grace. The table was a mess. Papers and crayons were everywhere; but in that moment, my world was perfect, I had been blessed with so much.

We moved to the home we still live in. It is where we call home. The absence of my mother tormented me. I blamed myself for years. I actually believed my mother was correct when she said I ruined our family. Trusting a man was not my strongest attribute either. Many times, in tenderness, Eric would put his arm around me in the middle of the night—only to be smacked with my elbow to his face. I never meant to hurt him. It was an instinctive reaction. Hormones and emotions got in the way of our intimacy. I think he started to believe I was not attracted to him, which could not have been further from the truth. I was physically struggling with my self-worth and my identity.

One of the best things I did for myself and my marriage was seeking professional help. I began to work out at the gym every day—six days per week. I loved running, cycling, kickboxing, aerobics, and weight training. My body and mind began to feel healthier. I read my scriptures every day and attended the Temple as often as I could. Through the trials, I never forgot God in my life. The scriptures began to be more and more of what I needed. I found my answers there along with comfort through prayer. I was the homeroom mom for all four of my children's teachers. I loved being involved in the elementary school, and I loved all of their teachers.

I overcompensated in areas I had missed out on in my own childhood. I baked cookies for teachers. I acknowledged their birthdays and volunteered time in their classrooms. I was an advocate for raising funds at the school. Simply put, I was enjoying life as a wife and mother to the best of my ability.

Every once in a while, we'd get a nasty note in the mail from Mom that would send me into a fetal position and cause me to regress. I'd wonder if I had handled the situation with my parents correctly. I questioned myself over and over again. I blamed myself and tricked my brain into thinking I should have done more. I should have told Mom every detail. And then I would remember that Mom was there. She saw so much of what was happening. Why didn't she stop him? She left my birth father when she found me hurt by his hands. Why couldn't she leave the stepdad? What kind of hold did he have on her?

When the sadness of wanting a relationship with Mom invaded my thoughts, I'd start a letter, but then I'd always call Sonya. She had taken over the maternal role for me. She was wise and would know what to say. Sonya would always tell me, "Don't do it, Monya. You're going to get hurt. She will never admit her faults, and you will be slammed back into depression. It's not worth it."

I always had this nagging feeling to write her back or explain how sorry I was in a letter. Sonya would always say, "What are you sorry for?"

After mulling it over for weeks, I always came to the conclusion that she was right. What did I have to be sorry for? Certainly not for asking for or initiating any type of abuse. I was a good child. I did everything right. I followed the rules. I was a little sassy at times, but I was a good kid. That was not what I was sorry for. I was sorry for how it was handled. I wished it could have ended with a better resolution. Who was I kidding? Facing those demons was far more complex than I'd imagined it would be.

In July, we often went to visit my birth father's family in Eagar, Arizona. I wanted my children to know my family. I wanted them to know my paternal grandmother and the rest of my aunts, uncles, and cousins. I wanted them to know my roots and where their heritage began. We usually stayed with Aunt Pam and Uncle Fred. My children loved the feeling in their home and we always had fun.

Every once in a while, I would stay with my Grandma because there was not enough room at Aunt Pam and Uncle Fred's home. One year, my birth father had unexpectedly moved to town. While I was staying with my grandmother I overheard a conversation between her and him.

He said, "I don't understand why my daughters won't stay with me. They must think they are better than me." My grandmother said nothing.

I immediately went into the kitchen and said, "I don't think I am better than you. I know I am. I don't want my children to stay in a home where their grandfather grows and smokes marijuana and I don't feel comfortable there either." I know it hurt him, I wash lashing out and the excuses he shot back at me didn't help. Once again, he'd vanish not be seen or heard from for years.

While visiting in Eagar a few year's later I found out my birth father was in jail again. It was within an hour's drive, and I decided to visit him. I welcomed anyone who wanted to come, but they needed to be prepared for what I was feeling.

Aunt Pam, Sonya, and I made the drive on the Fourth of July. The building was old and withered. It looked as though it may have been built in the forties, which was not what I expected. It looked abandoned, lonely, and decayed. The officers told me it wasn't a visiting day. I explained who I was and how far I had driven, and they allowed me to see him.

He was in a very small cell, alone, with no windows. It was dark, humid, and depressing. The only way to communicate was through a very small slit in the door where they slipped him his dinner. Sonya and my aunt waited in the car, giving me my privacy. It ended up not being so private when my voice rose.

He looked terrible, and he immediately started to make excuses for why he was in jail. He was blaming anyone and everyone else. I didn't go there for that, and I really didn't care. I said, "You have not been a dad to me or a grandfather to some amazing children. You dumped me when I was a baby girl. You handed me over to a predator. You should have protected me. You have popped in and out of my life each time, leaving me with hope for a father-daughter relationship. I wanted a dad I could count on. You failed in all of those areas. I will not be around for you to walk in and out of my life anymore. I feel nothing for you— no love, no remorse, no empathy, no sadness. More importantly, you are not—and never will be—my dad. I am leaving here today, and I do not want you to contact me again. I will not allow you to sporadically come in and out of my life."

He started saying he was sorry for what he did to my ear as a child, but it only added fuel to my fire.

"I've told you over and over again that I have forgiven you. I never blamed you. I'm tired of you hiding behind that regret. You need to forgive yourself and move on." I walked out of the jail—proud of who I had become, grateful I had the bravery to face him, and finally able let go of the anger and disappointment.

Breaking the Cycle

Our children were growing so quickly. Eric and I decided before we were married that four children would be a good number. I joked when he said he wanted another child. "If we have an odd number, then one person will be left out on a ride at Disneyland." This seemed perfectly reasonable. I guess that's why Eric asked if we could have two more. We discussed it and decided not to make a permanent decision yet.

Months later, I told him I wanted to get my tubes tied. He supported the decision and agreed that we could move forward as a happy family of six. I could not imagine having two more children. My life was so busy, and Eric was incredibly overwhelmed with work. We rarely got to see him before our children went to bed.

Emotionally, I could not handle one more child. I was already in a panic trying to keep up with what I had. In the back of my head, there was an open wound that would not heal. Would those scars of being abandoned by my mother ever leave? I wanted them to quietly exit my memory and allow me some peace. I tried every day to move forward, hoping Mom and the step dad would call to acknowledge what had happened in our home, take responsibility, and get the help that was desperately needed. It never happened. I tried my hardest to let my children know how much I loved them. I showed them by being there for them in all they did. I needed this cycle of dysfunction to end.

I had four children under the age of six. Week after week, I never missed taking them to church. On holidays, I bought them matching outfits, and they were always so adorable.

On Easter morning, a woman came up to me and said, "Your family is darling. You always dress them perfectly. I admire you. I wish my life was as easy."

I smiled and thanked her for her compliment, but I felt fake. She had no idea the turmoil I was going through. I learned a great lesson that day: what you see is not always what you see. That day took me back to the years when people would say, "Your mom and dad are so great. I wish I had parents like them."

I was not a good mom because I dressed them reverently for church each Sunday. I wanted them to know they were loved and would always be protected by my love. During that time of my life,

I became obsessed with whether or not my children were being touched by babysitters. Before we left the house, I would say, "No one is allowed to touch your privates." When we got home, I would wake them up and ask, "Did the babysitter touch you?" I realized it was unhealthy, but I could not get the thoughts out of my head.

A wise and kind therapist helped me get it under control since it was doing more harm than good for my children. I learned to take them twice a year on individual date nights. I would quietly and calmly talk to them about abuse. I let them know they could always come to me if anyone ever did something to make them feel uncomfortable. I was very open with them about this subject without revealing the details of my childhood. This seemed to work. My children were open and honest with me, and to this day, they have said they are glad I talked to them about that subject.

The weeks, months, and years seem to fly by. When Haleigh was in sixth grade, I took a job with America West Airlines. I wanted to get back into the travel field, and since my baby was going into seventh grade where they did not allow parents to help in the classroom, it was the perfect opportunity to start a new adventure. I worked early mornings after the kids left for school and was home before they arrived home. Those were such fun times with my children. We took advantage of visiting the world together.

I loved being needed, being wanted, and I never let my children leave the house without telling them "I love you." They also said, "I love you" freely to Eric and me—and to each other. To some, this may seem insignificant. For me, it was more than significant. It was more than a way of life; it was true. I loved them with all my heart, and it came naturally as their mother. Our home was not without arguing or raised voices. We were not model parents by any means. Eric and I loved our children. We truly cherished every moment with them.

I loved having teenagers. My experience was not what everyone had warned me about. The only thing that was true was they grew up way too fast. Their friends gathered in our home and I always appreciated having them all around. Since my children were so close in age they had many of the same friends and I loved them all.

Eric's dad was getting older and more frail. Ray was a great man and I loved him dearly. Our children adored him and loved spending time with his quirky, funny personality. He and Betty were happy and complimented each-other well.

We celebrated Thanksgiving every year in our home with Eric's family. Ray was always attentive and whispered to me about how much he loved me and how grateful he was that Eric and I would host dinner in our home so the family could be together. I always told him it was my pleasure and I wouldn't have it any other way. Ray would call me three weeks before Thanksgiving to give me his order for pies. His request was the same every year. He wanted pecan pie and would be satisfied to try all the others if Betty would allow him to. She kept him alive for more years than we expected. She made sure he was eating healthily, but she always gave him permission to eat whatever he wanted on Thanksgiving. He had no idea what joy it brought me to have the extended family over to our home. It was—and is—a privilege and honor for me.

One year after we had eaten our feast Ray told us he needed to have heart surgery. He wanted us to help him make a decision. We had two options; he could have the surgery and take a change he would be too weak to make it through, or if he decided not to have the surgery, he would probably live a few more years. The mood was quiet and sullen, but we all made the decision together: no surgery. Ray and Betty were in agreement.

Over the next few years, he had a hard time breathing. He would go on and off the oxygen machine. He fell a few times and proudly showed us some ugly bruises. My children took the time to call him, and he would always call them with crazy jokes or ideas. They really loved him and I enjoyed seeing the interaction between my children and their only grandfather.

Raylani's children were so great about going to visit Dad and Betty every Sunday. Their dedication and love for Dad and Betty was so sweet. Eric and his dad spoke on the phone just about every day. We could see him getting weaker by the years and then months. One morningBetty called to let us know he had fallen and was in the hospital. Everyone went to the hospital to say our good-byes. Everyone in my family was there except for Blake. My sweet boy could not handle death, especially his granddad.

For me, it was a very spiritual experience, it was difficult to see Betty in pain but more difficult to imagine him alive and in pain.

Vi and Ray taught me a new way of living and loving; because of them I was able to break the abusive cycle in my life. Knowing his spirit was going to leave his body and that Vi would be waiting on the other side to embrace him gave me great relief. With that comfort, it was easier to say, "See you later" instead of good-bye!

Chapter 7

The Stepdad Dies

*I*n February 2009, I received a phone call from my mother's friend.

"Monya, this is Susan. How are you doing?"

"Oh Susan, it is so good to hear from you. How are you doing?"

"Well, I have some bad news. Your dad fell in the parking lot where he works and was rushed to the hospital. He has been in a coma. Your mom is going to let the doctors take him off of the ventilators on Saturday, and I was wondering if you could come to the hospital to be with her?"

The rush of anxiety and apprehension in my body was overwhelming. I tried to stay composed but immediately said "I will be there. What time and what hospital?"

She told me the details and asked if I could get in touch with Sonya and Kris. I told Susan Kris was living in Louisiana. I didn't think she could afford to come on such short notice. I knew what Sonya was going to say before I even got her on the phone.

When I called Sonya I told her "Susan just called and asked if I could come to the hospital. Dad is dying, and they are pulling the plug on Saturday. I want to be with Mom. Maybe this will be the time to start mending and healing."

Sonya said, "Oh geez. Monya, please don't go. You are finally in a good place. This is going to send you backwards."

I replied, "No. This is going to be good."

"I'm not going with you, and I'm really worried about you going. I'm in a good place, and I don't want to be there when he dies. If Mom wants a relationship with me, she will contact me."

I really was not surprised by her reaction. Sonya was always the levelheaded one.

I called Kris, and she was not interested in being there either. She also asked me not to go. Kris expressed her worry about me going into another depression when it didn't turn out the way I expected it to. One thing I learned through all of this dysfunctional, sometimes comical life we had led was that Sonya, Monya, and Kris all had different ways of processing emotions. I was usually not as smart as they were.

I pulled my children together and asked them if any of them would go with me. Right away, Blake said, "Yes. I'll go with you, Mom. I won't let you go alone." The girls were a little incredulous, but in the end, they agreed to support me. It was an awe-inspiring moment for me. I always knew their loyalty was to me, but I had no idea they were so willing to be vulnerable alongside me. Mom had not seen my children since Kaitlyn was a year old, and she had never seen Haleigh. Kayla and Blake didn't ever remember seeing her or the stepdad.

Unexpected waves of anxiety shot through my veins. Was I doing the right thing? I had become an expert at second-guessing myself—and now was no different than any other time. The night before we left, I said, "Eric, I've decided to go to the hospital tomorrow."

Eric stopped brushing his teeth and said, "I don't think it's a good idea, but if you feel it's important, I'll support you. I'm just not going with you."

"It's okay. The kids are all going with me."

Eric's head whipped around. "What? No they are not. Are you serious, Monya?"

I stared at him and said, "I need them there. I want them to come. I—"

Eric threw his toothbrush down on the counter, leaned against the vanity, and said, "Monya, why are you doing this to yourself? Why do you want to see the man who defiled you, almost ruined our marriage, and never admitted to anything? Why would you want to watch this man die in front of you and our kids? You never listen to me. You always think the best about what I can already see is going to throw you into depression, guilt, and pain." He took a deep breath. "I know you, and I know you are going to go there no matter what advice I give you. I just didn't think the kids would be involved. Now I have to worry about the kids too?"

"But what if this is the only time I have to repair this relationship with Mom? I'm not willing to take that chance. Eric, please let me do this my way. Maybe this is finally a way that Mom and I can get past all of this. Maybe she will finally admit what he did to me. What if this is the time for us to heal and finally hear her say I love you?"

"Monya, I'm telling you to do what you think is best, but no matter what happens, that woman is not going to come and live with us. I won't allow it." Eric never really said much about my parents, but he was standing his ground.

"Mom is not going to come and live with us. Why would you even think that?" I could feel his dissatisfaction. My body and mind were in complete conflict with what was rational and what my heart wanted to be real.

In preparation for Saturday, I contacted Susan told her my children and I would be coming. We figured out logistics and times. Susan reassured me that I was doing the right thing. She and her husband would be there, and she knew it was going to be hard for me. Susan was always a friend to Mom. They spoke often, and Mom seemed to have a special bond with her.

Growing up, we lived in the same neighborhood. I called Susan the night my brother died. Her son was Lance's best friend, and our families were intertwined in a strange but comfortable way.

Shortly after I confronted the stepdad and Mom called me in denial, Susan let me know she believed me. She was trying to convince Mom she was making a big mistake by walking away from her girls. I remember exactly where I was standing in my kitchen when Susan called. The walls were covered in mauve wallpaper with white pinstripes.

"I'm just so sorry," she said.

"Susan, I need to go now. Maybe we can talk another time. I just can't do this right now."

"Okay—just know that I feel so badly about all of this."

"Okay. Thank you. Good-bye."

I hadn't talked to her since that phone call.

Saturday morning came quicker than I wanted it to. Before the hour-long drive to Phoenix, my son offered a prayer for a safe drive and peace in my heart. In the parking lot, I introduced Susan and Ron to my children. I'm sure it was uncomfortable for my children, but Susan and Ron were happy to meet them. Susan made some small talk about remembering Kayla and Blake being born.

On the long walk through the halls of the hospital, I was beginning to feel anxious and sick. I felt the blood rushing through my veins, and I thought I was going to faint. We cautiously entered the room, and my eyes were searching for Mom. Other people were in the room, but I did not recognize them. Maybe she was in the restroom.

Susan nudged me and pointed. No, that can't be my mother. Mom is young, vivacious, and beautiful. That thin woman was hunched over and reminded me of the witch from Snow White. I could tell that my children felt the same way, but they were gracious enough not to react.

Mom turned to look at me. When she spoke, it was as if no one else was in the room. The room was spinning. I needed to get my thoughts in order. I wanted to control the conversation. "How are you, Mom?" I gave her a cold and distant hug and stepped back to hear her response.

Her voice was shaky and cold. "I'm good. We are going to turn off the machines on your dad soon. If you'd like to talk to him, he can hear you. Go to his bedside if you want to."

Is she serious? She honestly thinks I am here to create a moment with the man who tortured me on a daily basis? I felt like a child again. "You are not good enough. You are too skinny. Hey boob-less. Forget about school. You're not smart enough." all of those demeaning words were coming back to haunt me.

Blake was standing behind me, and he squeezed my shoulders trying to shake me out of the slight coma I was in.

I introduced Mom to my children.

She said in a matter of fact voice, "I know who they are. I know their birthdays. I know everything."

I said, "Oh good. Well, you've never met Haleigh. I just assumed you'd like to meet them personally."

Haleigh was sitting on my lap.

"I know who you are," she said. "I sent you all birthday cards and Christmas cards, but I never heard back from any of you."

The mama bear was awakened in me. "Wait a minute. They did receive your cards, and I gave them a choice to call you. They didn't know you. Surely you can understand why it would be difficult for a child to call a grandmother they don't know? Please don't do this. They didn't know any better."

A voice in the room said, "You have a daughter?"

"Yes. I have three daughters. This is my middle child, Monya."

"You've had daughters who live in town all this time? Where have they been?"

I believe Mom had never mentioned us—or that what she had mentioned was to benefit herself. She had not changed at all. She still wanted to be the martyr.

Out of the corner of my eye, I saw a man nudge the woman who was so boldly stating her unwanted opinion. Not wanting to make eye contact with anyone in the room, I kept still at the feet of the man who had violently abused me. I didn't necessarily want him to die, but I wanted him gone before Mom. It seemed fair for him to go first so I could repair what was left of a relationship—if any—with my mother.

The nurse came in and asked if anyone had anything else they wanted to say. It was time for any last good-byes. She would return in ten minutes to start the process. No one made a sound. Mom just sat there—no emotion, no tears, nothing. Who was this woman? Was this the woman who gave birth to me? She was acting like she was okay with him dying. She said no good-byes.

What happened next was one of the most horrific things I have ever witnessed. The nurse came in, shut down all the machines, and told us it would only take minutes before he would be gone. Having gone through this with Eric's mother and father, I was expecting a much different exit from life. He suddenly started gasping for air, and his body went into complete warfare. It was not normal. His head reared back, and his body convulsed as if he were fighting to go to the other side. There was something on the other side that he didn't want to face.

The noises and movements of his body were more than I could handle. How could I let my children sit through this? What kind of mother was I to do this to them? Everything was going so wrong and so different from what I had expected. I wanted to shield my children's eyes and cover their ears. I wanted to run from the room. It seemed to go on forever. Those minutes were some of the worst moments of my life.

Blake squeezed my shoulders, reassuring me of his love and connecting with the warmth of his hands. It could not end soon enough, and I wanted out of there. Once he was gone I walked out into the hallway and was greeted by a church leader. He introduced himself as Mom's bishop. "I'm not sure what your relationship is with your mother, but I want you to know that you don't have to do this."

I looked at him and said, "Do what?"

"Be here. Stay here. I know a troubled spirit when I see one— and you are obviously struggling between right and wrong— what to do or not to do—am I right?"

I wanted to unload on him, but I said, "I have not spoken to my mother in seventeen years. I came here today because I thought it was the right thing to do. I want to help her with any funeral arrangements."

Without hesitation, he took my hand and said, "I don't know what happened or what went on in your home, but obviously if you have not had a relationship with your parents for this long, it was a serious situation. I would never judge you or blame you for not wanting to be involved. Please, if this gets too much for you, let me know. Our congregational members are prepared to pay for the funeral and expenses."

I said, "I'd like to help with whatever I can. I want this to be a healing and forgiveness time between my mother and me. I want my kids to see life like it is and know they can forgive. Please let me help. I need to do this." He was compassionate and kind.

I saw Susan talking to my children, excused myself from the bishop and went back into the room. I told my mom I was willing to help with whatever arrangements needed to be done.

She asked me to help with the program design for the funeral.

I said, "I'd love to. Anything else?"

She asked if I could meet her at the funeral home on Monday to help her make some decisions.

I agreed we would touch base the next day.

When I got home from church the next day, Mom left a message and asked me to call her so she could explain how to get to the funeral home.

I phoned her back and asked if I could pick her up, but she said my Suburban was too high for her to get into. Susan would drive her there to meet me. We decided on a time. I was ready to say good-bye.

She said, "Wait, I have one last thing I need to say."

"Mom, please don't do this. Let's just get through the funeral, and then we can consider it."

"You ruined our lives. Your dad has been forgiven for everything he has ever done—"

"Stop. First off, Mom, what was he forgiven for? Please just say the words. Tell me, what did he do? What did he need to be forgiven for? Last time I spoke to you or him, he didn't admit or say sorry for anything—and neither did you."

"I'm just telling you, we went through hell because of you. It is none of your business."

"Seriously, Mom? It's none of my business? You have no idea the hell I have been through my entire life. This is not about you. Can't you just get out of your own misery for once and admit that these things did happen so we can move past all this?"

My son-in-law was in the living room with me. I could see the worry in Jeremy's eyes as he watched me begin to cry.

A sudden feeling of peace came over me, and I calmly said, "Mom, I refuse to go backward. It has taken me so long to get on the road of recovery. Learning my self-worth has taken years. All I wanted was to help you. I was hoping to rebuild a relationship with you, but obviously this is not a place where I can go to heal. I'm sorry, but I will not be coming to the funeral home to help you." I hung up, went to Sonya's house, and told her what had happened.

Sonya took me in her arms allowed me to cry it out. I was so grateful for her that night. She didn't cast any stones or hold any dark shadows over my head. Having her live close by has been a saving grace for me.

She was trying to understand the excruciating pain I was feeling. Sonya knew, she had been there and done that years before I had. I firmly believe only those who have cried themselves to sleep—wanting so badly for life to be different, someone who has walked the road of redemption—can understand the devastating pain of rejection from a parent. Sonya and Kris understood, we had each other; I still rely on them for strength, unconditional love and fortitude to push through any circumstance.

Once I was composed enough to drive myself home, Sonya called Mom. I don't know exactly what was said, but I know she gave my mom a piece of her mind. She said she let loose on her. Sonya took the next couple of months to help me heal. I will always be so indebted to her for that.

I did not go to the step dads funeral. It took time for me to get over the rejection, but once again I turned it over to the Lord in merciful prayer. I knew I would eventually be okay. I had come too far in my self-development to allow myself to go backward, this was just a minor   setback. I would not let my mom define my character any longer.

Six months before the stepdad died, I had an overwhelming feeling that I needed to let him know I had forgiven him for all he had put me through. I sent him a very short e-mail.

Dad,

I want you to know I have forgiven you for all you did to me growing up. I forgave you many years ago. I also want you to know Eric and I are very happy. We live in

Gilbert and are very active in our children's lives and in the gospel of Jesus Christ.

Monya

The reply:

Dear Monya,

Thank you for your e-mail. It meant a lot to me. I would like to ask you to please consider having a relationship with your mother.

Dad

I never responded. I always felt if Mom wanted a relationship with me, then she would let me know. She had proven that the past was still haunting her. If she were to admit anything, she would have to do something about it. For Mom, that was not an option. It had taken me years, but I had finally forgiven Dad for all of his transgressions against me. I was done with letting him occupy space in my brain.

I forgave the stepdad, but forgiving and forgetting was not possible for me. Forgiving is a choice. I decided the best way to move forward would be to take responsibility for my own actions and not allow the transgressor to continue to be my reason for anger, hatred, or envy. A part of me felt sorry for him. A very wise man taught me that there are basically three reasons we fall into trials.

- A choice you make causes you to live with the consequences of your own actions.

- Another person makes the choice for you, and it affects your life. Moving forward is devastating and can change your life—for no reason and through no fault of your own.
- Life challenges, chronic health issues, loss of job, or the death of a loved one.

Forgiving and forgetting is next to impossible. Forgiving is essential for your own well-being. Forgetting is ignorant in some ways. If a man touched one of my daughters, I could probably eventually get to a place of forgiveness, but I would never invite him into my home for dinner. Forgiveness does not mean you need to resume a relationship with the offender. In my particular situation, I had done all I could do to repair a broken relationship with my mother, it was now in the Lord's hands.

Seeing Mom old and withered at such a young age opened my eyes. I believe she allowed pride, envy, hatred, and anger to take over her body. Like a cancerous tumor, it invaded every functioning cell in her being—and she was swallowed up by pride. Instead of softening her heart and opening up to the possibility of change, forgiveness, and pure love, she chose self-pity.

Within a few weeks of the stepdad dying, my birth father also died. I tried my hardest to make it to the hospital before he passed, but I was not successful. Sonya, Kris, and his brothers and sisters were all with him. Sonya said he mentioned me and wondered if I was coming. I didn't feel guilt for not being there, but I knew in my heart he had not forgiven himself for so many things he had done while he was living. All three of his daughters spoke at his funeral, I knew he would have been proud of us, I know I was proud of us. It was a loving tribute to the man with the huge and hands and delicate heart.

I had to believe his spirit was in a good place and that God would give him another chance to take what was wrong and make it right. I wanted my birth father to be in a place where he could finally feel the sweet peace of the Savior's arms around him. It was pleasing to know he would finally be able to forgive himself and fully repent for all his wrongdoings on earth. With no shadows to hide behind, he could finally walk down a road of restitution and be healed.

One day, I will have a sweet reunion with him. We will both be in a perfect state of body and mind. I look forward to that tender embrace

Chapter 8

Refuge in Rainbows

*S*hortly after the deaths of the stepdad and my birth father, I made the decision to fulfill a lifelong dream of running a marathon. When I was a teenager, I would run for therapy. It took me to a place where my heart could regenerate—and I could process my thoughts and feelings. Running has always been an excellent outlet for me. It's been my way of escaping the negative forces of life. Running purified my mind and soul for an hour or two.

I started training for the marathon by running the track at Highland High school and sometimes Gilbert High school. It was therapy on steroids for me. The more I thought about my feelings, trying to process the heartache of what my mom had done, the faster and stronger I ran.

At Gilbert High School's track, there is a huge mural of a tiger on the wall at the end zone. Every time I turned the corner and made eye contact with that tiger, it gave me strength. I was lighter on my feet than I ever imagined I could be. It was as if that tiger was saying, "You can do this. You are strong. You are a fighter."

With my headphones on, I'd listen to uplifting music or motivational affirmations to build myself up. I'd been beaten down so many times that it sometimes felt like the world was on my shoulders. Running helped me to lift that burden. One night,

I'd gotten up to twenty laps on the field. I was alone on the dark track as I took my last lap. I cried. I smiled. I laughed for the first time in years. It was happening. I was beginning to love myself and had finally learned how to drop the baggage of my past . I was allowing myself private moments of accomplishment that helped me move forward healthy—physically and mentally.

In June 2009, I wanted to take my training to the next level. Eric and I went to our condo in Mexico. I ran my first ten-mile run on the sandy beach of Rocky Point in Puerto Penasco. I felt a huge amount of pride in myself. After that run, I said to myself, "What the heck did I just do?" It was an amazing feeling. I was pushing my body to a place I only imagined it could go. I wasn't out of breath. In fact, I thought I could keep going forever.

The marathon I wanted to run was going to be in November that year. I knew if I was going to be successful in running it I needed to run a half marathon between the months ahead. I ran back to our condo and began searching for half marathon's. There was nothing more in life I wanted at that time than to fulfill a goal I had set at age ten.

While I was searching, Eric walked in.

"Eric, I did it. I ran ten miles without stopping. It felt so good."

He said, "Wonderful. I'm really proud of you. I tried to follow you with the binoculars, but you disappeared out of sight. I knew you could do it."

I expressed my gratitude to him for believing in me and for the support. "I'm excited. I can't wait to cross that finish line and see you there."

Eric knew the significance of my run and was in full support of me. "You can accomplish anything you want to."

One day while I was doing a five-mile run, I started to bleed. I had always had regular menstrual cycles, so this was an unexpected bummer, especially while I was training. I didn't let it stop me. I continued to train, but the bleeding didn't stop. In fact, it was so annoying that it forced me to go to the gynecologist—the last place I wanted to be.

My doctor examined me and said, "Well, you are forty-six years old. Maybe your body is premenopausal. You also have some cysts in your uterus. Why don't we take those out?"

"Uh … like a hysterectomy?"

"Yes. I think it would be best."

"Absolutely not. I'm training for a marathon. I don't have time for that."

"Okay, well let's go in and aspirate out the cysts. If you don't mind, I'll do a technique that will stop your periods—so no more bleeding."

"Yes, of course. I'm done having babies. Those eggs are hard-boiled anyway. How much time for recovery?"

He laughed and said, "Maybe a week?"

"I'll give you four or five days." I was determined to not let this slow me down.

I had the surgery, went home, healed, and started my routine. I registered for a half marathon in September. I continued my track running, cycling classes, weights, and kickboxing. It only took me a week or two to get back up to a thirteen-mile run. I was ready. My mind was focused. Blake had gotten his mission call. Kaitlyn and Brian were engaged to be married in November. Haleigh was starting her senior year of high school. It could not have been a better time for me.

Within a few months I started to bleed again. While I was running my final lap, I felt it running down my leg. "Dang it. Not now," I screamed.

I had a decision to make: go back to the doctor or ignore it and live with it. I didn't tell Eric, but the pain was too unbearable to hide. My gynecologist said the ablation didn't work and there were more cysts that needed to be removed. He again suggested a hysterectomy.

"No, no, no. I am not having a hysterectomy. I'm right in the middle of my training."

When I woke up in recovery at the surgical center, my surgeon told me how sorry he was that my cervix was scarred shut. He was unable to get the cysts out. I had no other options but the hysterectomy. He immediately made an appointment for a mammogram. The hospital would not allow me to be admitted until I had that done because of my age, and I had not had one in quite some time. My begrudging attitude made it difficult to get to that appointment, but I did it. It would take at least six weeks to recover from the hysterectomy. I would not be able to run the half marathon, and the possibility of running the November marathon was fading.

It was now July Kaitlyn had moved to Utah. Kayla and Jeremy were living in Mesa and expecting their first baby. Blake had a girlfriend who was attending BYU, and he spent most of his time before his mission with her in Utah. Since Haleigh was going into her senior year of high school, she and I decided to take a last-minute trip to Hawaii. We had so much fun, we stayed just a couple blocks from the beach in Waikiki.

We spent a day on the North Shore and stopped and ate at just about every roadside stand. She took surf lessons, and I have to admit she was pretty darn good. I loved watching from the sandy beach as she rode the waves with such grace. Is there anything this girl cannot accomplish? She had devoted more than twelve years to the dance world. I looked at her with admiration for the woman she was becoming.

On the drive back to Waikiki, we rounded a corner on the highway—and saw the most breathtaking rainbow. It was brilliant. Until that day I had never seen a full double rainbow. Our eyes were blessed. I could not get over the astonishing colors. It looked like we were close enough to drive through it. The rainbow's beginning was a little hazy and lingered over the homes on the hill but the end was precise and clear. This seemed to parallel my life. I explained to Haleigh how rare it was to see a full double rainbow; I felt it was a beautiful sign of hope. I told her to breathe it in and enjoy every minute of it because they don't come along very often. In my forty-six years, it was the first one I had ever seen. It was exquisite and calming.

Haleigh laughed at me and even called her dad to tell him how excited I was about the rainbow. I was a little weird, but I couldn't get over the beauty of it. I've always found refuge in rainbows. Over the years, they had become symbolic to me. I had a fascination with rainbows intertwined with an angelic ending to every turbulent outcome in my life.

For many years, dark clouds lingered over my head, but looking into the future, I could see a bright and pleasant ending. I had a breakthrough. Going through storms in my life I'd learned to see the glorious rainbow at the end. This impressive rainbow was my happily ever after. I said, "Haleigh, if ever I'm not around or when I die, you'll find me in the rainbows."

As a child, I watched The Wizard of Oz every year. The story gave me hope. The first time I watched it was in black and white. The year it came out in color, we watched it as a family on television. I was mesmerized. I felt much like I did with Haleigh. It was bright, precise, and beautiful. I have always been fascinated with the words to "Somewhere over the Rainbow." Judy Garland sang them so eloquently. That is one of my favorite songs; I'd love it to be sung at my memorial. As a child, I would sing it over and over, anticipating change for my future. I often thought about the words. "Can I wish upon a star and have all my dreams come true?" "Can my troubles melt like lemon drops?" "If happy little bluebirds fly beyond the rainbow, then why can't I?" I wondered if I had dreams or if they had diminished over time. In so many ways, that song helped mold my philosophy of life. In times of trouble, I let my mind wander to better places. I dreamed of living in better places. Little did I know I was being prepared throughout my life with the words of that song; they would soon become significant on a whole different level.

At home, the lab left a message. They wanted to do an ultrasound for a small spot they found on one of my breasts. I wasn't worried. Up until a few years before, I was regularly getting my mammograms. Each time, they would call me back for an ultrasound. I always endured the ultrasounds and followed up with the doctor to find out it was just cysts that needed to be aspirated. Before the doctor passed away, I think he had aspirated fifteen cysts from my breasts.

When I received the letter saying he had passed away, I stopped getting the mammograms. There was no reason for me to believe this time would be any different. I went to the lab and waited patiently for them to call my name. When they did, I walked back and put on the robe.

Two anxious ladies were talking in the waiting area. I tried my best to calm their nerves. I said, "I've had to do this so many times. It's always just a little cyst. Of course you need to get it checked out. It's just so inconvenient, but have no worries—everything will be great."

The technician told me my doctor would follow up with me, and I left. I didn't have any doubt or fear leaving that office. I knew I was healthy. I felt great. I just wanted to train for my race.

Eric and I were excited for Blake. In six weeks, he would be leaving for a two year   mission and as difficult as it would be to say good-bye to him I knew this was something he had prepared for and wanted to do. We wanted to spend as much time with him as we could. Since Kaitlyn was living in Utah and Blake spent so much time there, we decided to fly up for a visit. Maybe we could get some shopping done for Blake's mission. Spending time with Kaitlyn was very important too; we were planning a wedding and I needed her input on decision making.

Blake was getting fitted for a new suit at Mr. Mac in Salt Lake City when my phone rang.

"Um … Mrs. Williams?"

"Yes, this is her."

"I am calling from Dr. Jones's office. He would like to see you tomorrow around three."

"Well, I'm in Utah with my family. Can you just give me the results over the phone?"

"No. Dr. Jones wants to see you."

I was completely perplexed. I didn't want to fly home to see him and have him tell me the same thing I had heard so many times. I put her on hold and asked Eric if we could fly home.

"Yes, I will be there, but I want you to know I am not happy about this. We are visiting with our children. Isn't there any way we can make an appointment for next week?"

The assistant replied, "He will be on vacation next week. Tomorrow would be best."

I sighed. "Okay. I'll be there then."

Flying standby we were not able to get on the flight I needed to be on. My plan was to get home early enough to take Eric home before my appointment. Since we missed the first flight, we barely made it to Arizona in time for my appointment. Blake flew home with us to also make an appointment he had, then he would turn around and fly back.

On the flight I noticed tears in Eric's eyes. "Are you sad about Blake leaving—or excited for him?"

Eric said, "Both. It will be hard to be away from him for two years, but I know he's worked hard to be spiritually and physically ready to go."

I asked Eric if he would mind going with me to the doctor so I wouldn't be late.

He said, "I was planning on going with you anyway."

At the doctor's office, all the lights were off.

I said, "Oh my gosh. Are you kidding me? Look at the office hours. They say his office is closed on Fridays. Today is Friday the lights are off. This is ridiculous."

Eric looked like he had tears in his eyes, and he wasn't paying attention to me. I think he'd been used to hearing me spout off.

We opened the door, and I walked into the dark waiting room. No patients were waiting. With every step closer to the counter, I became more agitated. "Why would you call me in on a day when the office is closed? Why is it so dark in here?"

She collected my co-pay, and I signed in. I was rude, looked at her and said "I guess doctors will do anything to take a co-payment. I hope that forty dollars helps him out." I couldn't believe I'd given up time to be with my children to fly home for this.

When I turned toward Eric, he was crying. Oh geez. What is wrong with him now? I could not believe he was still crying about Blake leaving.

I told him to stop. "Blake worked hard to be worthy of serving a mission. Get over it." I didn't even have time to sit down when the receptionist called us back.

We were in a cold room, Eric was still crying, and I was ticked off. This was the last place I wanted to be.

It didn't take long before the doctor came in. Before the door shut behind him, he said, "Mrs. Williams, you have ductal carcinoma."

Shaking my head, I said, "Wait. What?"

"You have breast cancer."

I realized that Eric knew. He had better intuition than I did. He was wiping tears from his cheeks. I didn't cry. I didn't respond. I couldn't let myself believe it.

When I asked Eric how he knew, he said, "I didn't. I just had a really strong feeling that it was breast cancer."

Over the next forty-five minutes, the doctor explained all my options. I did not hear a word he said. All I could think about were my children. Blake is leaving in six weeks. Nothing is going to get in the way of him serving the Lord, especially not this. Kaitlyn is very close to her wedding date. Kayla is having our first grandchild in December. Haleigh is so young. She needs her mom to help her through her final year of high school.

The doctor explained that he wanted me in the hospital on Monday. Seriously? No way.

Eric was wise and announced we were going to get a second opinion.

Walking out to the car, all I could think about was how it was interfering with everything. It had to be a mistake. I was in shock or maybe denial.

On our drive home, I first called Blake and asked him to come home. I knew he was at the airport on his way back to Utah. I knew if I caught him in time, he could catch a later flight.

"Blake, we are going to have a family meeting. We'd like you to come home."

"Mom, what's this about? Put Dad on the phone. I'm not coming home." I handed the phone to Eric.

"Son, we need to have a family discussion and would like you there. Can you please come home and fly to Utah later?"

"No, Dad. Is this about Mom's doctor's appointment?"

"Yes, but we'd like to talk to the family together."

"No. Tell me now," Blake urged.

"Mom has cancer."

I could hear Blake on the other end. He was so upset. "You and Mom knew this—and you're just now telling us?"

"No, son. We just left the doctor's office five minutes ago. We had no idea." Blake went to Utah, and we could not get in touch with him for a week. He didn't return text messages or phone calls.

By the time we got home, Haleigh was there. Kayla and Jeremy were on their way. They all sat at the table.

I was at the sink and blurted out, "I have breast cancer." With no emotion or thoughts of how it would affect them or how it sounded, it just came out. Kayla began to cry. I assured her that it was going to be okay and that we were getting a second opinion. Jeremy gave me a hug, but he didn't say anything. Haleigh asked a few questions, but she didn't cry. Eric explained as much as he could with what little information we had.

After Kayla and Jeremy left, I called Kaitlyn. She didn't seem too upset. I found out from Brian and his mother that Kaitlyn was really worried, but being the most like her mother, she had a hard time expressing it in the moment.

I called Sonya and Kris, and they both cried. I didn't understand why everyone was upset. My body was in shock, and my mind was frozen.

I said, "Sonya, this is so inconvenient. I have way too much going on right now." Sonya knows me so well, she immediately knew I was in shock and needed time to process everything; she was quite worried about my lack of empathy for my own situation. Kris was completely overwhelmed with the information and immediately wanted to fly home to be with me.

I asked Haleigh to call Mysti Brown one of my dear friends. I'm not sure how that conversation went. I'm sure Haleigh was composed. She doesn't cry much. In fact, she seemed like she was in shock too.

I went to my room in complete and utter shock-I felt nothing.

Chapter 9

Consumed

*L*ater that night, I did one of the worst things a newly diagnosed cancer patient can do: I went to the Internet and began to search everything I could about breast cancer. I was hopeful and thought *maybe we've caught this fast enough, and the doctor is overreacting.* The images I saw on the Internet were horrifying, and the stories I read were sad. I didn't know my prognosis or stage of cancer yet, which made it difficult to determine where I was on this ugly scale of staging they kept talking about. I spent so much time on the Internet, considering alternate remedies. I'd get so worked up over words I'd either never heard before or cared to know about: white and red blood cells, chronic pain, acute, benign, malignant, lymph nodes, chemotherapy, radiation, hormone production (I didn't even know women had testosterone) bilateral, biopsy, BRCA gene, lumpectomy, segmental mastectomy, BSE, reconstruction, and nipple sparing. The list went on and on.

Life soon became overwhelming. I was consumed with the C-word. It was so confusing to think about cancer and how it was going to affect my life. I worried every day about my children. I didn't want them to have any fear. I wanted life to be normal for them. Eric was my rock. This news was more real for him. I couldn't imagine what he must have been thinking. I tried to comfort him and tell him breast cancer is not a death sentence. Many people actually fight it and win. Medicine has come so far since his mother passed away. I was confident I would survive and thrive with an abundant life, coming out of what seemed a black hole to a paradise of light.

Eric began calling people. Hal Walker was the first. I heard Eric talking to him about my diagnosis and asking him if he knew a good oncologist or surgeon. Hal happened to own the lab where my mammogram was taken, and he is a great friend of ours. We were grateful he was able to actually see my screens. We gave him permission to discuss them with us. Over the course of a few days, Eric spoke with several people he knew, and we decided the Mayo Clinic was a great place for us to get a second opinion.

One of the best decisions I made was allowing Eric to be a part of the decisions, especially about the doctor and or clinic I would eventually be going to. He needed to be a part of what was going on. I wanted him to feel in control of what he could be. I knew there would be things he could not regulate in the future and I know him well enough to know he likes to fix what's broken or damaged; this was the one thing he could oversee, and I liked it.

Since Eric and I are both natives of Arizona, we know a lot of people here. The word of my diagnosis did not take long to spread. I was paralyzed as the text messages started to come in. I didn't want to talk to anyone. I wanted to be strong and brave. If I talked about it with more than my doctors and Eric, it would be overwhelming. I'd have to face the C-word, I'd have to own it and deal with it. I was not ready for those conversations.

A phone message I will never forget came from Jenny, another dear and steadfast friend. "Moaners, please call me—if you just want to cry. Please don't leave me out. I want to be here for you. I love you." I listened to it over and over again, but I would not allow myself to call her. I felt guilty as I listened to the message. Why was everyone so concerned? Why were they all able to cry so easily?

What is the protocol for someone newly diagnosed with cancer? How am I supposed to act? How do I comfort others?

When Jenny didn't hear from me, she called Eric. He walked into another room. "Yes, I appreciate the phone call, but this is still shocking. She really doesn't want to talk to anyone. She seems fine though."

I wasn't fine. I was terrified. I wanted to crawl in my bed and pull the covers over my head, hoping it was just a nightmare. I did a really good job of covering my fear of the unknown. At a young age, I learned the art of faking it until it goes away. Iv'e learned since then, until fear is faced straight on, it will never go away. I didn't want to be a prisoner of my past and allow the poison that had penetrated my brain to continue to consume me. I decided I had a couple choices. I could either curl up in bed, withdraw from friends family and life, and drown myself in self-pity—or I could learn from the experience and be constant and true to all I believed in. I chose the latter. I felt I was being watched over in so many ways. I felt the love of my family and close friends. I knew my journey was going to be the hardest thing I had done. Looking back, I can see it wasn't the hardest trial I have gone through.

What is a normal life? I felt like we had conquered so many trials throughout our marriage, but there was never any relief. I was finally in a place where I felt safe. I loved my job, working out every day, and being involved with the youth of our church. Life was exactly how it should be. I started to ask what I was supposed to be learning. Patience? Faith? Endurance? Love? All of those are awesome attributes, but was cancer the venue to teach me? Quite honestly, I didn't want to learn about cancer. I had a marathon to train for.

I hadn't broken down or cried and I felt bad when other people cried because I didn't know how to comfort them. I wasn't feeling what they felt. The tears wouldn't come. When they finally did, was I going to really have a meltdown? Hopefully, it would be in private.

I knew I needed prayers. In my heart, I felt comforted, but something was missing. This was not a reality I had time for. If I hid my fear, surely this would all go away. As much as I didn't want this to consume my every thought, it did. Not a minute went by that I didn't think about this villain, growing inside of me.

Walking through a mall one day, I looked in the eyes of every woman I passed and wondered how many of them were walking around with breast cancer but weren't aware of it. The waiting between my original diagnosis and the second opinion was insufferable, but I really   believed this was a simple error when reading the scans. The Mayo Clinic was a reputable hospital. They would surely give me the thumbs-up … I really felt this was all a mistake.

Just before Haleigh and I went to Hawaii, I decided to join the blogging world. I've always loved journaling and felt it was a great way to share life stories. After the cancer diagnosis, I started to blog my feelings regularly. It was easier than writing. It was also easier for Eric and my children to send people to my blog instead of being on the phone and constantly answering questions. I was raw and unscripted when I wrote; for people who were close to me it was difficult to read; for me it was a release I needed to get me through some hard days and nights.

For the first few weeks, I was in shock. I wanted to protect my children; no child likes to see a mother cry. If I could just be strong, they'd see it was not going to be a big deal. It would be over before they knew it, and life would be back to normal. I always believed Eric would be the one who would get sick or need my help. His dad and all of his siblings had heart issues. Since Eric's aunts, uncles, and father had heart issues, I assumed he would too. I've always been in good physical health, eaten right, and exercised.

As I was facing the villain, I wondered if the Lord was trying to teach me to rely on   others, especially my husband. I wondered if I had done something to deserve this. Maybe I hadn't kept my part of that agreement Heavenly Father and I had made. He was supposed to get me safely out of that toxic house I grew up in, and I would follow Him. I racked my brain, wondering where I went wrong. What could I have done differently?

The cancer had been growing in me for years. The Mayo Clinic called several times and requested all the labs, notes, and scans from the original doctor. I asked Blake if he would like to drive me out to the Mayo Clinic. I wanted him to see where I would spend a lot of my time while he was gone on his mission. I thought it would help him to have a visual, but I was completely wrong. He agreed to drive me to Mayo, but he refused to talk about it.

I asked, "Do you have any questions or anything you'd like to know?"

"Nope."

I asked if he'd like to come in with me, and he shook his head. "I'll wait in the car."

It didn't take long, and we were on our way home. I was really worried about him. How could he focus while he was on his mission? He'd always been a sensitive mama's boy. He was raised with three sisters and no brothers. He quickly learned how to respond to women's feelings and hormones. I worried so much about him leaving in a few weeks. I wanted to spend time with him to help ease his pain.

After weeks of waiting, it was finally time to go to my first appointment at the Mayo Clinic. I was a little nervous, but I was grateful that Eric was there with me. The night before we went, I told him the waiting was the hardest part. I was ready to get going and move forward. I wanted to get the cancer out of my body.

Tuesday, August 18, 2009

We left the house nine thirty to make the drive to Mayo Clinic in Scottsdale. Eric and I went to the third floor to check in at ten thirty. The reception area was like a bank. We waited in line until the next teller was available to check us in. We filled out a ton of paper work. We walked to the breast clinic, where we met the surgical oncologist.

I was impressed with Dr. Pockaj's knowledge. We spoke with her for about forty-five minutes. I had to go through more testing and have an MRI. I was especially grateful since it was a second opinion. It seemed natural that they would want to do their own testing. One of the things that Dr. Pockaj wanted to order was a genetics test. I needed to get the history from both sides of my family for the test. It was going to help determine if I had the BRCA gene.

Not wanting to face my mother, I asked Sonya to call her. There was no way I could call Mom. I couldn't deal with her, nor did I want to hear her voice. Sonya told me she was cooperative and actually showed some emotion, hearing my diagnosis. Eric told Sonya that he did not want my mother to call or visit me in the hospital. A visit from Mom was the last thing on earth I needed.

I called my birth father's oldest sister. Aunt Nana knew all the cancers on his side of the family. She was so easy and fun to talk to. Aunt Nana has always been special to my sisters and I. She was the oldest daughter, and my birth father was the oldest son in the family. She wanted to keep a connection with us after Mom and my birth father were divorced. When I called her about the family history, she just cried and said how sorry she was.

Friday, August 21, 2009

Eric and I went to the Mayo Clinic for a follow-up appointment. They wanted me to have an ultrasound because of something they found on the MRI. The ultrasound confirmed that I had another lump in the right breast and one in the left breast. *Three lumps? Both breasts?* We would not know if they were all malignant without a biopsy. The news was really hard to hear.

Eric and I walked silently to the car. I was trying so hard to hold in the tears and not be a big baby. When I looked over at Eric, he was crying. This was my first breakdown, and we shared it together. We embraced, and I said, "I just feel so bad for you. I don't want you to go through this. I am so sorry. I never thought this would be something we would experience."

He looked at me and said, "I'm going to be with you every step of the way. I will hold your hand through the good and the bad. We can survive this together."

When we arrived home, there was a gift on the table from a friend. She was a cancer survivor and knew the feelings I was experiencing. The framed gift could not have come at a better time. I needed to hear it.

What Cancer Cannot Do

Cancer is so limited … yet in all these things
It cannot cripple love
It cannot alter hope
We are more than conquerors through Him who loves us
It cannot corrode faith. It cannot destroy peace
For I am persuaded that neither death nor life,
It cannot kill friendship. It cannot suppress memories
Nor principalities nor powers, nor things present, nor things
to come, nor height, depth

It cannot silence courage. It cannot invade the soul …

Nor any created things, shall be able to separate us from the love of God

In cannot steal eternal life, it cannot conquer the spirit Which is in Christ Jesus our Lord.

Monday, August 24, 2009

The Mayo Clinic is an interesting place to observe people. While walking from my car to the concourse level for check in, I noticed most patients were carrying their patient itineraries and studying them intently.

I was going in for a biopsy on both breasts. All I knew was to check in at eight o'clock. My people-watching skills kicked in full force as I contemplated. Why are they visiting the Mayo Clinic? Were any of them there for the same reason I was? I looked into some of their eyes and wondered what their journeys were. To this day, I have pen and paper in my purse and write what I observe. When I get home, I quickly write in my blog or journal so I do not to forget the fresh raw feelings I experienced.

While I waited, I read an article entitled "The Influence of Righteous Women" by Dieter Uchtdorf, a German aviator and religious leader:

> I hope women throughout the world—grandmothers, mothers, aunts, and friends—never underestimate the power of their influence for good, especially in the lives of our precious children and youth! They must begin in their own homes. They can teach it in their classes. They can voice it in their communities. Because their potential for good is so great and their gifts so diverse, women may find themselves in roles that vary with their circumstances in life. Some women, in fact, must

fill many roles simultaneously. I invite you to rise to the great potential within you. But don't reach beyond your capacity. Don't set goals beyond your capacity to achieve. Don't feel guilty or dwell on thoughts of failure. Don't compare yourself with others. Do the best you can, and the Lord will provide the rest. Have faith and confidence in Him, and you will see miracles happen in your life and the lives of your loved ones. The virtue of your own life will be a light to those who sit in darkness.

I was inspired. Reading this made me want to be a better woman. It helped me understand I am being the best I can as I live my daily life with all its challenges. I have the potential to rise above earthly circumstances. My name was announced over the intercom, and I went for the biopsy.

Cheryl was a petite nurse with a lot of compassion and spunk. This was the beginning of learning the standard operations at the Mayo Clinic. Cheryl handed me a hospital gown and asked me to undress from the waist up and keep it open in the front.

Dr. Lincoln came in and explained what was going to happen. I took my right arm out of the gown and put it over my head as he began the exam. The needle core biopsy was guided by an ultrasound. He and Cheryl watched on the ultrasound screen as he guided the needle to the spot that needed to be biopsied.

First, they sterilized everything, including my breast. Then they deadened the area with several shots from a needle. An incision was made where the needle would go. He said, "You will hear a pop. Don't be alarmed." The needle plunged into the breast and grabbed a piece of tissue four times on the right side. The anticipation of the pop was far worse than the actual penetration.

On the last shot, he hit a blood vessel, and it started shooting blood in a stream. It took about forty-five minutes to get under control. He and Cheryl had to trade off putting all of their body weight on my breast to get the bleeding to stop. This was not fun. With my arm up over my head, my fingers were asleep by the time we were done. Dr. Lincoln felt so bad. I assured him I was ok and this was not his fault. We then started the same procedure on the left side.

After we completed both breasts, it brought me to tears to bring my arms down. By the time I left the Mayo Clinic, I felt like if I had been in a frenzy of violations. These people were so accustomed to squeezing breasts, poking, probing, and intense examinations. Although they were compassionate and kind, it still felt like an infringement on my privacy.

Arizona has two Mayo Clinic campuses. I had to be at the Mayo Hospital in Phoenix for an appointment with Dr. Magtibay, a gynecology oncologist and surgeon. It was time to undress from the waist down. I've always been uncomfortable with gynecology appointments. Even at forty-six and four children, it wasn't any easier. Dr. Magtibay was very compassionate and knowledgeable. He advised me it would be best to have the hysterectomy at the same time I had the mastectomy. I knew I would have some decisions to make. A hysterectomy seemed radical and nothing I wanted to even think about.

By the time I arrived at my car, I had already made my decision. If I was being forced to lose both breasts and my hair, there was no way I was considering a hysterectomy. It meant   losing all of my femininity. I was totally confused and not ready to face the inevitable.

"Undress from the waist up and put on this gown. Undress from the waist down and put on this gown." I heard those orders so many times. I felt vulnerable and alone. I walked out to my car trying to comprehend the horrible things that were about to happen to me. There was no way I could keep it a secret. I did not want it to be a secret. I was ready to see prayer work at its finest.

After my appointments and procedures, I sat in my car with my head perched on the steering wheel. I tried to gather my thoughts and received a text from Haleigh: "Good luck today, Mom. I love you so much."

I started to cry. I couldn't stop. I read it over and over again. Tears dribbled down onto my shirt. My children were going to be affected. They already were. I wasn't quite sure I was handling this appropriately. Was there a book on parenting your children after being diagnosed with cancer? Could I endure this with grace?

On the long drive home, all I could think about was being strong and being courageous. I'd failed in so many ways as a mother. I was completely out of my comfort zone. I began to feel isolated. How could I console my children if I didn't have the stability or physical strength myself? Amazingly enough, even at my age, I still hadn't realized my potential as a woman of integrity and faith. It was time to take responsibility for my own actions. It was time to let go of the past, begin to understand who I was, and not be who I thought people wanted me to be. It was time for me to turn all the burden and hurt over to the Lord and let Him teach me how to overcome this hurdle with agility and confidence.

Over the next few weeks, I met with a plastic surgeon. Dr. Peter Kreymerman gave me some hope. I loved the simple way he explained my options for reconstruction. He took out a pen, drew a picture on tissue paper, and exposed my breasts again. I was beginning to feel some guidance; another fantastic doctor was on my team.

He said, "Your breasts are sisters—not twins." He explained just because you are diagnosed with breast cancer in one breast does not mean you will necessarily be struck with cancer in the other. Therefore, it was not necessary to have a bilateral mastectomy unless symmetry was what I was looking for. Dr. Kreymerman was easy to communicate with and answered every question.

"Are you married?" I asked. I'm pretty sure he wasn't ready for that question.

"Yes. I was just married a few months ago."

I added, "You should wear a wedding ring." I continued "If I was your wife, what option do you think would be the best?"

He said, "Well, first off, I don't wear my wedding ring when I'm in clinic sometimes   because I come straight from surgery where I never wear it for obvious reasons. To answer your question, if my wife were in the exact situation as you, I would recommend nipple sparing with expanders."

I chose to go with Dr. Kreymerman's suggestion, and this is how he became my "nipple repair man." I left his office with a sense of accomplishment. I appreciated him allowing me to joke with him.

When I thought all was good in Cancer Land, I picked up a phone call from Dr. Pockaj. She said the biopsy came back positive for another malignancy. Seriously? Dang you, Cancer. I was losing control, and I was feeling powerless.

When I arrived home, I was grateful to be alone. I lost my composure and cried out of control. I went into the bathroom and threw up several times. It made me sick to my stomach. I just want it out of me. How can I go on like this?

That night, while I was alone in a quiet place, Eric and Haleigh were in bed. I wanted every feeling and every emotion I was experiencing recorded; I went to my blog and began to type. Then I knelt to pray. I was aching from the inside out. I felt like I was being buried alive. I tried to turn all my fears, hurt, and sorrow over to the Lord. I had learned through the years when I prayed, I was never alone. However, I wanted some answers.

At a young age, I learned to feel that awe-inspiring spirit as I knelt to pray; but now I was fighting to understand why I was not being heard and why my prayers weren't being answered. I was trying to be positive. As I prayed, I spoke reverently and quietly.

I was trying to navigate my way through this new test of my faith. I had to believe the dread I was facing—every lonely hour and every tear—were for a reason. I was going through my own Gethsemane. It was agonizing and painful. I knew there was a why in all of this, but when my prayers weren't answered, I felt alone. I begged and pleaded to be rescued from the darkness I was feeling. I have now learned that the Lord doesn't always answer our prayers the way we want them to be answered. He has a plan for us, and I soon learned He definitely had a plan for me one that would take years to understand and be ok with.

Just when I felt like I was losing it—reaching the edge of nothingness—I could feel Him reaching down, taking my hand, and lifting me up. After all was said and done, I hadn't been forgotten. I felt it once again—like I had so many times in my life.

I was learning to rely on a higher power for my comfort. That amenity could not come from my husband (as wonderful as he is) The sense of understanding couldn't come from good friends or my children. I needed to allow Him to catch my fall.

Peace filled my soul that night. I let the exposure of His light and spirit swallow me up. I knew I'd never be the same. The type of exposure I was beginning to experience was deeper than taking my clothes off "from the waist up or the waist down."

Chapter 10
Cheerfully Coping

O nce I was away from the insanely dysfunctional world I was raised in, I believed I had crossed the finish line—and a shield would surround me. I would never have another trial or wrestle with another demon. Looking back, I can see my naive and premature presumptions. I was blessed to be married to a man I adored and loved. I felt he had rescued me. Had our marriage always been perfect? Yes, it had. To me, a perfect marriage is understanding each other. Even if we don't always agree, we've been willing to hear the other side and respect each other's choices as individuals. We have been able to work out any differences by including the Lord in all our decisions. We have learned to forgive each other for our shortcomings and love one another through good and bad times. Is it hard at times? Absolutely! Who said it would be easy? I have always believed anything worth having is worth working hard for.

As we faced this new trial, I wondered if I had enough fight in me to push through it. Would I be able to do it with dignity and poise? Was it possible to be cheerful during this mess? I'm not the easiest person to live with. I'm stubborn. I like things to be my way. I wanted to be kind, patient, and loving, but I knew I would fall short. It scared me. I wanted to have a laid-back, no-big-deal attitude and maintain it during the good times and the bad. In sorrow or in joy, I wanted to be fearless, but I was so afraid of failure.

So many people said, "You know the Lord will not give you any trial He knows you cannot handle?"

My brain always said, "How cliché is that? Seriously?" My heart wanted desperately to say, "I can do this." Then doubt engulfed my thoughts. "Can I be the wife and mother I want to be—with a cheerful heart? Can I find joy in this journey?" I worried all the time about Eric and how he would tackle this new battle. Technical difficulties were going off in my head as I tried to process everything. I immediately turned to my scriptures for assurance:

- "Wherefore, if ye shall be obedient to the commandments, and endure to the end, ye shall be saved at the last day. And thus it is" (The Book of Mormon, 1 Nephi 22:31).
- "Be patient in afflictions, for thou shalt have many; but endure them, for, lo, I am with thee, even unto the end of thy days" (The Doctrine and Covenants, 24:7–8).
- "Behold, we count them happy which endure" (James 5:1).

I love the Olympics and healthy competition. I often research stories of victory and defeat. I read a story on a night I was looking for an inspiring story to help me through a worrisome time. This is a true story about the greatest last-place finish in Olympic history:

In 1968, John Stephen Akhwari represented Tanzania in an international marathon competition. A little over an hour after (the winner) had crossed the finish line, John Stephen Akhwari … approached the stadium, the last man to complete the journey. (Though suffering from fatigue, leg cramps, dehydration, and disorientation,) a voice called from within to go on, and so he went on. Afterwards, it was written, 'Today we have seen a young African runner who symbolizes the finest in human spirit,

a performance that gives meaning to the word "courage."
For some, the only reward is a personal one. There are no
medals, only the knowledge that they finished what they
set out to do." (*The Last African Runner*, Olympiad Series,
written, directed, and produced by Bud Greenspan, Cappy
Productions, 1976, videocassette).

When asked why he would complete a race he could never
win, Akhwari replied, "My country did not send me five thousand
miles to start the race; my country sent me to finish the race."

I loved this story. Not all of us come in first place in everything
we do. However, finishing what you said you would is far more
commendable and impressive to me. I knew getting out of my
own world and serving someone else would help me to finish
my own race. However, trying to intentionally help others when
I could see a need was difficult.

I was feeling physically defeated and drained. I tried to
concentrate on what I could do rather than what I was unable to
accomplish. This seemed to help. One thing I could do was write
thank-you notes. I am a visual person. I needed something to look
at, something to give me hope.

When I was diagnosed, it didn't take long for the word to
spread. We were inundated with cards, letters, flowers, and
gifts from neighbors, family, and friends. I tried to keep up with
thank-you cards, but there was no way I would be able to thank
everyone.

I remember an inspirational talk about a group of children
whose teacher had taught them about giving service to others.
Every Sunday, when they came to church, they could put a warm
fuzzy in a jar to represent a service they had accomplished during
the week. The warm fuzzies were small fuzzy balls from a craft
store. After one year, they had filled the jar. I loved this idea so
much. I decided to start putting a warm fuzzy in my own jar
every time someone performed a service for our family. I didn't

tell anyone about it. I just did it. I keep this jar on my dresser in my bedroom where I can see it every day and never forget.

We have some really good doorbell ditchers in our neighborhood. We would open the door to see salsa and chips or some type of treat, but no one would claim the service. I could see children running down the street, hoping not to get caught. The parents were teaching their children to serve others without recognition. I loved it. This jar of warm fuzzies represented all the people who had unselfishly served our family. Visually seeing this added a level of inspiration and hope. It was the first thing I saw in the morning and the last before retiring to sleep. I now have two full jars with hundreds of warm fuzzies to remind me of how far I have come—and all those who have helped make our journey a little lighter along the way.

A mixture of emotions flooded my head. In the back of my mind was the nagging fact that I would be spending time with my surgeon soon. It was time to get my surgery on the calendar. I was apprehensive, but I felt like the bad news was finally behind us. It was time to move forward. I decided I was going live each day the best I could and be happy. This was an opportunity—not an accident—and I was determined to find optimism one day at a time.

No matter what happened, I decided I would have no regrets. I made a list of people who I knew I had offended or hurt, and I decided I'd go to them individually to tell them how sorry I was. The list was long. Had I truly been a person who offended and hurt feelings? Never purposefully but I do have a tendency to say it like it is. People who know me know if they want a truthful answer, I will always ask, "Do you really want the truth? Or do you want me to tell you what you want to hear?" Over the years, this has gotten me into trouble.

I was busy getting Blake ready to leave and working on the final plans for the wedding. These tender mercies were distractions with a meaningful purpose. Random thoughts about   cancer were constantly running through my head, and I'd have to stop myself go to my bedroom, kneel down and pray, giving thanks for the energy I was being blessed with.

I tried to keep my brain occupied with thoughts other than cancer. I'd think about people who were going through other trials that were so much worse than mine. I often thought about other trials I had endured in my life. Is this new trial because I didn't learn something? Is it a new chapter in my life? It was going to be a new learning experience meant to expand my mind and toughen up my spirit. I pictured myself every day as completely healed from the inside out. This daily meditation gave me vitality to take each day moment by moment and helped me see the good in all things.

Neal Maxwell, an LDS leader, said, "Rather than simply passing through trials, we must allow trials to pass through us in ways that sanctify us." I tried to comprehend the meaning of it for days. It's simply worded, yet it has such depth. My little brain took a while to absorb it all. How can I be sanctified as I allow this trial to pass through me? When will the cleansing come? In my trials, I've tended to leave people out and shut down. This time would be different. I had a will to conquer with grit, and my family became my focus. I constantly reminded myself that I still had a lot of life to live and share.

"He that shall faithfully endure unto the end, the same shall be saved and return with honor to our Heavenly Father" (Mark 13:13)..

I decided I was stubborn and determined to be happy and cheerful in whatever storms were coming my way. I had learned from personal experience that my disposition—and not necessarily my circumstances—determined the greatest part of my misery or happiness.

I believed I was worthy of returning with honor, but it was hard to imagine I would have to put my family through so much to get there. Little did I know at the time, my trials were just beginning to unfold. My intellect and perspective on life were going to change drastically.

Chapter 11

Risk Factors

Tuesday September 1, 2009

*I*t was an interesting day at the Mayo Clinic. Dr. Pockaj explained the surgeries I needed to have. *Surgeries? As in plural?* She wanted me to have all of them in one day, which would mean eighteen hours of surgery. *Eighteen hours of being under anesthesia? I don't think so.* I told her I would have to decline. "My son is leaving to go out of the country for two years. We won't see him during those years. It's important for me to spend some time with him." I also didn't want him to see me after surgery. "My daughter is getting married on November 14. I still have a lot of planning to do."

She was looking at the calendar to find a time for surgery.

I said, "Oh, and my oldest daughter is having a baby in December. She would like me to be in the delivery room with her."

Dr. Pockaj looked at me and chuckled. "What the heck? Who are you?"

We both laughed.

She agreed it would be way too much surgery and recovery with everything I had going on in my personal life. She believed the wedding and baby were more important right now. She explained that I would be having another surgery in five or six months. At that time, we could do the other procedures I needed. She mentioned it would include the hysterectomy. I deposited that little idea in the back of my brain. I was not ready to consider any more than what I was currently coping with.

September 29 was marked on the calendar for my bilateral mastectomy and beginning of the reconstruction surgery. After the surgery, she would be able to tell us more about what stage the cancer was. She explained there were three lumps and two different types of cancers. They know for sure that one of the three lumps were in stage two or three. This seemed unusual to me, but so did hearing the words "You have breast cancer." It didn't alarm me. I didn't have the luxury of worrying about it. Eric and I felt like we were led to an uplifting, compassionate surgeon, and we loved her.

There were so many points of view and warm sentiments coming at us. I heard from people through e-mail, text messages, and social media. It seemed they all knew someone who was cured of this nasty villain by simply drinking this or that, taking this vitamin, or trying that all-natural remedy. The list went on and on. We had remedies left on our doorstep on a weekly basis. I tried so hard to listen and discern, but I fell short in so many times in my efforts. It was overwhelming.

Eric and I decided our answers were leading us to the medicinal path. I've always been open to natural remedies, but not this time. My oncologist has given me the answers I feel are appropriate for my body. My oncologist believes natural and medicinal worlds can coexist. However, I know women who've decided to strictly take the natural path, and a year later, they were back in an oncologist's office—past the point of chemo to help them fight. They ultimately did what they thought was best for them, but unfortunately, their remedies were not strong enough to fight off the cancer cells. They eventually died.

We had clear and precise answers. Whatever path a person decides to take, medicinal or natural, friends and family need to support and love, not judge and criticize. I'm not being negative; this is just my opinion.

The pharmaceuti-cal/governmental world became more clear and precise as I ventured through it. One of my pills was new to the market and designed to help breast cancer patients block hormones. It was not an option for me; I had to take it. Imagine my shock when I went to pick it up, and with my insurance, it would be $300 per pill per day. Without insurance, that sweet little pill was $800 per pill per day. Within six months, it went generic—and is now available for $15 a month. We have been blessed financially, but what about the elderly woman I watched tearfully advising the pharmacist she could not afford it? I helped her pay for it, but I knew I would not be there to help her the next month. Cancer cells are in every one of us. I've learned from research and personal experience that there are methods and resources to help us all avoid those cells manifesting themselves, but there is absolutely nothing we can do about the price we pay for medicine.

Some of the risk factors for breast cancer are obesity, alcohol intake, smoking, starting your menstrual cycle before ten, not having children, family history, and a few others. Two doctors asked if I had any trauma in my childhood. When I heard this from different doctors who were in no relation to each other—one from the Mayo Clinic and one from another facility—it blew my mind. Constant worry and stress are a huge factor for many breast cancer patients. Different cancers have different risk factors. For example, exposing skin to strong sunlight or tanning beds is a risk factor for skin cancer. Smoking is a risk factor for cancers of the lung, mouth, larynx (voice box), bladder, kidney, and several other organs.

Risk factors don't always tell the entire story. Having a risk factor, or even several, does not mean you will get the disease. Most women who have one or more breast cancer risk factors never develop the disease, while many women with breast cancer have no risk factors (other than being a woman and growing older). Even when a woman with risk factors develops breast cancer, it is hard to know how much those factors might have contributed to her diagnosis.

Some risk factors, like a person's age or race, can't be changed. Other factors can be linked to the environment. Others are related to personal habits or behaviors (smoking, drinking, and diet). Risk for breast cancer can change over time (due to factors like aging or lifestyle). I believe my risk factors were family history, trauma, and stress. I have never had a drop of alcohol or a puff on a cigarette. I had never tried any recreational drugs, and I exercised every day. I changed some of my eating habits, but up to that point, I considered myself to be a pretty healthy eater.

According to the National Breast Cancer Foundation 200,000 new cases will be diagnosed each year—and 40,000 lives will be ended due to the diagnosis. In 1960, one in twenty women were diagnosed with breast cancer. Today, that number has risen to one in seven women. Breast cancer is the leading cause of death in women from the age of forty to fifty-five. The good news is if you are keeping up with your exams and mammograms, they have found 80 percent of lumps are noncancerous. Why is there such a huge difference in the percentages over the years?

I have my own theories, but they are not backed by any scientific testing. There is a debate among doctors and scientist about mammograms. Some think it is adding useless radiation to your body. I believe the amount of radiation you intake for a mammogram is less than the X-rays you allow when you go to the dentist office. If I had not gotten the mammogram when I did, I believe I would not be writing this book. I would be long gone.

I regularly advocate for mammograms and breast self-exams on social media. I've shown my three grown daughters and daughter-in-law how to perform their own BSE (breast self-exam). I advise this be done every month (not during your menstruation). I also believe early detection saves lives. My other theory is that families are far busier than they were when I was being raised. I don't remember eating out like young families do now. We occasionally had a pizza ordered, and I once ate tacos from Jack in the Box, but other than that, my mother cooked dinner every night. Fast food, while convenient, is laced with preservatives and fillers. These are not healthy for our bodies, and they should not be regularly fed to young, growing bodies.

You need to do your own research with reputable books or websites. I got most of my information from www.mayoclinic. com. An even better solution would be to ask your doctor or specialist in the area of interest. I also believe you should always consider getting a second opinion.

Chapter 12

Bilateral Mastectomy

The time for Blake to leave was quickly approaching. He was to report in for his mission on Thursday, September 23, 2009. I promised him I wouldn't cry. I did so well until … he walked away. I saw my little boy walk into the mission training center in Provo Utah. I cried all the way back to the Salt Lake City Airport.

The night before he left, I said, "Please don't worry about me. The Lord will take much better care of you the next two years than I ever could. He will consecrate me with health and happiness. Our family will be blessed for your service. I know you are scared to leave, but it would be much harder on me for you to stay home and watch me go through this than to know you are out serving other people. Never forget how much I love you. I'm so happy for you."

With tears rolling down his cheeks, he hugged me tighter than he ever had. "Mom, please don't send me any pictures. I just want to focus on my mission, and pictures of you bald and sick would be such a distraction."

I said, "Okay, this is your time. I want to respect what you need." I never sent him a picture of me while he was gone. In every e-mail, we talked about positive, uplifting happenings in Gilbert. My son left for his mission at age twenty-one, and as much as I knew living in the   Dominican Republic serving other people was going to turn him into a man I wanted to believe he would always be my little boy.

The days after Blake left were both a blessing and a heartache. I was so grateful he was not around to watch me prepare for surgery. There was a void in our home without him being physically around to hug every day. Blake has always been the best hugger, and he still is. I went into his room every day, sat on his bed, and was reminded of how much I was going to miss him. I wanted to go back in time, hold him a little longer, lower my voice, and listen better. There were times I'd sit in his room and have snapshots of him being born, taking his first steps, playing baseball, going through elementary school, and graduating from high school. I had so many memories, and the time went by so quickly. I wished I could make time stand still.

Eric had pink shirts made that read "Monya's Team" and pink silicone bracelets that read "Live Free." All the family and close friends had them. When other people saw them, they wanted one too. We made them available for anyone and everyone. It was reassuring to see the support coming from people I wouldn't have expected. I think the entire football and basketball team at Highland High School wore them. Strangers came up and asked where we got them. I'd just pull one out of my purse and hand it to them. I still wear my bracelet today. I have the original that is now sun-bleached white.

While the family waited patiently to hear from my surgeon on the day of my mastectomy Eric took a picture of them all wearing the pink shirts. He hung it on the wall at the foot of my bed, when I arrived in my hospital room after surgery it was a sight for sore eyes.

Monday, September 28

In just a few hours, most of what I have always defined as femininity will be taken from me. Forever, never to return. In a few months, I'd have to face a hysterectomy. I contemplated this over and over again. I was forced to think about having a surgery I never imagined having. I was overwhelmed by what was happening to my body. I began to cry. It was difficult to work through. It all happened so fast. Trying to comprehend all that had transpired in such a short time was intolerable. *How would my family react? How would Eric ever see me the same again? What about the scars?*

Eric and Jeremy gave me a beautiful blessing the night before surgery. I appreciated every word of it. But the bottom line was my breasts were being removed the next day. Not by my choice, cancer had decided it for me. After Jeremy left, I asked Eric for some alone time. I lay back on Blake's bed, and tears rolled down my cheeks. I'd never been so afraid. The possibility of leaving my family and never seeing Blake again was extremely bothersome. Did I do my best as a mother? Do they know without a doubt that I love them more than life itself?

I trusted my surgeon and had no fear in her skills. I sincerely liked her. I knew she had performed this exact surgery on many women. The problem wasn't about her it was about my self-doubt. I couldn't embrace the awareness I had, knowing a part of my womanhood was being taken from me. Would I want Eric to look at me? How long would it take for me to look at me? I tried not be vain, but I wanted to look pretty for my husband. I didn't want things to change. We still had not talked about the loss of breasts, the scars, or the side effects of intimacy.

It was hard for me to sleep the night before surgery. I ran my fingers through my hair, knowing my long blonde hair would be gone soon. I touched my breasts, knowing I would never have feeling in them again. When I woke up, it'd be time to go to the Mayo Hospital and begin a terrifying journey. I was not ready. I still had housework to do and wedding plans to get done.

I read the first letter from Blake. He was trying so hard to learn the language. He only had two hours of sleep one night because he wanted to study. It was the most beautiful letter and testimony in English and Spanish. His words calmed me and made me feel better about what I would be facing. Blake has so much faith, and on the days when I was feeling like my well needed to be filled, the people in my life filled it up with words of encouragement. Blake's faith would fill the void when I needed it. I knew the Lord would pick me up and carry me when I wasn't strong enough to do it myself. I knelt next to Blake's bed and instead of asking for anything I thanked Heavenly Father for all that I had.

Tuesday, September 29, 2009

There was not much conversation between Eric and me as we drove toward the unknown. We arrived at the Mayo Hospital and checked in at 7:30. The waiting was the hardest part. Once we checked in, we took our seats in the corner. The room was full. I looked around at every single person and wondered what type of surgeries they were having. Once agin I found myself wondering *Did any of the women have breast cancer also?* The waiting was insufferable. I had a panic attack.

I'm not sure Eric knew what to do. He tried to calm me down as I paced back and forth, crying. I couldn't breathe. It was if my heart was about to burst from my chest. My hands were shaking. I was startling the patients who were waiting. Finally I was taken back and given some medicine to calm my nerves. Dressed, prepped, and marked up with the purple marker, it was time. I kissed Eric and said, "See you later."

I know he wanted to cry. Instead, he smiled and said, "I love you. Everything will be okay."

I was horrified. I calmed myself down by closing my eyes and thinking about Blake. Tears rolled down my cheeks as I was wheeled into surgery. "Everything will be okay." I held onto Eric's words as I drifted off into sedation.

Friday October 2, 2009

After being told by Dr. Pockaj that the cancer had spread, I was ready to go home for the weekend. I held Eric's hand, crying off and on the entire way. I just needed time to cry, be sad, disappointed, and try to internalize all the news. *"I'm sorry. The cancer has spread"* were words that cut like a knife. I was so blinded by the marathon I wanted so badly to run that I forgot about the potentially life-threatening disease I was facing. My heart had been like a stone for years, but it was time to feel something, anything.

I will returned to the hospital on Monday to have the lymph nodes removed and the port placed. *Lymph nodes? Port?* Two months ago I had no idea what those were. It was like going into a deep dark hole—and I wasn't sure I could find light at the end of it.

I spent two nights in the hospital and came home on Wednesday. The drugs took a toll on my body and made me nervous. I didn't like not having control over my own body. Taking a shower was difficult with the drains hanging out of my body. If one dropped, gravity would pull them from my skin—and it hurt. I finally found a way to holster the drains by setting them on the bar in the shower.

Raising my arms above my head was excruciating. Washing my hair was quite an event. I eventually sat in the shower and took my time. I used my left hand to gently wash my hair and rinse it. I was careful not to disturb the drains.

Chapter 13

Becoming Teachable

I will never forget the day I got brave and stood in front of the mirror naked. It took me a few seconds to stop shaking and drop the towel. This would be the first time for me to really examine my breasts. It all happened in slow motion. I stood still, heard the towel hit the tile, lifted my head, and walked toward the mirror. My eyes had a hard time focusing on anything but the scars.

Tilting my head to the side, I examined the nipple sparing Dr. Kreymerman had performed so skillfully. I realized they might not take. I was sure the newly sewn on nipples would not last through the burns of radiation. I ran my finger across the line of stitching. I inspected the indention where breasts used to be—the ones the stepdad used to joke about.

Looking at my chest was horrific. It was just like the pictures I'd seen on the Internet. I examined the port in my chest. Another scar. How can I ever let Eric see these? Would I still be beautiful to him? Eric is so kind. He will never tell me the truth. I stared into my eyes and watched as tears streaked my cheeks. Why is this happening to me? I'd give anything to be a normal boring housewife and mother. My life was forever changed. I was allowing the scars, at that moment, to define me. What would happen when I lost my hair? How would I handle the stares? Would I wear a wig? All these questions were running through my mind as I stood naked in front of the mirror with pure transparency. I've heard time heals all wounds, but at that minute, those wounds were deep. They were much deeper than I thought I could live with. Every insecurity I'd ever felt came rushing back to me. I was so conflicted.

I was allowing the bitter words of the stepdad to predict my future. I needed to get out of the dark place and cope cheerfully. I closed my eyes and tried to think of Vi. How would she handle this moment? Did she have these times of doubt? Oh, how I missed her. I would have to rely on my own strength to catapult me over this next hurdle in my life.

The lymph node removal surgery made it difficult to have full use of my right arm. Lifting anything was really painful. I quickly learned I had taken for granted being able to wash and blow dry my own hair or put on my makeup. Reaching for anything above my waistline was impossible. I no longer could sleep on my side. I missed not being able to go to the gym.

Working out had always been a daily routine for me—like drinking water or sleeping. When I started physical therapy a week after surgery, I was determined to do exactly what I was told. I wanted to push myself as hard as I could physically handle. The mind is a powerful tool that we don't always access properly. I told myself—no matter how much it hurt—I would get through it. I would be back in the gym to work out with my friends. I set realistic goals to do just that. There were days when I felt exhausted, but I pushed through. Soon, the therapy was paying off. The drains were getting in my way. I was looking forward to seeing Dr. Kreymerman and getting them removed.

When Dr. Kreymerman said they needed to stay in another week. I seriously wanted to kick him. "PK, I need these out. I can't stand them, and they are getting in the way of moving forward."

With a sigh, he replied "I am your doctor. Do you trust me?"

What a dumb question. "Of course I do. Why?"

"Those drains are not coming out for another week. They still have a significant amount of fluid draining into them."

I left his office a bit disappointed, but I knew Dr. Kreymerman had my best interests at heart. I genuinely cared for Dr. Kreymerman and his PA, Heather Lucas. I appreciated how well they took care of me. I looked forward to my visits, knowing I may get some comic relief.

I still got emotional when I thought about my life and the turn it had taken. It was important to breathe deep and know it was okay to feel sad or disappointed in my situation. I've always been able to recognize trials, deal with them, and get over them by knowing a better day was coming. Through prayer and personal meditation, I could get myself back to a spiritual place and cope. I allowed myself to cry at times but chose not to stay in that realm for too long.

Eric and I had a discussion about the proper protocol when we saw each other crying. I told him if he ever came home and found me in tears, it was okay to just let me cry. I promised him the same. When I saw him shed a tear or two, I would not ask questions. He needed to cry sometimes too. He didn't understand what I was going through as a cancer patient, and I certainly did not understand how it felt to be the caregiver for someone going through a potentially terminal illness. We just had an understanding—no questions. We just let the crying happen. It was empowering and fair for both of us. I talked to a friend about how he and his wife handled it. Sheldon was my only friend who could truly understand what I was feeling. He was diagnosed with cancer in 2008. I remember when I found out, thinking it was so sad.

A year later, I found myself wanting to connect with someone who had been through some of the emotions I was feeling. Sheldon said he did not understand what his wife Kit was feeling either. She didn't understand what he was going through. I believe the role of a caregiver is so critical. I'd rather be the one going through the trial than the one watching. Kit and Eric were incredibly strong and patient care givers.

Talking to Sheldon always put things into perspective for me. I love Kit too and knew she was trying her hardest to understand the journey Sheldon was going through. I've learned the human eye cannot understand another's agony, accomplishments, or defeat unless they have had the experience themselves. I didn't understand the caregiver role, and neither did Sheldon. We discussed our children and wanted to do all we could to comfort them. I will forever be grateful for the tender mercy of Sheldon in my life. I finally had someone I could relate to. I looked forward to Sundays when we would have a few minutes to talk about our week ahead.

I had a really hard time sleeping, and it was becoming an unbearable problem. I started experiencing extremely sharp pains in my right breast. When I would lie down or turn over in my sleep, it felt like a sharp knife slicing down the middle of my breasts. It took the breath out of me, and it sometimes lasted up to thirty seconds.

Eric didn't know what to do for me—and there was nothing he could do. I had to work through it myself. Once I'd get myself up, I was so afraid to lie down again. I'd go downstairs and sit up straight on the sofa to sleep. That approach didn't work either. I sometimes would not get to sleep until three thirty in the morning or later.

I finally had to call Dr. Kreymerman's office. Heather called me back right away. She told me the pain was normal. The expanders were settling into place. She was so sympathetic and understanding as I blubbered.

Becoming teachable is a process of learning line upon line, precept upon precept. When I embraced this process, I could convert thoughts and feelings into actions. When I don't follow up, the promptings eventually diminish, making it difficult to rewind. I was beginning to discover that becoming teachable meant changing my attitude and reassessing wants versus needs. I soon realized that everyone has something I can learn from. Every day, there is something new to learn. No matter if it is positive or negative, I learn and benefit from my experiences.

Chapter 14

Dr. Northfelt

October 19, 2009

*I*met my oncologist for the first time. My friend Tamy went with me. She's been my friend for more than twenty years. I was so glad I took her with me because she knew what to ask. She'd been a scrub nurse and took great notes.

When Dr. Northfelt came in the room, I instantly felt comfortable. He made me feel like I was his only patient. We talked for about twenty minutes, asking and answering questions. I was worried about all our questions, but he let us know none of them were silly or insignificant. In fact, he loved that we asked the questions we did, and he was thrilled with Tamy coming.

A lot of what he had to say was not pleasant. He told me that my attitude was everything. "Do you want to know statistics?"

"No. I just want to do what is best for me. I trust you. When you tell me what to do, what is best for my body, I will do it. I really don't want to know statistics."

He smiled and replied, "Perfect. You have a great attitude." He told me the cancer was in stage 3C*. Dr. Pockaj had told us the same thing. Even with the research I had done, I had no idea what that meant for me individually.

He explained to us that some people who have stage four live twenty-thirty years after a diagnosis, and some who have stage one or two die because they give up and don't want to fight.

I am a fighter, and he could see it. I would be one of the survivors!

He excused himself and stepped out of the room to get the rest of my team of doctors and the physician assistants I'd be working with over the next year.

I looked at Tamy and asked, "What do you think of him?"

"I love him."

Tamy and I had tears in our eyes as we discussed how warmhearted he was toward me.

When he came back in, he introduced me to the team. They were all awesome. He knelt down in front of me, looked me straight in the eye, and softly touched my knee. "When you go home tonight, I want you to tell your family that I am the doctor who is going to get you through the next forty years—not the next few months. In forty years, you will be alive and thriving. I am going to help you every step of the way."

With tears rolling down from my eyes, I told him I was going to hold him to that promise.

He gave me a huge hug. On his way out the door, he hugged Tamy a little tighter and a little longer. He whispered, "I'm glad you were here for Monya today. You had all the right questions."

Chemotherapy would start on November 16. That was just two days after Kaitlyn's wedding. Dr. Northfelt agreed I needed to enjoy the wedding. He thoughtfully and kindly told me I would lose all my long blonde hair. Oh dear. Was it time to enter the side-effect world? He assured me that I would not need to worry about most of them.

I had kept myself in good shape, but I could not ignore the feeling of my stomach coming up to my throat as I studied and pondered the potential side effects from chemotherapy. I had friends who never had any side effects and were happy to let me know. In retrospect I wish no one had told me not to expect the side effects. I experienced almost every one of them, and I still have lymphedema and neuropathy. Lymphedema is an abnormal collection of high-protein fluid just beneath the skin. Many cancer patients are diagnosed with secondary lymphedema. This type of lymphedema occurs as a result of damage to the lymphatic system. Specific cancer-related surgeries such as surgical resection of melanoma, breast, gynecological, head and neck, prostate or testicular, bladder, or colon cancer may require the removal of lymph nodes. These surgeries put patients at risk of developing secondary lymphedema. Radiation therapy can also enhance the risk of lymphedema. When you see a person with a sleeve on an arm or leg, more than likely, they have lymphedema. I always wear my sleeve when the swelling begins. When I go on an airplane, the high altitude kicks the swelling up a notch too. Peripheral neuropathy is a result of damage to your peripheral nerves. It often causes weakness, numbness, and pain in your hands and feet. It can also affect other areas of your body.

Your peripheral nervous system sends information from your brain and spinal cord (central nervous system) to the rest of your body. Peripheral neuropathy can result from traumatic injuries, infections, metabolic problems, inherited causes, and exposure to toxins such as chemotherapy.

People with peripheral neuropathy generally describe the pain as stabbing, burning, or tingling. In many cases, symptoms improve, especially if they were caused by a treatable condition. Medications can reduce the pain of peripheral neuropathy. For me, the neuropathy during chemo was excruciating. It felt like I was walking on glass. Many times, I crawled to the bathroom. My hands tingled and made it hard to hold heavy objects; even the smallest of handheld items hurt to hold.

In the process of killing cancer cells, chemotherapy drugs can also damage other rapidly dividing healthy cells, such as bone marrow and the digestive tract. The results may include:

- Hair loss. Every bit of hair on my body fell out.
- Loss of appetite. Eating was limited to soup and oranges.
- Nausea and vomiting. Hugging the toilet every day was my reality.
- Diarrhea. Sometimes I threw up at the same time.
- Mouth sores. The sores were very painful and lasted throughout chemo.
- Fatigue (due to fewer red blood cells). I have never been so tired and gotten less sleep in my life.
- Increased risk of bruising or bleeding (due to fewer blood platelet cells that help blood clot). I experienced bruising easily.
- Increased vulnerability to infections (due to fewer white blood cells that help fight infection). Wearing a mask was normal for me.
- Heart damage. My heart had some skipping, but I did not get damage to my heart.
- Nerve damage. Neuropathy feels like the nerves are being exposed to the air. When I walked, it felt like needles in my feet. My fingers became numb, and it felt like my nerves were being exposed to the air.

Eric and I attended a class the Mayo Clinic offered about side effects of chemo. While I was in the classroom, I could feel myself wanting to vomit. The information was overwhelming.

Eric was affected by the info too. He had huge tears in his eyes.

I've always had compassion for cancer patients, but I'd never really researched or experienced it with anyone close to me (other than Vi). I am the type of person who will pray for those who I know need the extra prayers, but I have a hard time talking to them. I've always been worried I'd say the wrong thing. Since my diagnosis, I've become much more open. I talk to people all the time at the Mayo Clinic. I ask them what type of cancer they have and let them know I care about what they are going through. For me, a simple hug says it all. A smile tells me that you are thinking of me. When you say, "I'm praying for you," I know you are because I feel it. Sometimes less is more, and nothing needs to be said.

I understand the effects of cancer are different for everyone. Maybe some people don't want to talk about it. I also understand that feeling. I sometimes just want my life back. Now I know that my life will never be "normal" again. For the rest of my life, I will see an oncologist. I feel blessed to be in the care of Dr. Northfelt and his assistant, Maryann. They will forever be a huge influence for me.

When I hear patients complain about their oncologists, my heart aches for them. Dr. Northfelt is the one I want on my team until the day I leave this life. There have been times I have emailed him with concerns and he is always compassionate and quick to respond. I appreciate and love this about him.

I asked Dr. Northfelt how long it would take for my hair to fall out. He told me about three weeks after my first treatment. In less than a month, I would have no hair.

On the way home, I said, "Tamy, I remember saying to someone who was going through chemo, 'Don't worry. It will grow back.' Just so you know, that is an ignorant thing to say to a cancer patient." She smiled and said "Perspectives change when you are the one living through the trial huh?" I agreed and wished I had never said those words to someone.

I know those words were not something I wanted to hear. I realize people will think those thoughts are vain or assume "it's just hair." However, unless you go through it, it's hard to say how you would react. I used to think the same thing.

When Dr. Northfelt told me I would lose my hair, I really had no reaction. He warned me that losing hair is sometimes the most devastating part for women. I ignored it at the time. I didn't think hair defined a woman. However, no matter how much I didn't want it to be true, I came to accept the fact that I had the same thought process as most other women. Hair was part of my identity. We usually get to choose how to style our hair, I've seen woman with curly hair, straight hair, long or short hair some choose spiky or blue hair. Mine was soon going to be gone and I hated that I didn't have a choice, cancer decided that for me.

*I have heard stage 3C from both doctors, but I have also seen on my medical reports that it was possibly 3A.

Chapter 15

The Bra

November 12, 2009

I drove for the first time in a month. I felt like a teenager who had just gotten her driver's license. I loved what little time I could get out and enjoy fresh air without cancer lingering around like an unwanted guest in my body. I constantly encouraged my mind to think positive thoughts. I imagine myself on a 150-mile bike ride again. I looked forward to the freedom of movement. I couldn't wait to feel the wind in my hair and the sun on my face as I ran. Allowing myself to think positive gave me hope for my future. On days when I needed a lift, those thoughts fueled me to endure one more day. Looking too far into the future was literally something my mind could not do. I lived day by day.

There was nothing better than opening up the mailbox and seeing a letter addressed to Mami y Papi Williams. Handwritten letters from Blake were few and far between. Missionaries don't always have time to sit and write out their feelings. I will treasure those letters forever. When the letters came, I couldn't get down the road and into the garage fast enough. I'd leave everything in the car, run as fast as I could to a quiet place, and read it several times before filing it away with the others. Every letter or e-mail I received from Blake would inoculate me until the next week.

Inevitably, he explained how he loved the Dominican Republic. The language was not always easy for him but he was trying hard to learn and communicate. He loved the food. He loved the Dominican people, and he wanted to help their families. He loved to teach the gospel to random people on the streets, and the best thing was that he wanted to be obedient. I could see all of these things, even the little ones, as graceful, thoughtful mercies from the Lord. My son was being blessed for his service.

My heart was so full. Words couldn't explain to anyone how grateful I was. The mention of Blake's name made me tear up. He was listening to the spirit and remembering the blessing he was given the night before he left. He was promised in the blessing if he was obedient, his mom would be alive when he returned home. He would be able to share with me the wonderful stories and experiences he was having. The next two years would bring such light and strength to our family as we watched him grow and turn into a man. I was looking forward to the day when he would hug me again.

I was sure I would look back at this time in our lives fondly, remembering how much we were consecrated. I was so happy that Blake had found a place where he could feel protected—a place that allowed him to build his faith. He is a strong person. His strength came from turning everything over to the Lord and trusting Him. He was learning to do this, especially on days when he had a hard time moving forward. God lifted him and carried him—just as He had me.

A month after my last surgery, we started getting the itemized bills from the insurance company. One of the items struck me as very funny. When I got out of surgery, they put an ugly white bra on me. It had huge pieces of Velcro down the front—something you might see at a dollar store. Well, that ugly bra costs me over $200. I was shocked—and even more shocked when I noticed they threw the first bra away during my second surgery and gave me a "fresh" one. Finding some humor in this, I decided to rhinestone it. Tamy, Kayla, and I had a lot of fun blinging it out with rhinestones.

Even in the rough times, it helped to laugh. It had been a rough week for me physically. I was certainly not looking forward to an expansion. During my mastectomy, Dr. Kreymerman inserted expanders. It's basically a balloon inserted under your chest muscle, which is gradually filled with saline over a period of several weeks or months. The gradual inflation of the balloon stretches the skin and tissue over your chest to make room for an implant. The filling process is very painful. For a week, I could barely move my arms without extreme pain.

When I went to my appointment with Dr. Kreymerman, I decided to give him a laugh. I hoped he would laugh and not think I was some kind of weird patient.

The nurse guided me to the exam room and asked me to put on a gown. Under the gown, I fastened on the newly rhinestoned bra.

Dr. Kreymerman came in and said, "So, how have you been doing?"

I told him it had been a tough week. Knowing chemo was coming soon, I was having some anxiety. We discussed that for a moment, and he told me he was sorry for what I was going through.

I told him I had received one of the itemized bills from the hospital. "Before I take off my gown, I want to tell you something." I could tell he was worried about what was going to happen when I took off the gown. I told him I could not believe the price of that ugly white bra he had put on me after surgery.

He looked at me and said, "Don't you have insurance?"

"Yes, but still $200 for that ugly bra. Are you kidding me?"

"I know. That seems expensive."

I laughed. "Well, I think if they are going to charge that much for those bras, they should be runway ready."

He looked at me with a smile. "Oh no. What did you do?"

I took off my robe, and he started to laugh. "Let me go get Heather to see this."

It was so fun. For a couple of minutes, it felt good not to think about cancer and just laugh at something silly.

Kaitlyn and Brian's wedding was sneaking up on me. So many friends and family helped us to prepare. I didn't want anything to go wrong. The wedding reception was held in our backyard. I'd always dreamed of having my children's receptions there, and it was time for our second. Looking back, I believe her wedding was the one I was most prepared and organized for. A few nights before the wedding, I couldn't sleep. I had so much on my mind. My breasts were aching. The pain never went away, yet they were numb to the touch. When I drank something cold, I could feel it going down my throat. The cold sensation penetrated the holes where my breasts used to be. It was like having a brain freeze in my breast cavity.

My mind was wandering in all directions: the wedding, the baby, the chemo. I ran my hand across my chest and felt the port that would feed poison into my body. I started to cry. I knew I couldn't control any of it, and I wondered again how it had happened to me. The emotional part of this journey was getting to me.

Sometimes when people would talk to me, I didn't hear them. The words were coming out of their mouths, but I processed nothing. It happened a lot, especially when someone started to tell me about their aunt's friend's sister who either died recently from breast cancer or didn't do chemo and was cured. Many times, I said a quiet prayer as I wandered off, hoping not to offend. I was scared and wanted only positive information about what I had chose be fed into my brain-the negative whether positive for them or not was hurting and discouraging.

On the day of Kaitlyn's wedding, all I wanted was for it to be happiest night of her life. I wanted the reception to be a cancer-free night with no villain talk. I knew I had a long road in front me, but Saturday, November 14, was Kaitlyn and Brian's day. I wanted to enjoy it. I needed them to look back fondly and remember it as a beautiful day. I wanted Brian's family to enjoy their time before, during, and after their son's wedding. I made a sign that read: "This is a No-Cancer Talk Zone." I posted it at the entrance to the reception. I also posted on my blog, I did not want to engage in conversation about cancer with anyone on that night. Surely everyone could understand. This was a special night, not about me but dedicated to Kaitlyn and Brian.

Kaitlyn loved her reception. I was pleased with what a beautiful night it was. I loved seeing everyone having an exceptional evening. Brian told us over and over again that he thought the backyard looked "magical," and he was right. It was extraordinarily enchanting. When the night came to an end, I was so happy for them. Kaitlyn had chosen a remarkable man. We love Brian.

On Monday, November 16, I woke up feeling okay, but I was not ready for chemo to start. Eric and I decided it would be too difficult for him to actually watch me being injected with chemotherapy. We asked Tamy if she could take me. I wanted to experience it without Eric there to see if I thought he could handle it.

When Tamy arrived to pick me up, I had already started pacing. The anxiety was more than I thought was reasonable. The tears would not stop.

Eric hugged me and reassured me that it would be okay. I was so mad. I threw everything in my purse as hard as I could. I kept saying, "I don't want to go. I just don't want to do this." The tears were flowing. "I'm serious. I don't want to go today—not any day."

With every hesitant step I took toward the car, I could feel my body, heart, and mind fighting me.

Tamy said a prayer when we got in the car. It helped me feel a bit of relief. We were introduced to our chemo suite where we would be sitting for the day.

My nurse came in to access my port. It was quite different from the needles used to draw blood from your arm. A Huber needle is used for ports. A Huber needle has a long, beveled tip that can go easily through your skin as well as the silicone septum of your implanted port's reservoir. These needles can be used for chemo, antibiotics, saline fluid, or blood transfusions. Huber needles come in different sizes, depending on what you are being treated for. The strong, tapered point of a Huber will be less painful than a non-tapered needle, and it will slice through skin and silicone clean.

When my nurse Kathy showed me the size of the needle, my eyes about popped out of my head. It looked like the circumference of a nail. It was suggested I put some numbing cream on my port an hour before accessing it. I used Emla cream.

Kathy whispered, "Take a deep breath when I count to three. One, two three." I took a deep breath, the needle was inserted, the port was accessed. There was some pain—but nothing more than a needle stick.

The first medicine going into the IV was bright red and very toxic. I could feel its warm poison spreading throughout my body. I closed my eyes and imagined the men I love in my life entering the port together. They were searching for cancer cells to kill. Eric enters first; he is cautious and reserved as he makes sure the coast is clear. He motions for Blake, Jeremy, and Brian to enter. Together, they fight the battle of their lives. Knowing it would be a long day and the war would last for months, they began fighting.

It was the beginning of a long progress. It was hard, and I hated every step of it. I was told not to let anyone use the same bathroom as I used because the chemo was so toxic. I needed to flush twice. That night, I felt tired and weak. The poison came out the same color it entered, and I urinated red. I never knew pee could look so pretty!

The next day, I went back to the Mayo Clinic for a Neulasta shot. It helps the bone marrow make new white blood cells. When certain cancer medicines like chemotherapy are used to fight cancer cells, they also affect the white blood cells that fight infections. Neulasta is used to reduce the risk of infection while you are being treated. I had to return every week the day after chemo treatments to receive this shot. It is sometimes referred to as the "day-after shot."

I was told my bones and muscles may ache, but some people do not experience it at all while going through chemo. I was certain I would be one who would not feel that pain. The next morning, I woke up with aches and pains I'd never experienced before. Every muscle in my body hurt. I'd take my medicine, and it would help—but then all I did was sleep. Since there are only three bathrooms in our home, I had a private one (Blake's). I spent a lot of time in that private bathroom. I didn't want to eat anything. Everything tasted like metal. I knew I had to eat some protein to keep up my strength. However, it didn't last in my system. Everything was purging from my body. I spent days sleeping on the sofa from the medicine or hugging the toilet.

I was ticked off about all the times people said, "Chemo would be a breeze." That's another dumb thing to tell people diagnosed with cancer. It's different for everyone. I was not one of the blessed ones, but I knew it was the beginning of the end. I was going to get through this. I was going to fully heal, and I was never going to take my life for granted—or anyone in it—again.

I have the highest respect and love for those who have gone through it and for the caregivers of cancer patients. I don't think people realize how hard it is on them. My family had to watch the pain I was in and listen to the gut-wrenching sickness—and they couldn't do a thing about it.

Chapter 16

Losing Hair—Attitude Is Everything

*D*r. Northfelt affectionately pointed out that my hair would start to fall out between the second and third round of chemo. As a forethought, he advised me that many patients with long hair cut it short before it started to fall out, which was sometimes less traumatic. With that advice, I made my final appointment with Kara. She had been cutting and styling my hair for ten years. I trust and love her. There was no one else I wanted to cut it, but I also knew it would be hard for her to watch.

Before my second chemo treatment, I made the appointment. I warned Kara how difficult it might be on me. As the appointment became closer, I was getting anxious, sad, and afraid. The fear of losing my hair had been lingering in my mind. I had been able to push it away with the distraction of Kaitlyn's wedding. Eric mentioned cutting my hair several times, wanting to tactfully discuss it with me. I pretty much cut him off at the knees when he brought it up. It was agonizing to allow myself to think about losing my hair. So many women have let society and the media dictate the meaning of feminine. I have learned that my hair has never—and will never—define who I am. Having big or small breasts says nothing about my character. However, this day was emotional. There was no sparing of tears. All week, I had been extremely sick. I didn't have much time to think about my hair. The side effects of chemotherapy hit me like a brick.

On the dreaded day of the haircut, I had my support team with me: Sonya, Kayla, Haleigh, Jenny, and Tamy. Kaitlyn would have been there, but she was off enjoying her honeymoon—as it should be. My body was so weak. I hoped my spirit would not give out on me. I was so angry; cutting my hair was not my choice.

Once again, the cancer had taken control. I was feeling very vulnerable. The pain I felt in my heart was starting to dribble out as tears from my eyes. Hoping and wanting it to go away, we drove to Kara's. There had been so many times I'd driven to Kara's over the years, but this was the first time I resented going to see her. My heart was beating a million miles a minute. Jenny was talking to me, and I was trying to keep up with the conversation. I felt like I was in a Charlie Brown scene where the teacher was speaking but the words were garbled.

I was thinking about Aunt Pam making chocolate and coconut cream pies for Thanksgiving. I'm not sure why my brain chose pies as a diversion. I've trained my brain, during hard times, to distract me with my happy places or people but never food. I enjoyed the thought of family being together for Thanksgiving. It was a quiet, almost reverent feeling to walk into Kara's salon. As I took my seat, it felt as though I was going to the electric chair. We began talking about hairstyle options. I couldn't hold back the tears.

Kara's eyes welled up with tears. I felt so bad. I didn't want to make anyone cry. I looked around the room, but it was too late. They were all crying.

"I'm so sorry. Thank you for going through this with me. Please help me make a decision. These are my options: Cut it short and have fun with a different style for a week or two (and maybe the transition will be easier when it all falls out). Shave it off and start wearing a scarf or wig (the transition would be obvious)."

My mind was being bombarded, and it was hard to make a judgment. As a group, we agreed to cut it short and enjoy it for a couple weeks. Kara pigtailed my hair, preparing for the dramatic cut. I stared at myself in her mirror, wondering when I lost control of my own decisions. Had I allowed the hatred for my dad and anger toward my mom fester so long it manifested itself into cancer? Had I allowed hurtful words to poison me like a serpent slowly kills its prey?

The first cut through the pigtail echoed loud in my ear. I will never forget the sound of my hair being chopped. The second ponytail was just as dreadful. In two quick clips, it was done. Sobbing, I had no control over emotions. With every snip, it became apparent that this was not about losing hair. It was an uncontainable, sorrowful weep becoming louder and stronger with every cut. I was letting go and surrendering. I was releasing a cancerous tumor of hatred I had felt for so long. I was beginning the sloughing off of layers, which would take years to completely heal.

Tamy was holding my hair in her hands, carefully placing it in a plastic bag, and trying not to lose one piece. Kara faced my chair away from the mirror and began to cut and shape it into a masterpiece only she could have accomplished. My girls were tearful. I could feel their compassion. I'm sure it must have been difficult for them to watch.

On our drive home, I wondered, What will Eric think? I had about fifteen missed calls from him. When I got home, he hugged me and told me I was beautiful. He told me everything I needed to hear and then some. I was learning to appreciate Eric. I've worked with cancer patients since then and discovered that some patients are not affected by their bald heads. For others, it is painfully hard to process.

I heard people say, "Well, just think ... you get a new set of breasts." Most people do not want to offend, but some people simply don't know what to say and vomit all over themselves. For me, it was much better for people to ask how I felt about it instead of telling me how I would react or how they thought they would deal with cancer if it were happening to them. Other breast cancer patients gave me their opinions, which did not coincide with how I felt. The bottom line is everyone's journey is different because we are all individuals who are experiencing life in our own ways.

Sheldon was always there to talk. I asked him if it was hard for him to lose his hair. I'll never forget his reaction. He smiled, rubbed the top of his head, and replied, "This is different for a man. We can be bald and get away with it. I'm sorry you have to experience the loss. I imagine it is much different for a woman."

He certainly brought that into perspective; for him, the baldness was no big deal. He was intuitive enough to know how sensitive it might be for me. Over the next few years, I loved sharing moments with Sheldon. I looked forward to talking to him. It was easy. He was the one who understood. Sheldon was real, and he understood when family, friends, and Eric couldn't. I wished Eric had a friend to share with too. Caregivers experience cancer in a totally different way, which I didn't understand. Sheldon and I didn't quite know how to comfort our spouses.

I began my expansion process during chemo. Tissue expansion is a process that stretched my remaining chest skin and soft tissues to make room for the breast implant. Dr. Kreymerman placed a balloon-like tissue expander under my pectoral muscle at the time of my mastectomy. Over the next few months, through a small valve under my skin, he used a needle to inject saline into the valve, filling the balloon in stages.

This gradual process allows the skin to stretch over time. I visited with Dr. Kreymerman every other week to have the saline injected. I experienced some discomfort and pressure as the tissue expanded.

After the tissue is adequately expanded, Dr. Kreymerman will perform a second surgery to remove the tissue expander and replace it with a permanent implant. The day after expansions, I literally wanted to slap someone—namely Dr. Kreymerman. My breasts were in extreme pain. I couldn't get any relief. When I coughed, they ached. When I breathed, they ached. When I moved on the sofa or bed, they ached. I couldn't turn over in bed the throbbing constantly reminded me of the villain in side of me.

November 23, 2009

On my second round of chemo, I tried so hard to think about Blake, his mission, and all the blessings I had in my life. This usually helped me endure the first hour. I'd get worn down when the red dragon hit my organs hard. My mind was all over the place. I turned on the TV for a distraction, but it just made me more agitated. Chemo was going to make sure I felt every drip going into my body. During the chemo infusion, I got text messages from Sonya. "I love you. I'm here for you." My sisters are incredible, and I love them so much. Their support comes from the heart. Eric and Haleigh called me and said, "I love you." Kayla texted, "I love you." There was no better distraction. I let them know I loved them too.

As Tamy and I made the long drive home from the Mayo Clinic, my hair started falling out. I ran my fingers through it, and chunks of hair fell into my hands. I looked at Tamy and apologized for ruining her clean car.

Without hesitation, she responded, "I want it in my car."

Seriously? Who says that? Tamy does. She loved me and was a great strength to me through all of my treatments. I was trying to be fearless, and Tamy was helping me laugh my way through it. The moment I got home, I ran to the mirror. I wondered what losing chunks of hair would look like. It was just a little thinner, but

I saw no obvious holes or bald spots. I decided to take a hot bath and get all my crying out. I sobbed, hoping no one in the house would hear. I needed to feel anger, sadness, and annoyance. I walked around with a baggie and scooped it all in so I could record it. I put each strand in a baggie and marked them day one, day two, etc. I still have the bags.

I was asked a lot of questions about hair loss. These answers may not be the same for every cancer patient, but this is what I experienced.

How long after chemo does it take for the hair to start falling out?

Dr. Northfelt told me it would be about ten days. It took up to three weeks for complete baldness.

Does all the hair on your body fall out?

Yes (eyebrows, eyelashes, underarms, legs, and anywhere else you have hair).

When does it grow back? Will it grow back the same as before chemo?

For some people, it will start to grow back after chemo treatments. For those who need radiation, it will start to grow back before radiation starts. And then it may start to fall out again because of the dosage of radiation. As far as how long it takes to grow back, everyone is different. My hair grows quickly. It took about a year before I could actually style it.

As more and more hair fell out, my head became sore. I often laid my head on Tamy's lap as she gently stroked my hair and massaged my temples. My skin was so tender. The hair follicles seemed swollen or weakened. I was not dealing well with the hair loss and did not expect the pain. After six days of carrying around baggies to collect my hair, I made the decision to have it shaved. My hair was constantly falling in my face, in food, and on the sofa, bed, and floor. I made an agonizing call to Sonya, and she agreed to shave it.

Sonya got out the clippers and shaved my hair as short as we could. She listened to me cry. I watched as the last of my hair fell to the ground. It was past the point of reality for me. Once I got myself composed, Haleigh put a scarf over my head and wrapped it up cute. Once again, the strength of family helped me overcome a huge milestone in my journey.

I was spiritually overcome with love from Heavenly Father. Kayla was induced on Saturday December 12, at 5:00 a.m. The thought of holding a new baby in my arms by Sunday was exciting. When I went to my chemo treatment on Monday, I would close my eyes and remember the moment he was born. Recker was born on Monday, December 14, 2009, just past midnight. This beautiful miracle would help me get through the next week. Little did I know at the time this little angel of ours would help me endure more than just a week.

I was trying to maintain a positive attitude during the transitional time of losing my hair. A friend told me a story she read about a woman who woke up one morning and noticed she only had three hairs on her head. She decided to braid it, and had a wonderful day. The next day she woke up, looked in the mirror and could see she now only had two hairs on her head. She thought about it and decided she would part her hair down the middle, the rest of her day was happy. The next day when she woke up she only had one hair on her head, she decided it would look best in a ponytail, and she had a fun, fun day. The next morning there was not a hair left on her head she looked at herself and said "Yeah, I don't have to fix my hair today."

Do you love it? Attitude is everything. I will not give up. This battle is not fun, short, or glorious, but I will fight and win. Deuteronomy 4:30 says, "When thou art in tribulation, turn to the Lord thy God." John 16:33 says, "In the world ye shall have tribulations, but be of good cheer." John 16:20 says, "Your sorrow shall be turned to joy." Romans 5:3 says, "We glory in tribulations, knowing that tribulations worketh patience."

We all have trials, and some seem harder than others. No matter what they are, I think we need to own them, recognize them, and accept our limitations while experiencing them. When we own them, we learn from them and become stronger. The tragedy would be to become unteachable and unlovable because of the trial. The bald head I was learning to live with was not perfect or beautiful, and I felt insecure in so many ways. The stares of people not knowing what to say made me uncomfortable. I was struggling with my own identity—mentally, spiritually, and physically.

My reality became authentic as I watched a mother hush her child when she pointed and asked "Mama, what's wrong with that lady?" The mother quickly took her child by the hand and hurried off. I vowed to never do that to a person with a disability or a bald head. I didn't blame the child or the mother. I knew how I felt, and I didn't like it. At one point or another, that child will surely run into a person with a disability or someone who looks different than the average person. It would do the world a great service if we'd take the time to talk to the person with the disability, acknowledge them with a smile, or discuss with our children how this person is not any less than you or me. He or she just looks different or acts different because of an illness.

Chapter 17

Chemotherapy

The weeks and months were dragging on, and the chemo treatments were exhausting. I was feeling weak and depressed. Chemo was knocking me out physically, mentally, and spiritually. I couldn't sleep, and the throwing up was debilitating. My body ached. The sleep deprivation was encouraging my body to mentally shut down. I did what I knew would help. I prayed for strength. When the energy didn't come, I started to doubt myself.

Depression is an awful emotion. It sometimes drained me to the point of believing I was not going to make it. There were days I just wanted to give up. Dr. Northfelt told me about people who gave up hope, and I didn't want to do that. Slowly but surely, I was losing strength. Just thinking about going back to chemo made me want to scream. I literally despised going. I thought about it every day. I also wondered how I could get out of it every day!

Everything had changed so quickly. In just one year, I had dealt with extreme happiness, uncontrollable tears of pain, heart-wrenching sadness, and complete self-doubt. I felt ugly at times, unaccepted in my own skin. The self-consciousness of having no hair was one of the toughest emotions I dealt with. Never before had I been so raw with emotions. It was liberating and healing for me to blog.

When I was feeling well enough to attend church, Sheldon approached me and said, "You look beautiful." For some reason, I believed him. I believed my bald head was beautiful. He was bald and had pale skin. I knew he was hurting, but he was kind enough to say those three words. I had heard those words from others so many times, but I normally just heard them say the words out of obligation. Sheldon meant it; I could feel his sincerity. He understood. Sheldon's cancer had come and gone several times. He and I often discussed the things people said. I relied on his wit and humor to get me through another week. I'm not quite sure he shared the same feelings about me. He was strong, and I felt so weak.

Eric and I decided in the beginning of this journey to take time once a month for ourselves. We wanted to be away from the worries of the world, away from the Mayo Clinic, and away from the constant reminder of cancer. We would take little trips to our condo in Mexico. I walked on the beach and took my hat off—just me and my bald head. The ocean and it's beautiful rippling waves has always given me a feeling of serenity. Many times I'd sit on the sandy beach of Rocky Point Mexico breath in the fresh air and feel the strengthening power of His love for me.

I walked the path where I normally ran. I imagined myself taking off running, sweating, and dodging a few sand traps. It was walking the beach I had my first ten-mile run on less than a year ago. A few tears fell from my eyes as I thought about the sand and that run. I had hit a sand trap that was difficult to get out of. I was on a whole new journey. I listened to the waves softly hitting the shore. The cool breeze was soothing I was grateful for a moment of reflection. It would get me through another round of chemo.

Dr. Northfelt warned me I would have four rounds of Taxol. It was a new chemo drug for people with breast, ovarian, lung, bladder, prostate, melanoma, esophageal, and other tumor-related cancers. The side effects were dreaded and unpleasant. I also had to deal with the expanders being filled by Dr. Kreymerman. When he first explained my options, I was completely confused. I was amazed then—and I still am—at the knowledge and talent of Dr. Kreymerman. My mind was so full of uncertainty, and I really did not care what he did. Who cares what my boobs look like right?

I've been asked several times about the different options I was given. I chose the expanders.

DIEP flap is a procedure that is very popular among surgeons and patients. DIEP stands for the deep inferior epigastric perforator artery, which runs through the abdomen. A DIEP flap procedure uses fat and skin from the lower abdomen, but it does not require removal of any muscle. The skin is grafted on your chest where your breasts were. When Dr. Kreymerman drew that picture on the tissue, my brain checked out. Are you kidding me? Another scar as a constant reminder on my abdomen?

Dr. Kreymerman also told me I was a good candidate for nipple sparing. During my mastectomy he removed my nipples, and then he stitched them back on after Dr. Pocki removed my breast tissue. Not every woman qualifies for nipple sparing, and I'm not sure what the qualifications are. This is something that should be discussed with your board-certified plastic surgeon before you schedule your mastectomy. I qualified, and I chose nipple sparing.

During the expansion process, Dr. Kreymerman was compassionate and gentle with me. Most of the time, I endured it well, but as time went on, I asked if I could stop the expanding process several times. The pain was not worth it. I wondered why I decided to do this. Suddenly "boob-less Monya" sounded inviting. Dr. Kreymerman was supportive, but he always encouraged me to finish what we started—and I did.

January 14, 2010

On my birthday, I woke up feeling awful. The poison from chemotherapy treatments was becoming unbearable. When I wasn't throwing up I was sleeping.

Eric woke me up and said, "Wait until I show you what the ladies from church made for your birthday." When I saw the quilt, I broke down crying. I was so overwhelmed. On each square, the women wrote personal notes. I had no idea so many woman knew me—let alone liked me. I was surviving some days because I wanted to be like those women. They were strong, worthy, incredible wives, mothers, and friends. How could I ever thank them for the time and effort it took to make this quilt—and for the message behind it? I think everyone wants to feel loved and needed. I felt the love from each of the messages. I knew the words would give me strength. I still read them when I am feeling down. It is honestly my favorite gift I have ever been given.

Dr. Kreymerman called to see how I was doing. It was surprising since most doctors don't take the time to do that. He cares about his patients even when they are not seeing him on a regular basis. I was not due to see him until chemo was over, but I was still experiencing extreme pain in my breasts. He said the aching would not go away until after chemo and radiation. Because I had no tissue in my breasts and the lymph nodes under my arm had been removed, I was not like "normal" women. My breasts were extremely hard, which caused pain, especially if I used my arms a lot. The low blood cells were being divided and taken away from my body, and there was nothing to protect my breasts from the aching and pain.

The side effects were beginning to ravage my body. I had a lot of pain in my hips, back, and legs. Lying on the bathroom floor next to the toilet was not my idea of fun. Knowing this was going to get worse before it got better, I was determined to make the best of it. While lying on the floor, I'd look at pictures of Recker, Blake, and places I wanted to visit. The distraction kept a bit of happiness in my soul and was something I could visually look forward to.

Food tasted like metal, and I continued to lose weight. Sometimes oranges were the only food I would eat for a week. Women from the church took turns bringing meals into our home. I was so grateful for them since Eric and Haleigh needed to eat something more than just oranges.

The aching in my breasts seemed to never go away. It was agonizing. I was eventually diagnosed with capsular contractors, chronic insomnia, fatigue, and arthritis in my lower back—all side effects of chemotherapy.

Capsular contractors is a response of the immune system to foreign materials placed in the human body. Medically, it occurs mostly in context of complications from breast implants and artificial prosthetics. For me, the expanders had hardened through chemo and radiation. I seriously thought if my grandson were to bump his head on my chest it was going to split his head open. My breasts were somewhat disfigured and felt like granite. I cried myself to sleep many nights because the pain was so severe. The pain medicine was not strong enough.

One day while I was grocery shopping, pushing the cart made my breasts ache. I left without buying anything. As I walked from Costco to my car, I let the rain hit my face. It was a private moment that brought me to tears. I imagined the rain was tears from heaven, letting me know He had not forgotten me. Cancer is a monster—a villain that preys on the weak. I felt as though the cancer had been preying on me from a young age. I would have spiritual uplifting moments, and then thoughts of inadequacy would flood my mind like a vicious beast. I sabotaged myself over and over again. My brain was in a full-on civil war.

I have always treasured a good dream. I love them and always write them down in my journal as soon as I wake up so I can remember every detail. I usually dream about the things I love and my family. Several times during chemo, I dreamed of heaven. In heaven, I am with Viola. It was hard to believe twenty-five years had passed since she had left this earth.

Heaven is beautiful. When I passed through the veil from earth to heaven, Vi was standing there with her arms open (like always) and ready to hug me. I will always remember her piercing blue eyes and rosy cheeks. She was wearing white and the most beautiful smile I had ever seen. Our embrace was soft and tender. I wasn't quite sure if it was the place that was so beautiful or if it was the peaceful feeling I was experiencing that was beautiful. We sat under a tree, and she asked me about Eric. Was he progressing in his life? Was he helping me to endure this trial with compassion? Was he a good father and husband? She took my hands and looked at them.

With tears in her eyes, she said, "These are the hands that protect, hug, and watch over my grandchildren. These are the hands that comfort my son, and these are the hands that have served others."

Vi told me how much she loves me and how grateful she was that I married her son. She asked me about each of my children. We laughed as I shared experiences about them. I told her that motherhood was the best and most rewarding experience. I love being a mom. I told her Kayla has her smile, Blake has her eyes and incredible love for the outdoors, Kaitlyn has her spunk and laughter, and Haleigh has her heart. She and I walked and talked for hours. She shared sacred things I recorded in a journal.

We stood in the most beautiful garden I had ever seen. The greenery was stunning. She gracefully wandered through the garden, showing me everything as if it was her task in heaven to oversee it. I was looking everywhere for Ray. I wanted to get a hug from him too, but he was nowhere to be found. She explained that this would be our last meeting for a while. This drew tears to my eyes. I didn't want it to end. She asked if I had done all I could on earth to be the best I could be. Had I forgiven those who had hurt me? Had I served others enough? Her last question left me confused. "Do you unconditionally love everyone you come in contact with? Your time on earth is not yet finished." We shared the best hug ever. I said, "I love you." When I woke, I couldn't wait to tell Eric about it.

He said, "Why don't I ever dream?"

I had no intelligent answer for him. I came to the conclusion that he didn't need to dream because he lived a dream life. He maybe even took for granted something I had hungered for my entire life. Just as he could never conceive of living in a home where disrespect, humiliation, or abuse took place, I craved living in abundance of love like he did.

Marathon Dreams

In the course of the chemo treatments, I spent a lot of time watching television. Every show I watched had a series about someone with cancer. I wished my life resembled one of the TV shows. One of the girls on the show found out two months ago she had cancer. She had already gone through chemo, lost all her hair, had radiation, and was now running for a Senate spot. And her hair had grown back! I wish it were that easy and fast! Actually, I'm glad my life is real. I needed to feel something. I needed to learn something. Hollywood was not where I wanted to learn it.

During chemo, I also had dreams about running. It felt so good. I realize most people would think that was a nightmare. I was so determined to fight the villain and be able to exercise again. During one dream, I was not in a race. I was just running in a park. I was happy, and all my hair was in a ponytail. I was keeping up pace and enjoying the scenery around me. The trees were beautifully green, and there were flowers along the path. I could see weeds and tumbleweeds ahead, and I wondered how I was going to get around them. They were completely covering my path. I tried to run straight through them, but they were so thick. The thorns were cutting my legs.

The tumbleweeds were starting to disappear, and the path was clear again. I ran back on pace, and the sky was bluer than I had ever seen it. Up ahead was the biggest mountain, and I wondered if I could make it to the top without being pushed from behind. As I started to conquer the hill, tears filled my eyes. I could feel the pain. I wanted to give up, and my legs were burning. You can't do this. The tug-of-war in my head was becoming oppressive.

When I was able to push the negative thoughts away and clear my mind, I was looking down from the top of the mountain. I was living in the moment, knowing and appreciating where I had been. I was looking ahead and knowing the road was still long and hard. I continued to run. I was now in a race. I stepped up my pace and smiled at the road ahead of me. I couldn't see the finish line, but I knew I'd finish if I continued. It wouldn't be easy, but it would surely be worth the fears and doubts.

Those dreams meant so much to me. Fighting the villain was my marathon at the time, and it was tough. I didn't get a chance to train for this marathon. Instead of being angry, I looked at it as a challenge. I needed to get healthy again and finish what I'd started.

I'd never noticed people running like I did during that time. It seemed like every time I left the house, all I saw was people training and pacing themselves. Were there really that many people who loved to run like I did? Sometimes I was jealous. I'd look the other way as if they weren't there. Other times, I'd honk and wave to encourage them. I was still climbing the mountain and trying my hardest to get the view at the top, but I also realized there were more tumbleweeds ahead.

The most uncomfortable and painful nights of my life were during chemo. My legs, back, arms, and feet throbbed. I felt like I couldn't get any relief. I had taken all the drugs prescribed to me and still nothing seemed to help. My bones and muscles were in so much pain. Eric held me in the fetal position and listened to me cry. "I don't want to do this anymore. I wish it was over." He didn't know how to respond. He'd rub my legs until I fell asleep. Thank goodness for him and Haleigh. They both rubbed my legs and held me, not knowing what to say. I'm not sure I could watch someone I love go through that. Haleigh was so sweet, she often came into my room and just lay on the bed next to me.

The pain from neuropathy was not easing up and I often thought "How am I supposed to run a marathon if this does not go away.?" I chose to believe it was just a little side effect for the moment. When people asked me how it felt, it was difficult to explain. My bones and muscles ached 24/7. When it hurt the worst, the pain penetrated my mind and body. It felt as if the nerves in my fingers, feet, and legs were exposed to the air. If you've ever had a tooth removed and the nerve was exposed to the air, the pain is sudden and quick. This pain was non-stop, and it felt like the nerves were constantly exposed.

At the Mayo Clinic, I asked the PA if I would be able to run or exercise again. She said, "Most people are okay with just walking a little every day. Give yourself a break. You're very sick."

"Seriously? I'm not most people—and it's good therapy for me."

"No running. Your bones are brittle. They could break more easily than you think."

I thought, I will run again someday—and I will cycle again someday. I felt as if it was just temporary. The pain reminded me of how hard I needed to fight to get my body healthy again and be the athlete I was born to be. It would have been easy to give up and say I'd never be able to do those things again, but I knew I would. I don't believe I was being naive about the situation; I was being hopeful and optimistic. Holding on to thoughts and dreams of running again got me through some of the hard days.

After what seemed to be never ending months of chemotherapy my last day was a milestone, and it was exciting. I wasn't feeling well, but I was ready to conquer. It was a cloudy, rainy day. After hours of chemo being pumped into my body, the nurse came in and told us the drip was over. I hugged all the nurses and thanked them for the service they had rendered me all of those months. Then something incredible happened. We saw a beautiful full rainbow like the one Haleigh and I had seen in Hawaii. The only difference was instead of the beginning being a little hazy the end of the rainbow was a bit blurry—much like how my life felt at the time. I still had some work to do before my journey was over, but the sight was the hope I needed to get through radiation.

I was in complete peace at that moment. The chemo was over, and the end was in sight.

Chapter 18
My Smile Experiment

I decided I would make eye contact with as many people as I could and smile at them. At the Mayo Clinic, a blind man with his guide dog got into the elevator with me. I smiled and said, "Hello. How are you today?"

He answered, "I am terrific. How are you?"

I smiled and replied, "I am terrific too. Have a great day."

"You as well," he said while stepping off the elevator.

In the beautifully decorated waiting room, I looked around and saw so many sick people. Everyone was in his or her own world. I wondered why each person was there. I overheard the lady sitting next to me telling her friend that it was the end. She did not have much time left; she was dying. My eyes filled with tears as I listened to her worry. When the intercom sounded her name for chemo, off she went. I looked into the eyes of a lady in a pink breast cancer baseball hat; her hair was gone. I smiled, and she smiled back with a nod.

When they called my name, I smiled at my nurse. Liz smiled and gave me a hug. "How are you? Why are you walking so slowly?"

I explained the neuropathy, and she hugged me with a sincere strong embrace. I teared up again. Although I usually chose to start conversations, I didn't always like what I had to tell others about my health. There were times I didn't want to hear what they had to say either. I was being intentional with the people I connected with, and it was emotional. They are in my world, and they understand what it feels like to hear those awful three words: You have cancer. I don't have to explain. I don't have to hide my feelings. A smile, a teardrop, and a nod are understood and acceptable.

I had an hour and forty minutes until my next appointment. I went to the cafeteria to grab some lunch. I listened as a lady yelled at the employee working the grill. She was upset with him because he forgot to give her a pickle. She looked at me and shrugged her shoulders, wanting me to agree with her disgust. I just smiled, and she looked away. As I walked to my seat, I saw a man and woman sitting together. She was in a wheelchair and couldn't hold her head up. I smiled at him, and he smiled back.

I watched couples and friends discussing their medical issues over lunch. One couple never talked or looked at each other. Did they forget how to communicate? Maybe they were dealing with too much and didn't know how to talk about it. How did I get here? Why didn't I take time before my diagnosis to seek out these people who needed to be heard?

In that room, there was not one person who was my age or younger. I watched an older couple sharing lunch. He was careful to split the cheesecake right down the middle and give her half. He made sure not to start his lunch until he knew she was comfortable and happy. I watched them laugh and enjoy their time together. I watched the Mayo volunteers walking around the tables, asking if they could take trays or if anyone needed water. A man walked by with a long ponytail. I wondered when mine would be that long again. I saw angry people, sad people, people with tears, and some with hair and some without.

I was restless and nervous about the lab results and my life. When I entered the building, I could smell ailment. It hit me when

I stepped off the elevator onto the third floor. I could smell it and hear it in the lunchroom too. It made my stomach turn. What am I doing here? I drank my water, but I threw away the salad, which was not as good as I thought it would be. Everyone in the room was sick and frail or caring for a sick loved one. A young guy walked in and sat close to me. His entire face was bright red. When he turned to look at me, he had a huge tumor on his face. For the first time since my diagnosis, I felt what so many others probably felt when they saw me bald. I wanted to look away, but I smiled instead and gave him a nod of reassurance. I was grateful for life, my life, my journey, and all that I had been through to bring me to this moment in the Mayo cafeteria. I knew I was where I was supposed to be. I was becoming who I wanted to be. That boy was probably in his twenties. Why was he alone? Where was his mother? Was the beginning of his journey or the conclusion?

I stared at the clock, and it moved so slowly. There were still twenty minutes until I could check in to visit with Dr. Northfelt. I felt like my life was moving in slow motion. I could hear the ticking of the clock. I always lived in a fast world. The diagnosis had slowed me down and given me cause to reflect on what was truly important in life. My family was my main priority; helping and serving others was another. In public, I look around at all the people who are healthy and try to remember what it felt like to be carefree with my time and body. I'd get jealous sometimes. This is the journey of my life, and I am learning to accept it. I left the cafeteria to check in for my appointment with Dr. Northfelt.

The nurse called my name, and I went with her.

Dr. Northfelt walked in with a big smile and said, "Your labs came back normal."

"What does that mean?"

"It means something we are doing is working. I had a whole new regimen lined up for you to start this week. I rarely see anyone go from such low white blood counts and platelets to normal that quickly. I am very pleased."

I left the office that day with a deeper love for Dr. Northfelt. I trust him. The first phone call I made was to Eric, and we both cried happy tears. It felt good to be empowered with good news. I love Dr. Northfelt for so many reasons. I believe he is my oncologist for a reason. Just mentioning his name makes me tear up. I know he has a tremendous load of patients and may not share the same emotions I do. I'm okay with that too. He is not here to love me; he is here to help me. He will never know the courage he has instilled into my heart. The compassion he shows always makes me feel as though I am his only patient. He reminds me of Eric's mother; she had the same ability. That precious gift is rare. I cherish it and believe those who are blessed with the capacity to make others feel special like Dr. Northfelt are meant to be in my life.

With all the good news, I was feeling hopeful and really happy. I was going to enjoy the time. I was blessed with great doctors, incredibly supportive friends and family, and a serenity of peace. I did not know the future, but I was in good hands with people who loved me. I was allowing myself to trust, especially with the male doctors in my life.

I came to some conclusions after my smile experiment: Most people smiled at me no matter what their condition, and some even indulged in conversations. The ones who didn't quickly looked away as if I had just injected them with some deadly disease. I'm not sure what makes people happy or sad, but I know it's curable because it's a choice. The hard times can make you stronger or defeat you.

I decided to be happy I was not the lady in the wheelchair who will never walk again, the woman who will never hold her head up to see the beautiful blue sky, or the man who walks with a guide dog. I couldn't imagine being the young man with the facial tumor. I will never again take my legs for granted. If you can walk or run with no pain, you are blessed. If you can hold a baby in your arms or write a letter, you are blessed to have hands and arms that work. If you have a mouth, you can smile. Maybe your smile will save the life of someone who is feeling depressed or lonely. There are so many around us who think they have nothing to live for. Every day, we all make a choice when we wake up. Am I going to be happy and serve someone else today? Will I waste the day doing insignificant things or being angry about people or circumstances?

At the end of the day, can we say we made a difference today? I want to make a difference—even within the walls of my own home. I look forward to tomorrow; it's a new day to make those changes. Wake up in the morning and do something worthwhile. Close each night by knowing you made a difference. Never let your knees tire of bending—and asking for the help you need.

Chapter 19

Radiation

I entered Mayo Clinic on my first day of radiation and wondered what was ahead of me. Waiting for my name to be called, I talked to a woman who was waiting on her husband. He was having his radiation treatment. Her daughter also had breast cancer two years ago; she told me her hair grew back curly and beautiful. It had been so long since I had hair. I wondered how long it would take. What will it look like?

I heard my name, and my stomach turned. I got up to meet Chris. He would become a major part of my life for the next couple months as I endured radiation. After getting my gown on, I was taken to a huge room. In the middle of the room, a table was connected to an incredibly large machine. It was cold and uncomfortable. I remember the echoing of the vault door closing as they left me. The door was about eighteen inches thick of pure metal. No one could be in the room while I was being radiated. The terror of that door shutting was something I will never forget. It sounded like a torture chamber being locked up. This can't be good. They left me to save themselves?

I now have five tattoos the size of freckles where they radiated. My right arm had to be up above my head. It was painful. I hadn't had my arm above my head for that long since before my mastectomy. With the lymph nodes being removed, it was hard to hold my arms in that position. Tears rolled down my cheeks when I didn't think I could keep my arm up any longer.

The technicians set up my body so all the beams would radiate exactly where they were supposed to. I was told not to move. When the lights went out and the technicians left the room, I felt like I was in a science fiction movie. The huge round machine above my head moved and made noises. Red and green beams penetrated my breasts. The technicians came in and out, rearranging the machine and telling me not to move. The machine rotated completely around my body. The beams radiated each spot a few times. When it was all over, I had been in the same position for forty minutes. It was difficult to straighten my arm and get off the table. My chest and face felt hot and red.

This is one of my journal entries:

I have not slept more than a couple of hours since Sunday night. I have been throwing up, and my stomach aches. I've also lost seven pounds. I'm not completely sure why. It is the worst feeling to stare at the ceiling fan all night just waiting for the sun to rise, three nights in a row. I'm not sure I can do this again; I might go crazy. Since I started radiation, I have been really depressed and lonely. Something inside of me is scared. Today, I didn't want Eric to go to work. I miss him when he's gone. The house is so quiet, and I feel sad. When Eric left for work this morning, I was crying. I told him I want my life back. I pleaded with him not to leave me. I stood at the top of the stairs and cried. "I'm afraid I won't be here for you when you get home. I can't do this anymore." He hugged me and whispered, "You're almost done. Keep fighting." He's always been an optimist in everything he does. But this time, he seriously doesn't understand. I want to die. He left with tears in his eyes "You will be okay. Recker is coming over. He needs you."

Recker saved me that day. His sweet tiny hand gripped mine. His smile filled me with hope. He needed me. I was the caregiver for this darling baby boy. I adored every second I had to inhale his baby smells and listen to his laughter. Having him around kept me from ending my life.

On my fifth day of radiation, Eric was off work and went with me. The radiation technicians took him back and showed him all the machines and let him watch while they radiated me. He said it was really interesting. As a caregiver, it was really hard on Eric. We were both experiencing the journey through different lenses. I worried about him. Constantly trying to be positive was in his nature, but it's not normal. I wished he'd open up to me. Maybe he needed to know it's normal to feel anguish and pain when someone you love is going through cancer treatments. On the way home, I asked how he was feeling.

"I'm so happy I got to be with you today. It seems like they are really taking great care of you."

"No, that is not what I'm talking about. I need to know how you are dealing with all of this."

Dead silence filled the air where I was trying to connect.

"Eric, I know you are always optimistic. You live in a world where nothing ever goes wrong, and I feel like you're seeing this as a failure on your part. Please talk to me. This is not going away."

"I love you more than anyone in the world. I hate seeing you go through this. I hate coming home and not knowing if you are going to be exhausted, throwing up, or depressed. I want to fix it, and I realize I can't. I hated watching them radiate you today. It made me sick to watch you on the monitor as they maneuvered that machine around. Is that what you want to hear?"

"It's exactly what I wanted to hear. If you were going through this, I would be strong for you. I know I would have quiet times of crying too. You were there when I was diagnosed. You cried through the entire thing while I was in denial. It's like we've changed sides. You don't always have to be strong."

"What do you want me to say?"

"I want you to know you can have emotional releases. It's okay for you to cry. It's okay for you to say my wife has cancer. This is not your problem to fix—and you're definitely not a failure for not being able to take care of everyone all the time."

"Monya, seriously? I do cry. I know I can't fix this, but I do believe it will go away. I don't want to think about your death—about my life continuing without you."

"Do you understand that there is not a day, an hour, a minute, or a second of the day that I don't worry about cancer? When I wake up every morning, it's the first thing I think of—and it never, ever goes away. It's scary. I don't want to think about it, but I also don't have a choice. I didn't choose this villain. My life seemed perfectly fine until cancer came along. I'm not sure how to communicate with—"

"And you don't understand how I feel either." he bellowed

We decided we both were right. It was acceptable to be okay with the awkward silence at times. I finally got what he was saying. The emotional roller coaster of sickness and desperation didn't necessarily need to be verbally communicated to be understood.

Getting ready for radiation one morning, I looked in the magnifier mirror. I had some hair growing in. It was more like peach fuzz, but it was starting to grow. "Eric, do you see the hair growing on my head?"

"Um, yeah sure."

"It's there. I promise. Look in my mirror."

Shaking his head, he said, "Oh yeah. Looks good."

I knew he was just trying to make me feel good. "Then feel it."

He ran his hand over my head and smiled. "It feels as soft as a duckling feathers."

"I told you it was there. That is worth celebrating, right?"

"Yes. If you're feeling like it, we will celebrate tonight. Dinner maybe?"

"That sounds great. See you tonight. Aren't you glad you felt it?"

"Um, yes. It's so great, baby. I'm happy for you."

I'd been told hair grows kind of funky after chemo. I have always been a true blonde, but it came in kind of dark. Time would tell. Waiting for your hair to grow back is like watching a plant grow.

The universe has a humorous way of making me smile. On the way to the Mayo that morning, I pulled up behind a car with a huge print on the back window that read: Got Hair? I laughed out loud, especially with all that had taken place with Eric. After thirty-six rounds, I finished radiation. It was so hard to say good-bye to the staff. I had never met people more compassionate and kind. What a wonderful experience it was. Five days a week for seven weeks, I was greeted by people who genuinely cared and understood. This staff treated me more like a friend than a patient. I loved them all. I was sure if there were a special machine to check the levels of radiation in my body, mine would light up like a Christmas tree. One of the techs told me patients who undergo radiation are known as the glow club.

My skin was so burned. It was sometimes excruciating to put a shirt on; anything rubbing against my skin hurt. Under my arm, chest, face, and breasts felt like second-degree burns. Everything was swollen, red, and painful. The Mayo Clinic has a little ceremony for patients when they finish radiation; it's like a badge of honor. The technicians surrounded me while I rang the bell. tears ran down my cheeks. I hugged each one of them like they were family. In the waiting room, I saw the other patients I had sat with every day for months. We shared stories, pain, and tears. I will miss them. A couple of us had gone through chemo together, and I hugged them all.

Driving home, I considered the thought that only those who have suffered from the atrocious side effects of poison, chemotherapy riddles the body with or the red and raw burning skin from radiation or the emotional and physical pain of surgeries and seemingly endless invasive procedures in an attempt to purge the body of cancer or it's ramifications truly know what it's like. The bond that I had formed with other patients, my doctors, and technicians in a span of a year was indescribable. It's my opinion only those who have looked into the fierce eyes of the disease get to be in the exclusive club. Membership comes at a cost much higher than any dollar amount.

Chapter 20

Curing Cancer Dancer by Dancer

May 2, 2010

*H*aleigh had her final dance recital at Highland High. Kaitlyn wanted to be here for it. I was on cloud nine with Kaitlyn and Brian in town. I was happily surprised when we all went to the school dance recital. Haleigh was a senior and also the president of One Image (the dance team) at Highland. She had been diligently working so hard on the recital. We had no idea exactly what she was working on until we got settled in our seats and the program began. The theme the class decided on was "Curing Cancer, Dancer by Dancer." Haleigh wanted us to be surprised.

It was such an emotional night for both Eric and me. Haleigh dedicated one of her dances to me and called it "Monya's Song." The actual name of the song was "It Feels Like Home to Me" by Chantel Kreviazuk. She danced with such grace and confidence. I was proud to be her mom. She told me later she handpicked the girls who would dance with her. I loved them all. She knew they would dance like it was their last dance, and it was beautiful. Eric and I were touched by her spirit. Her senior year of high school will always be the year her mom had cancer. I could tell my journey had really affected her. In the program, she wrote as a dedication to me:

This dance is dedicated to Mom who was diagnosed last year with breast cancer. She is the strongest person I've ever met, and I look up to her so much. Thank you for being the best mom in the world. I love you!

—Haleigh

It was overwhelming to see her with such courage and strength. She cried while she danced. She is not an emotional person. Was she processing everything that had happened? She just wanted to be strong for me. Knowing what was happening in our home and observing her tears was actually reassuring. She was processing her emotions—on her terms. It's amazing the love families can have for each other. The support my children give to one another has always touched me.

One of the positive things that have come out of my diagnosis with cancer has been the opportunity to meet some of the strongest, bravest people I know. Every time I go to Mayo Clinic, the grocery store, or the mall, I am blessed to meet people who will forever stay in my prayers and my heart. I met a man at a pizza shop in Tempe, and I think about him often. He noticed that we had a relay for life cancer sticker on our car and that I was bald. He approached Eric and asked about my cancer. He and Eric talked for a few minutes while I was waiting. I could tell they were talking about me so I joined the conversation.

The man introduced himself to me and immediately started to cry. I hugged him, and he told me of his two-year-old son who was diagnosed with a rare cancer when he was only three months old. He told me that Brady was the youngest to ever be diagnosed with that type of cancer. He talked about the struggle of watching his child go through agony for two years. They hoped the next surgery would be the one to get Brady out of the hospital and home where he belonged. Brady had been put under anesthesia more than eighty times in his short life. He had a breathing tube through his nose, did not know what it was like to run outside and play, and would never be able to do the normal things in life that we all take for granted. My heart ached for this man. Eric and I got emotional and cried as he spoke. It's a lot easier to handle when adults are diagnosed. A child that young does not understand what is happening.

For Brady, this is his life. He has never known anything different. The man took a bracelet off his arm and gave it to me: B is for Brady. B-Strong! While thinking about Brady, it made me think about the Savior and the agony and suffering he went through in the Garden of Gethsemane. Heavenly Father had to watch his Son go through the worst pain any person has ever endured. Heavenly Father could have taken it all away and stopped it at any time, but he didn't because it was all part of the plan. I'm sure that God suffered along with his Son, knowing the pain he was going through.

As we go through our trials, Heavenly Father looks down on us all and wants to take away the pain. He feels our anguish, and he has the power to take it all away. He doesn't because this is part of his plan. How we endure and who we become through our trials is all part of his plan.

Brady has since passed away and is in heaven with no more pain, leaving a legacy of faith and hope for so many of us. I will always remember this special father who tried so hard to take his son's pain away and couldn't. For me, "Curing Cancer Dancer by Dancer" was dedicated to him and all the children who suffer with the villain and are not able to live full, complete lives. We will never understand the suffering these children go through, but they seem to have an understanding and peace about not living the life of a typical child. They have a different journey. I believe they are too perfect to be in the world.

Chapter 21

Ditch the Hats

r. Northfelt walked in and rubbed the top of my head. With a huge smile, he said, "Looks good. I love the new hair."

I asked, "When will you be able to tell me I'm cancer free?"

Dr. Northfelt said, "You were diagnosed with an advanced stage of cancer. I won't feel good about saying you are cancer free until I've seen you for another thirty years."

This was an interesting discovery for me.

He explained if he thought just removing my breasts would 'get rid' of my cancer, he would have told me long ago. He would never put me through all of the chemo and radiation if he didn't think it was absolutely necessary. Because of the lymph node invasion if even one cancer cell was able to get through it could manifest itself at anytime, or perhaps never.

Chemo killed my ovaries and threw me into post menopause. That explained the night sweats and hot flashes. Hormone therapy was not an option for me. The type of cancer I have is estrogen fed. My naive small mind actually thought the cancer was removed with my breasts. It makes sense to me now. He gave me a big hug, told me to keep fighting, and asked me to read The Anti Cancer.

I went home and did some research online about remission and breast cancer. Everything I found said Dr. Northfelt was right. I may have some cancer cells in my body that will show up later. I made the decision to stop thinking about my limitations and concentrate on the things I could accomplish. I couldn't treat it like a bout of pneumonia or a broken bone either. It was not a thing of my past; the cancer was a part of my new life. I was realistic enough to know if Dr. Northfelt could not tell me I was cancer free I had a responsibility to do all I could to help prevent it from returning.

Not long after chemo and radiation were finished, my lower back and right hip started to really hurt. I began to limp, trying to relieve the agonizing pain. Dr. Northfelt referred me to the pain clinic at Mayo Clinic. I would now be seeing Dr. Freeman for any pain issues.

When I finished reading Anti Cancer, I was thoroughly intrigued by the information and wondered why more oncologists didn't suggest it to their patients.

The author, Dr. Servan-Schreiber MD, PhD, was a clinical professor of psychiatry at the University of Pittsburgh School of Medicine and cofounder of the Center for Integrated Medicine. He also serves on the board for the Society for Integrative Oncology; there is a lot to learn when it comes to preventing cancer. His research comes from his own diagnosis with cancer, world-renowned cancer centers and oncologists, the World Cancer Research Fund, and Food, Nutrition and the Prevention of Cancer (A Global Perspective, London World Cancer Research, 2007). These are just a few of the resources he used; it would take twenty pages to list every resource, but I will do my best.

- Cancer feeds on sugar cane, beet sugar, corn syrup, etc.

- Cancer feeds on bleached flour, including white bread, white pasta, etc.
- Cancer feeds on vegetable oils such as soybean oil, sunflower oil, corn oil, and trans fats.

These three sources contain none of the proteins, vitamins, minerals, or omega-3 fatty acids we need to keep our bodies functioning properly. They directly fuel the growth of cancer. The tests also concluded that women with high blood sugar levels (or who are diabetics) are seven times more likely to develop breast cancer.

We have become a nation of people who do not want to take the time to prepare home-cooked meals for our families. It is much easier to get takeout food. We need to get back to basics and be aware of what we are putting in our children's mouths. Processed foods, which are in every fast-food restaurant in America, feed cancer cells.

Anyone with a family history of cancer should take note of this information and consider establishing a new way of life. We could all probably improve our lives and our families' lives by changing a few things we eat and introducing some new foods to our children.

Young parents have the control to give their children water instead of sugary soda's. If they have never tasted sugar, they will never know they are missing it. I never drank soda until I met Eric, but I'm not blaming him. When we were dating, he drank a Big Gulp every day filled with Dr. Pepper. I told him if he kept that up, the name of the doctor he was visiting was going to change. Who thought of naming a sugary, brain-fogging drink after a doctor?

I finally ditched the hats. It was a little bit harder than I thought it would be. If I heard one more person say, "At least you have a perfectly shaped head," I was going to throw up. I knew—and everyone knew—that I looked weird and funny, but it was getting so hot. The hats made my head sweat. Going out in public without the protection of my hat to hide under was hard, but I got used to it. Long before I knew I had cancer, I said, "I would never wear a wig if I got cancer." After my diagnosis, I talked with Eric about it.

Eric said, " I really think you should get a wig."

"No way. Why?"

He joked "I think it would be fun to have a brunette or a redhead for a wife. Think about how much fun we could have walking through the mall or at a restaurant. Someone might see me with a redhead or brunette and instantly text you to let you know I am cheating on you."

"Ha ha. Okay. As fun as that sounds, for one thing I don't think brunettes or redheads are better than blondes. Second, if someone we knew saw you with another woman, I doubt that their first inclination would be to text me. I'm glad you think you could get caught so easily though."

"I'm just kidding. You are the love of my life."

"Good answer, but I am not wearing a wig."

I knew I'd look scary to little children—with or without a wig. It was kind of funny to see their reactions. Children stared as they walked, following their mothers some even ran into things. My favorite was a lady who walked up to me and said, "Did you do your hair like that on purpose?"

I was so shocked but was witty enough to come right back with "Why? Does this shirt make me look bald?" I was wearing a breast cancer T-shirt for the American Cancer Society. All I could do was laugh, and it is okay to laugh. I made fun of myself all the time. Maybe it was my way of coping, but it did help. It was sad to say good-bye to all of my hats, but I was happy about the prospect of new hair and a new life.

I had some funny and interesting things happen during my journey. At one point, my hair or lack of was completely consuming my thoughts. After chemo and radiation, I didn't think about it too much.

I started having hot flashes, the fatigue and insomnia were not any better. I decided it was time to get out of the house and get a pedicure. The chemo had killed my big toenails. I wanted that covered. I needed to go grocery shopping. On the way into the store, I noticed a lady with a huge bouffant hairdo. I couldn't help but think about the early seventies. Mom had hair like that. I thought how nice she feels comfortable enough to go out into public.

She went to the east entrance, while I went to the west entrance. I was getting the ingredients I needed. I looked up as I was putting some diced green chilies in the cart to see the lady walking straight toward me. I had a feeling she was going to say something to me.

"Whoever does your hair doesn't do a very good job." She pulled out a business card and handed it to me. "Here is the business card of the lady who does my hair."

Seriously? She has got to be kidding me. I started to laugh and looked around to see if my silly kids set it up. When I realized she was serious, I smiled. "Um, I have cancer. I didn't cut my hair this way."

"Oh, well, I didn't know." She stomped off as if I was the one being rude. It was very, very funny.

That's what I get for judging her hair in the parking lot. I would have never said anything to her, but I wonder if she had been introduced to 2010. Maybe that style was coming back. What do I know?

Haleigh called and asked me to get her Subway on my way home. When I walked in, the lady behind the counter said, "Oh my goodness. I love your hair."

"Thank you. I appreciate you saying that."

"Are you attracted to females?"

"Um, no not really."

"That's too bad. You'd be a huge turn-on at the club I go to. I was going to ask you to go with me tonight." She was so excited and smiley.

I couldn't help but smile too. "Sorry." Are you kidding me, Monya? That's it? All you can say is sorry? I just wanted to get in my car and get home.

"Let me help you to your car. Are you sure you won't reconsider going out tonight?"

Do Subway employees usually walk their customers to the car? Wow. That was uncomfortable. It was the third time I was hit on by a woman since my hair loss. I have several friends who are lesbians. I'll have to inquire about this. Eric and I got a great laugh out of it. I loved that we had been blessed with the ability to laugh during that time.

Not long after Haleigh graduated from high school, she and I went on a bike ride. It was beautiful and the weather in Arizona was incredibly soothing after the sun went down. We were talking, laughing, and really enjoying our time together when two boys passed us on their bikes. The first boy mumbled something under his breath. The second boy yelled, "OMG. Look at the dyke." I felt so embarrassed for them.

Haleigh was so upset. She turned her bike around and was ready to take the kid on. They rode as fast as they could, but Haleigh was faster. When I caught up to her, she was engaged in a conversation with the boys. I'm still not sure what she said, but when I arrived, they took off. This could be a great teaching moment. I should talk to her about turning the other cheek. Something told me to keep quiet, and I did. I wondered if she was embarrassed to be with me. The fact that she stood up for me and defended what she knows to be right was impressive.

I'm not shocked by what people say anymore. Ditching the hats meant I'd sometimes have to ditch and dodge the fiery darts being thrown my way. The struggle between right and wrong and when to confront and when to ignore has always been confusing for me. My vulnerability took on a new form. Most of the time, I was too mentally exhausted to feed into the curiosity of other people. Life is so short, and we spend so much time worrying about what others think and do. If we concentrated on being kind in every circumstance—with the mindset that you have no idea what someone else is going through—life would be so much more abundantly appreciated.

Chapter 22

*Defusing Fear /*PTSD

fter reading Anticancer: A New Way Of Life by David Servan-Schreiber, I decided I would try a new way of life by cutting out sugar, white flour, and all processed foods. It took a week to completely detoxify my body of the poison I once called dessert. I had no problems giving up chips and salsa, breads, and pasta, but the bakery items were going to be a challenge.

Our kitchen has always been a gathering place. Even as a child, my mother had Sonya, Kris, and I learn how to make and prepare meals once a week. Baking has always been her specialty, and now it was mine. We had a garden while growing up, but we cooked most of those vegetables with a lot of margarine and bacon grease—two ingredients I no longer use. I was beginning to empower myself. It was like learning how to walk again, but I was doing it with food and shorter, less structured exercise.

Dr. Servan Schreiber is a clinical professor of psychiatry and also the author of The Instinct to Heal. He has counseled thousands of cancer patients and knew a lot about depression, anxiety, and post-traumatic stress disorder. He hit on many of the feelings I had encountered over the years. He said trauma could actually feed cancer. This research came from his experience with patients and research for his book.

Many people with life-altering experiences believe they have healed. In reality, they have never dealt with the underlying calamity. It weighs on the brain of the innocent until an explosion of emotions takes over. It may not manifest itself with a diagnosis of breast cancer, but the havoc it creates in the mind and body will eventually rear its ugly head. Many times, I had to shut the book, walk away, and breathe. How was I going to claim this one? How did this doctor know what I was feeling? It was my life he was talking about. Although I had forgiven my perpetrator, if I was honest, I'd have to admit not too many days went by that I didn't recall painful events in my life. Even small things I witnessed could trigger bouts of fear and anxiety. To this day I will not allow golf tournaments to be played on the television in our home. The reminder of my stepdad watching endless hours of it brings back terrible memories. Certain smells or songs will also bring back terror in me.

There was something unnatural about having Mom living within an hour—only a phone call away—yet not having a resolution we could both live with. I continually questioned myself. Had I tried all I could to mend the bridge of communication that had so terribly separated us?

I'm deaf in one ear because alcohol and drugs altered the thinking of a man who could have been an incredible daddy. His addictions were bigger than he was. I forgave my birth father for abandoning me, but I spent most of my life in anger and fear because of it. The tragic death of Lance was still an open wound with a temporary bandage on it. I had forgiven the abuse that was allowed in my home by constantly remembering that if I didn't forgive the stepdad, he ultimately was still in control of my life. I wanted to be free of that thinking. It took a lot of meditation, prayer, and self-control to forgive him.

I needed to come to grips with the fact I was suffering from PTSD. Was that even possible? A therapist I'd seen years ago had diagnosed me with PTSD, but I didn't believe it. I was in complete denial and thought it was an inaccurate diagnosis.

According to the Mayo Clinic and personal therapists:

- PTSD is a mental health condition triggered by experiencing or seeing a terrifying event.
- Can't be cured, but treatment may help.
- If it's chronic it can last for years or be lifelong.
- The condition may last months or years, with triggers that can bring back memories of the trauma accompanied by intense emotional and physical reactions.
- Symptoms include flashbacks, nightmares, and anxiety.
- Treatment includes different types of psychotherapy as well as medications to manage depression and anxiety. In the United States, there are more than 3 million cases per year.

Psychological Intervention Improves Survival for Breast Cancer Patients was a study done by Barb Anderson, a professor of psychology at Ohio State University. She observed 227 breast cancer patients for eleven years. They all had stage two, three a, b, or c. They all had received conventional treatments. They were all told about nutrition and exercise, and they all learned how to avoid stress in their lives with simple yoga exercises. The results were remarkable. The group of women who practiced all they were taught and made lifestyle changes had a 56 percent lower mortality rate.

According to BreastCancer.org, nine out of ten women who have breast cancer (out of four thousand women interviewed) had some type of traumatic event happen in their lives, and 80 percent of women are diagnosed with PTSD after a breast cancer diagnosis. That was a huge discovery to me. When I looked at the risk factors for breast cancer, I had none of the traditional causes. I could understand stress, anxiety, and helplessness.

How could I completely purge myself of all the trauma I had experienced in my life so I could live a stress-free life? Was it possible? It was time to stop detaching myself from the realities of what actually happened to me. When I was seeing a therapist during one of the sessions, the doctor asked why I always referred to myself as a third person. For example, I might say, "Then the little girl went to her room and cried." I had no idea I was doing that, it was difficult to face the reality and much easier to refer to the third person as someone other than myself.

Fear had paralyzed me for too long. I was ready to defuse the disabling worry and move forward by taking responsibility for my life. I just wasn't sure how I was going to be successful in doing it.

I first needed to admit PTSD was real and it was part of who I was. The sudden and shocking flashbacks were no longer going to throw me into a fearful panic. I chose to be proactive and taught myself how to defuse those moments of fear by immediately writing down a good memory instead of dwelling on the negative reality. I'd love to say fear has completely diminished but that would not be true, every once in awhile I get a fear of someone hurting one of my grandchildren and it turns my whole world upside down for a few minutes-I'm not proud of it but it is something I will probably have to work on for the rest of my life.

The word cancer is no longer a death sentence for everyone it strikes. It does suggest a dreary shadow. For so many patients, this dark cloud of cancer has given us the time to think about life, what we want to do with it, and how we want to spend the rest of our lives. I have had the wonderful opportunity to meet cancer survivors who are realistic. They know the odds of survival, but they are positive and have made great changes in their lives. They have lived far beyond what the statistics or what doctors have told them they would.

I have had a fear of unfinished stories. I truly believe the best way to prepare for our final farewell is to make one last try while we're still alive. Do something for someone else daily. Write the poem you've always wanted to write or take a trip you've dreamed of. Spend quality time with the ones you love. Forgive those who have offended you. Forgive your own imperfections.

When we turn the page to a new life, we leave behind some old habits and look to the future with eyes wide open and a heart full of love and appreciation far beyond what we ever thought we could. I may die earlier than I could have foreseen, but it is possible that I'll live much longer. Whatever happens, I'm going to live happy. My story is unfinished. It will end with: "She lived happily ever after."

Chapter 23

Je t'aime' Paris

*D*r. Northfelt mentioned that it would be a good time to get out and do something I'd always wanted to do. It would still be a few months before my next surgery. I went home and started to make a list.

I was going to call it a bucket list, but I was thinking that bucket lists always imply the thought of death. I called it my to-do list. They are in no particular order, and I realize it may change.

- Go to Paris With Eric—a lifelong dream.
- Give more than I've been given (not sure if this is possible but worth a try).
- Run a marathon. I'm running it now—just not on a track or trail
- Write a book.
- Attend the Olympics.
- Live long enough to hold all of my grandchildren.
- I love giraffes. I'd love to go on a safari and see them gracefully commanding the ground they inhabit with such grace.
- Learn to play tennis (I don't even know the rules).
- Learn to use my camera on manual.
- Take my entire family on a Disney cruise.
- Go to Tahiti—Bora Bora would be a great start.

- Visit Savannah, Georgia.
- Help change the life of just one person

Although my future was unsure, I was the happiest I'd ever been. Eric came home and gave me a card:

> Monya,
>
> My wonderful wife. I am so blessed to have you. I love you with all my heart. I feel very privileged to be able to spend time with you. Will you go to Philadelphia with me? It's not where we go, but being together … I know we both love history and art. Will you go with me? Yes ☐ or No ☐
>
> I love you.
> Love, Eric

Philadelphia was nothing I would have guessed he would have chosen, but who was I to complain? I would get to spend ten days alone with my sweetie.

A couple of hours later, Eric walked in with a beret. He handed me another card

> Rain or Shine
> I'm so glad you're mine!
>
> Monya, I love you, I am so glad you chose to go to Philadelphia with me. I forgot to mention that we are only having a layover in Philadelphia—and then we are going to the most romantic city in the world! I always promised we would visit it together. I never want to have any regrets (like Mom and Dad not going to Hawaii together).

I am so in love with you and would like to spend the next ten days with you in Paris. Bonjour, Je t'aime'.

Love,
Eric

After a lot of hugs, kisses, and tears, I said, "Are you kidding me?"

We both cried, and then we went to Costco to buy a video camera and a new digital camera. I could hardly wait. I was so excited. I have the best husband in the world, and the Paris trip was on my to-do list. A few years ago, Eric took our girls on a daddy-daughter trip to Paris. I wanted to experience the enchanting city. Eric speaks fluent French and served his mission in France. I wanted to visit the place where he had lived for the two years he was away from his family.

I had less than twelve hours to get packed and ready for Paris. I was given strict instructions to only bring one bag. I was not sure how that was going to work out, but it did. We flew first class from Phoenix to Philadelphia, spent the night, and then headed to Paris the next day (again in first class). I blogged, took pictures, and smiled for ten days. It was so interesting to see a different culture. I'd been in other countries, but Paris was extremely close to my heart. To make it more fun, I made up a game we played every day. Like every game, there were rules. We each had to find the most interesting person we could and take a picture.

Rule #1: They could not be defined as interesting if they had physical disabilities.

Rule #2: We had to take a picture.

Rule #3: They had to be interesting because the person chose it (wacky haircut, clothes, or lack of clothes).

At the end of the night, we compared notes and pictures. I won every time, Eric is competitive but he didn't like 'pretending' to take my picture of me when in fact he was really taking a picture of the person standing beside me or behind me. I on the other hand had no problem this was the most fun I'd had in over a year. I walked right up to people , complimented them and asked if I could get a picture. Another little game I played was called Favorites—Less Favorites. I wrote down my favorite smells, sounds, tastes, and sights of the day. I shared them every night before bed. We laughed, made silly faces, gagged, and had a lot of fun with this one.

While we were gone Eric wore a beret, grew a goatee and I never tired of hearing him speaking French. I gave him a new name, Frenchie. He fit in perfectly.

We visited the Eiffel Tower, Versailles, Notre Dame, Le Sacre' Coeur Cathedral, Moulin Rouge, the Champs Elysees, and the Louvre. I tasted Nutella for the first time on a beautiful crepe and visited the exquisite Sainte Chapelle. The Arc de' Triomphe is a must-see landmark. Saint Michel was fascinating, and we watched the street dancers. We enjoyed Luxembourg Castle and its beautiful gardens. The Catacombs were a little freaky but historical. We walked to the top of the Pantheon. I was exhausted, but the view was breathtaking. Visiting Disneyland in Paris was only worth saying we've been there. Disneyland in California is cleaner and more updated. Disney World in Florida is the ultimate clash of fun, excitement, and exhaustion. Paris Disneyland was boring to us.

The entire trip was worth finding a secret heavenly place. I will forever refer to it as my Happy Place just outside of Paris. The natural beauty of Porte de Jaune is stunning. We rented bikes and rode through gorgeous tree-covered bike lanes and picked wild berries. We rode over bridges and ate lunch next to the lake and creeks. It was the most romantic, beautiful place I had ever been. We saw people holding hands, kissing, and enjoying the beauty of the earth. Children with berry-stained faces were laughing and picking wild berries with their grandparents. There were local groups of men who gathered to play chess, throw horseshoes, or visit with a hot cup of coffee or tea. I was intrigued with their lighthearted wit and charm. I don't speak any French. I just imagined they were all dear friends from childhood, growing old together. They could have been saying awful things to one another, but it sounded fascinating and whimsical. We could not have custom ordered a better day. The weather was exceptional with sunshine on our faces and a breeze on our backs as we strolled along. It made me sad to leave. As we walked toward the train stop, I took one more look back—just in case I never had a chance to return. I closed my eyes, got my visual, and knew exactly where I would go next time I needed a "happy place."

As our plane was descending into Phoenix, I looked out the window and heard the pilot say, "Welcome to Phoenix." Tears ran down my cheeks. I could not control the emotions. How would I return from such an unforgettable experience to my real life? Thoughts of Mayo Clinic, doctor's appointments, and medications flooded my brain. I realized what an amazing opportunity my husband had given me. What a blessing it was for me to truly live in the moment enjoying every minute without the thought of cancer lingering. I had forgotten what it was like to be carefree and 100 present. We all have to face hard times in our lives, but every once in a while, it's nice to check out.

The day after we arrived home, I went back to work at US Airways. It had been over a year since I had worked. Now it was time to return from my sick leave and get back into a daily routine that didn't involve the Mayo Clinic. By then end of the day I was exhausted from the mental stimulation. I sat at my computer with tears in my eyes on several occasions. Did I always know how to do this? I am so grateful for my job. I never would have said that before. I now had a different perspective, and I would never take my brain for granted. It is an amazing gift.

Chapter 24

Patience

October 6, 2010

A friend asked, "If you knew at age twenty exactly how your life would end up, would you change the course of it?" I said, "No." She was a little surprised by my answer and told me that she would change a lot if she had the chance. I think all the trials and pain I have seen in my life have molded and formed me into who I am. It's hard to imagine any other life. Patience is a virtue, but it stinks. I believe patience is not a passive word; it's a word showing action. Unless my patience is tested, I can never master it. In other words, don't pray or ask for the energy of the world to give you patience without expecting to have struggles that will try your patience.

Why is patience a virtue? Why was it chosen as one of the seven virtues?

Remember the story of the tortoise and the hare? I've been confused about why the tortoise always wins. I get it now. The tortoise wins because of his sure-footed, slow pace. The tortoise learned to slow down and enjoy the moment. I guarantee he has a much better story to tell as he slowly inhaled the beauty around him. Crossing the finish line was not a race to him. He was learning along the way and breathing in every experience. Seeing the big picture was his goal. The hare was me. I had rushed through so much of my life. With all the hurry and scrambling around, I missed out on great lessons in life. My diagnosis taught me that my body and my brain were not working in harmony; they were working independently. Being an athlete, I knew I had to have discipline and practice. The only way for me to become faster and stronger was to go slower, take the strides, and slowly build up my cadence.

I took a class once on how to run properly. There is an art to running. It shows in your confidence, your posture, and your breathing during your stride. I could control these things, and they weren't a stretch for me. Being forced to slow down, I became perfectly aware that patience was not a virtue I possessed. I wanted to work on it. For the first time in my life, I was coming face to face with the fact I was not in control of my body. It was a reality I wasn't familiar with. Patience is hard. It takes inner strength. It means allowing yourself to release fears, letting go of any preconceived expectations, and granting yourself permission to be vulnerable.

We often complain about our lives and some of the decisions we've made. Why do we do that? After all, they were our decision to make—we have to sometimes live with the consequences. I'm glad we get to choose the paths we will take, but those choices are not free. They usually come with ramifications. When agency is taken away by someone or something else, we develop strength, patience, and endurance. This has been when my true character is tested. How the trial will affect your life is still your choice.

You can choose to learn and grow from it or let it fester and grow into an evil disease that takes over your life. The villain is my adversary, but I have learned that our enemies can become our choicest friends. The secret is learning what to do with the conflict. It's like the old saying "Keep your friends close, and your enemies closer." I've studied and learned all I can about cancer and the possible prevention of recurrence. I'm no longer angry about my diagnosis with the villain, it has proven to be a sweet tender mercy teaching me so much about my inner strength and ability to overcome hard obstacles in life.

During the first year after my diagnosis, I slowly became distant from friends. It was no choice of theirs or mine; it simply was not the time or season for me to frolic with friends. I was in a battle for my life. I became exclusive and kept to myself and my family. I knew it was important to concentrate on my health and leave some of the negative influences of the world   behind.

I continued to journal on my blog and had a very large following. Men and women who were dealing with cancer stumbled across my blog when googling a hospital, a doctor, or a diagnosis. I loved these people. Most of them connected with me through e-mail, and some have   remained good friends. I may never meet them, but I know them on an intimate level since we shared similar circumstances. For the most part, I was inundated with e-mails from kind, gentle people who were experiencing some of the same feelings. We supported each other. As with most things in life, there is good and bad. I sometimes received e-mails that were not so nice. Someone asked me, "When are you going finally let this cancer thing go?"

In the book Wherever You Go There You Are, Jon Kabat-Zin said, "When people say 'let it go' what they really mean is 'get over it.' That is not a helpful thing to say. It's not a matter of 'letting go.' I would if I could. Instead of saying, 'Let it go,' I chose to say, 'Let it be.' I will never let it go …'it' meaning cancer is a part of my life story now. To say it never happened would be foolish, to watch me learn and grow from it is astonishing.

My blogging was becoming more and more popular every day. For the most part people were kind and understanding but I also received unwanted advice and negative attitudes. I   usually asked them to simply not read my blog if they didn't like what they were reading. I would be lying if I said those comments didn't effect me. The added hurt and stress were still my life. At the end of the day, I was still dealing with the circumstances of my life. That part was not going to go away—no matter how many times I wished it. I've learned to discern the good from the bad. I was severely hurt and disappointed by a person who I thought I knew; since that encounter, I have learned to guard my heart from the evils of the world. A person with good intentions who chooses to live an authentic life will always come under attack from those who were jealous or insecure. I had to find out this sad truth the hard way.

Thomas S. Monson graduated cum laude from the University of Utah in 1948 with a degree in business management said, "Life is full of difficulties, some minor and others of a more serious nature. There seems to be an unending supply of challenges for one and all. Our problem is that we often expect instantaneous solutions to such challenges, forgetting that frequently the heavenly virtue of patience is required."

I was learning to possess patience through difficulties in my life including finding the capacity to be humble and poised. Some people will never quite understand unless they actually experience it. I didn't want anyone else to have to experience this. I show tolerance toward those who just don't get it.

Chapter 25

Spiritually Speaking

Religion is for people afraid of going to hell.
Spirituality is for people who have already been there.
—Unknown

I love this quote because it somewhat describes how I feel. I think the person who wrote it might have meant it to scare people into believing in something. I understand it and connected with it on a different level. I have become more spiritual because I have lived through hell on earth. I am not afraid to die. I consider myself a spiritual person living in a religious world.

While blogging, I have had the opportunity to meet people from across the globe. Most of them are going through cancer treatments or are caregivers of loved ones. I have enjoyed most of the interactions. There are two common questions in each e-mail:

- How do you have so much faith and hope?
- What church do you belong to?

This always opens a door for me to share what I believe and ask, "What are your thoughts on spirituality?" The opportunity to expand my thinking and my heart around cultures and differences of worshiping across borders has been an unexpected treasure I will take to the grave.

I've found strength over the years through complete faith in a God I have never seen. I've learned through my experiences with support groups, volunteering, and listening with my heart that not all of us worship in the same way. I've learned to be inclusive. Many of my acquaintances and friends have completely contrasting ways of finding spiritual awareness. I reverently respect the beliefs of others. In fact, I find it fascinating and refreshing. I am going to try to explain both of these questions with sincerity in my heart. I hope you will respect and honor what is so precious to me. I believe your way of finding peace is important and sacred to you. If I were to be judgmental, it would be inconsistent to everything I authentically believe in.

1.   How do I have so much faith and hope?

My life has been truly blessed—beyond what I ever thought it could be or deserved. I know without a doubt that God lives. I have felt him touching my life many times. He has taken the pain away when I thought I could not go on. He has lifted me to new spiritual heights. I have never been more in tune with who I am. I will never deny the spirit I feel. My heart has been touched and healed because of this spirit. The stillness helps me know heaven is real.

Spirituality means having faith and love for my life and the world around me. The trials and tribulations in our lives can be hard and sometimes seem to never end, but I have learned to rely on God for guidance and strength. I have daily practices. Some have been saving graces for me. Without doing these simple practices, I could not have gotten to where I am today. These are simple and have been a part of my everyday life since I was young. Doing them daily has collectively brought me to a spiritual height that has pulled me through some really rough days and long nights.

I take time each morning to have silence, ponder be still and pray. I ask for help and give thanks for all that I have been blessed with. There have been times I have been prompted by a spirit or intuition to help someone in need. I intentionally do acts of kindness daily.

I keep a journal, and I write everything down. In each entry, I write something I am grateful for. It is so instinctive for people to see the gloom of each day. For me, living in that manner would be draining. I try to find the good in small things. I may be grateful to see the sunrise or be strong enough to brush my teeth. Those gratitudes change from day to day, depending on where my strengths and weaknesses are.

I read from a good book for at least thirty minutes per day. When our children were in living at home, we began every morning with scripture and having prayer before school. With technology the way it is now, I listen to personal development audio books and scriptures as I drive. I believe feeding my mind, body, and soul with uplifting words of affirmations balances me out and helps me to move forward with a positive feedback. I look in the mirror or rearview mirror at stoplights and tell myself I am beautiful, I have a good heart, I am smart, and I am fun. I always end with I love who I am.

I pray each night and give thanks for all I have. I don't always kneel, but I do pray. I learned this ritual on my own at a young age.

2. What church do you belong to?

I am a baptized member of the Church of Jesus Christ of Latter Day Saints. I am a Mormon. I don't belong to any church. I choose to live the LDS lifestyle. When I hear belong, it implies that I am owned by someone or something. I am a Christian. I attend Sunday worship services every week. This gives me a chance to renew covenants I have made with God and quietly repent for the small thoughts and feelings I may have had since the last Sunday.

Nothing about the LDS church has ever made me feel uncomfortable or forced. I love the wisdom of eating healthy, balanced meals and not drinking alcohol or coffee or smoking. These have all been proven to be addictive and potentially toxic for your body. The simplicity of the culture has always been comforting to me. I have never attended a church service and heard a bishop or members talking bad about other religions from the pulpit or in a classroom unless it was with absolute respect.

As members of the LDS church we concentrate on what we believe in we don't worry or talk about what other religions are doing or their beliefs. We are inclusive and never belittle, although we may not live the same lifestyles of other religious sects we respect and love them. We are all daughters and son's of God no matter what our lifestyle or belief.

Eric and I have attended church in other cities, states, and countries while vacationing. It doesn't matter where we are; nothing changes. Their beliefs have proven to be steadfast and immovable. Every meeting is conducted exactly the same—from China to Los Angeles. I never exclude people from my circle of friends because of religion, spiritual beliefs, or skin color. I love everyone who treats me with respect. It would have been easy to blame the Baptist Church for the abuse I received from the stepdad. There are people of every religious belief and every race who are products of their own inner struggles. They sometimes take it out on the innocent; unfortunately, I was one of them.

Too many people do not really know what Mormons believe in. They listen to other people's opinions or get their "facts" from excommunicated members of the church. I have been asked about polygamy, racism, and the book of Mormon being my "Bible." One time a person asked me if the LDS church gives us a Suburban after we have our fourth child. I'm usually shocked by some of the things people ask me about mormonism, but I would rather be asked instead of being told what I believe in. Like I've said many times throughout this book if you don't live it, you simply cannot understand it so ask an active member or go to LDS.org for the correct answers.

All I know for sure is that we are born—and one day we will die. What we do with the time in between is the most important thing. Live, learn, and share with no regrets.

Chapter 26

When Pink Was Just a Color

Every October is National Breast Cancer Awareness Month. When I had my bilateral mastectomy, it was the beginning of October. I woke up the next morning to a talk show host showing off her very large breasts on television. I think she thought she was honoring the wounded and breast-scarred women who had endured mastectomies. I will never forget how sick it made me feel as she wore her pink sweater and had her studio completely decorated with pink.

I remember thinking I'm lying here without any breasts. I could careless about implants.

She was flaunting her fake breasts and pronouncing implants as a bonus for being diagnosed with breast cancer.

A year later, Dr. Kreymerman would finish what we started with reconstruction. I remember when pink was just a color, but now it means so much more to me. I had never really given the breast cancer pink ribbon much thought. I hadn't donated money or let it penetrate my mind.

I started to see pink everywhere I went. It was like someone had thrown up Pepto-Bismol on every shelf in every store in America. The endorsements came from major corporations. I saw them on toothpaste, toilet paper, pencils, pens, paper, mascara, candles, gum, candy, and even the shoes, helmets, and gloves of athletes. Had I been ignorant for all these years—or was it something new I was just discovering? One of the boys from the Highland football team, Josh Menden, brought me the pink glove he wore during football season. I still have it. On October 1, I put it on my dresser to remind myself of the meaning of pink and the people in my life who deliberately and intentionally kept me in their thoughts.

Every time I see a pink ribbon, I think about my three daughters. When they were little, I loved to braid their hair. I always finished it off with a ribbon. The ribbon may not have always been pink, but the ribbons of October remind me of those days. In those innocent days, I had no thoughts of breast cancer. The only things I worried about were what was for dinner and if the clothes were washed. During those days, our home was filled with pink ribbons, pink pajamas, and pink bikes. Pink, pink, pink for my sweet girls. That was when I thought pink was just a color that divided the boys from the girls.

During my radiation treatments, our family attended a breast cancer awareness race in Salt Lake City. There was a time in my life when racing and running were just for fun. I didn't think about running for a cure. I ran without a care. We're racing time now and hoping for a cure. We hold tight to the thought that our children will not have to endure this terrible villain we like to sugarcoat and call breast cancer. I was in a sea of pink shirts that day; some were honoring their grandmothers, mothers, sisters, aunts, wives and friends who have survived cancer. Some were honoring family or friends who had lost the battle.

Since that day, I've thought about the phrase "lost the battle." It has never sat well with me, and I finally figured out why. Does the patient actually lose a battle? I think not. The patient no more loses the battle than the cancer wins. When the patient dies, the cancer dies too. No one wins. There were too many women who looked scared and lost as they wondered what the future would hold for them.

On that day, pink took on a whole new meaning. I stood proud with thousands of survivors in our pink shirts. With tears running down my cheeks and my bald head exposed, all I could see was my family. My eyes focused on my girls and Eric. At that very moment, pink was no longer a color; it was more like a new best friend.

During the last couple of years, I have educated myself about donations. October will always be National Breast Cancer Awareness Month. Although breast cancer is the leading cancer for death among women I believe every cancer deserves to be recognized and mentioned as much as breast cancer is. Some of the largest moneymakers out there are making money and putting it in their pockets. In my research, I was shocked to find out most money donated does not go toward the cause. Very few nonprofit organizations give 100 percent back to the cause. In fact one of the largest "nonprofit" organizations made over $300 million in 2010—and only 20 percent went into actual research or programs for breast cancer patients.

When people ask me about supporting Breast Cancer Awareness Month, I always say, "I support it, but I always check where my money is going before I give to a nonprofit organization." The American Cancer Society supports all research, and 100 percent of all money made through fund-raising goes right back into their programs for cancer patients and their families. This is the only nonprofit donation I will support. Pink? Well, the color pink has become a signature color during the month when black, orange, yellow, and white should be prevalent. It's somehow become a novelty. For me, the month of October, pink month, will forever be a sweet memory of when my journey to loving myself began.

Chapter 27

Dr. Magtibay and Dr. Kreymerman

On December 9, 2010, I entered Mayo Clinic hospital to have Dr. Kreymerman finished up the breast reconstruction. Sitting and waiting was difficult. I watched doctors escort family members into a private room to discuss the outcome of surgery. Eric and Dr. Kreymerman would be doing that in a few hours.

I spent the night in the hospital. Dr. Kreymerman and Heather came to visit me. I was extremely nauseated and my bladder was not working. They gave me something for the nausea, and I was finally able to sleep a little. Around 6:00 p.m., they showed up again. Because of the nausea, they decided I needed to stay one more night. The next morning, I felt a little better. At least my bladder was working. The nausea was still there but I felt as though I could go home and have nausea so I decided not to tell them about it. I also started to bleed, but I decided they did not need to know about that either. I was released from the hospital, and I got home around five o'clock just in time for Recker's first birthday party.

The truth is while Eric and I were in Paris, I started to bleed and have cramping. There were a couple of times I fainted or vomited. I tried to ignore it thinking part of it was the after effects of chemo and radiation. I knew the bleeding was not normal and I had ignored it for too long.

When Dr. Kreymerman came into the room for my postoperative appointment, I had   severe cramping and was doubled over in pain. He urged me to see Dr. Magtibay. I did not want to face the inevitable. I knew he would suggest a hysterectomy. Had the cancer returned? No matter what the answer was, I didn't want to face it. Things in my life were finally back on track and going as planned.

I was scared. I didn't want to go through any more. Cancer had taken my breasts and hair—and now it wanted to take my uterus? I would rather be in pain than go through another surgery, but I also knew the risks.

The night before I went to see Dr. Magtibay, I researched him. I watched a video he had done for Mayo Clinic. I had seen him a year ago when he suggested having the hysterectomy at the same time as the mastectomy. I was so particular about seeing a man of integrity, a kind and gentle man for this surgery. Watching the video, my heart was immediately put at peace. The words that came out of his mouth were captivating.

He said, "First and foremost, my family, wife, and children come first in my life. Second are my patients." I felt an overpowering comfort. I knew he would be the doctor who would see me through another heartache. I went to my first appointment of many with Dr. Magtibay. He was in the same office as Dr. Kreymerman.

Dr. Magtibay asked a lot of questions. He wanted to do a biopsy of my uterus. I agreed and tried to relax. He inserted the needle and said, "You might feel some pain." I immediately threw up, which was unexpected and embarrassing.

I became light headed and fainted, He had to stop the exam because I was in too much pain. My cervix was scarred shut from all of the other surgeries. Dr. Magtibay was so sweet. He stepped out and got a bottle of water for me. We discussed the possibility of uterine cancer. We decided to have an ultrasound.

I ran into Dr. Kreymerman and Heather at the clinic. Dr. Kreymerman made me promise I would do everything Dr. Magtibay asked me to do. I confessed I didn't want to have a hysterectomy. He looked at me and said, "You promised me, and I need you to keep that promise." He had no idea the anguish I was feeling or why. I walked away thinking, If he only knew. I wonder if he would react differently?

December 29, 2010

I was a little sad about my last appointment with Dr. Kreymerman. Most patients looked forward to this day, but I felt sad. Dr. Kreymerman and Heather had become endeared to my heart forever. They had been with me from the beginning of my journey, and that part of my journey was over. It was going to be hard to leave his office since I felt safe and valued as a woman there.

I told them I didn't believe in good-byes but I did say "I'll see you later—and I love you both."

I cried a bit on my way home, thinking about what a big part of my life they had been. I would miss them and appreciated how compassionate and kind Dr. Kreymerman had been. I hope every cancer patient experiences unconditional love and care from their surgeons and physicians.

January 3, 2011

I was waiting to be called back for the ultrasound Dr. Magtibay ordered. My bladder was so full, but I was told to wait until after the exam. I glanced over at the restrooms and decided I needed to reposition my body so I didn't have a bird's-eye view of the women's bathroom. There was no one else in the waiting room under the age of seventy. I couldn't help but hear the conversations going on all around me.

"Oh, I hated radiation."

"My prostate is on overload right now."

"Yeah, I got a UTI and was put on meds right away."

"You should have seen my wife. Two weeks ago, she started chemo. It's gonna kill her—I just know it—but the doc won't listen to me."

I sat listening and thought to myself Please don't ask me anything. Please don't make eye contact. I don't want to engage in conversation. Today, I just want to be entertained.

Saved by the loudspeaker, my name was called. My bladder was ready to burst. I had three different types of ultrasounds. The agreement to have a hysterectomy was a fight. I was in total conflict with what actually needed to be done versus what I wanted to be done. The surgery was significant in so many ways. My fears were based on these words: "When I get done with you, no man will ever love you—and no doctor will ever be able to fix you." After coming so far, why was I allowing those words to penetrate my mind? The stepdad had used those words as a defense mechanism to keep me quiet or tear me down. I guess they worked. I never talked, and I never believed I was worthy of real love.

I texted Heather and asked if she was able to meet me in the cafeteria for lunch. I broke down and told her a bit about my childhood abuse. I know she was shocked, but she could not connect the dots. She asked, "What does this have to do with surgery?"

I explained how I was fearful of being put under anesthesia, having no control, and   waking up feeling like the stepdad was right. She asked if she could tell Dr. Kreymerman. I agreed, but I didn't want to talk to him about it. Before my appointments were done for the day, I went by to see him. He didn't have much time, but hugged me. "I'm so sorry, but you need to have this surgery. Dr. Magtibay is a fantastic doctor. He will take good care of you. Just talk to him."

I said, "Why can't you be there? Why can't you do the surgery?"

He smiled and said, "That part of the body is not my specialty. You need the best. I believe Dr. Magtibay is the best."

He was right. After explaining my anxiety to Dr. Magtibay, he looked at me with concerning eyes and said, "Well, the man who said that to you was wrong. Eric loves you, and I am the doctor who is going to fix you."

We scheduled my next surgery.

After my appointment, I met Haleigh for lunch. When I got up to refill my water cup, a woman said to her son, "Look at that lady's hair." I looked over to see that they were talking about me. The mother turned her head away when she realized I heard. The son just laughed.

As I walked back to my chair, the mother said, "Does she seriously think her hair looks good?"

Tears filled my eyes. It really hurt my feelings. Normally, it would not have bothered me. I understand some people are ignorant when it comes to the social ability of tact. I'm not sure where I heard this or who is responsible for the quote but I love it: "Tact is the ability to tell someone to go to hell in such a way that they look forward to the trip." I was feeling a little sensitive, but I let it go and enjoyed lunch with my sweet daughter.

January 6, 2011

On my way to Mayo Clinic, Dr. Magtibay called to talk about my upcoming surgery. I was so happy to hear from him. I explained some of my restlessness, and he listened with a sincere heart. I felt so blessed to have such incredibly caring doctors. Dr. Magtibay is a really good man.

As I drove down the Beeline Highway toward Mayo, the mountains were the most beautiful I had ever seen them. They were bright red and completely clear to the eye. Behind the red mountain, another mountain was topped with snow. It was an awe-inspiring, magnificent view. Never before had I been so attuned to the beauty of the earth. The desert had always been dreary to me, but I saw beauty and a heavenly closeness. I had achieved awareness at that moment. Everyone and everything has a time and a season. I was experiencing my season in alignment with the season of this angelic landscape.

January 11, 2011

Walking from the car into Mayo Clinic hospital for surgery with Dr. Magtibay, I told Eric it felt like walking the Green Mile. The sitting, anticipating, watching, waiting, and pacing were always heinous. I felt like I needed to throw up. The Mayo smelled of sickness.

I wore my comfy jammies with my breast cancer blanket wrapped around me. Eric was rubbing my back and reassuring me. I went into the operating room with two wallet-sized pictures: one of Eric and me in Paris and one of Recker.

They finally called my name and told Eric he could come back in about forty minutes. I didn't want him to go. I needed him today. I knew the routine, but I was uncomfortably panicked. I was shaking in a fetal position with my blanket over my head when Dr. Magtibay came in to see me. He reassured me that it would all be okay.

As soon as he left, I pulled the blanket over my head and cried like a baby. I heard nurses coming in and scurrying around, but I didn't take my head out until one asked if I was okay. I sniffled and said, "I'm fine." While going into the O.R., the nurse told me she liked my blanket and said that Recker was such a cute little boy. Those pictures helped take my mind off of what was about to happen. I kissed Eric and watched him walking away. I grieved for him in that moment. It was heartbreaking to watch him fade into the halls of Mayo Clinic.

When they rolled me into the operating room I heard the door open and quickly looked to my left. It was Dr. Kreymerman. Knowing this was going to be a difficult surgery for me he came from his office to hold my hand and talk to me until I drifted off into sedation. Technically I was no longer his patient since I had finished my treatments with him. His familiar face was the last one I saw, and his voice was the last I heard. Thinking back on that day I am in awe of him leaving his office coming to the hospital taking the time to put on a sterile gown and come into comfort me. I don't believe most physicians would take the time to do that. I'm going to miss him.

I woke up in recovery and was ready to go home. I just wanted to get out of there. I have this love-hate relationship with the Mayo Hospital. Where is my husband? Where is my uterus?

The nurse said, "Are you in pain?"

I responded, "Yes."

"On a scale of one to ten, how would you rate your pain?"

"I hate pain meds. I put them off as long as I can, but it's time." My post-op nurse was so nice and stayed with me until I went to my room on the seventh floor. Room sixty-four.

I woke up in the morning, and Eric was in a bed on the floor next to me. I watched him sleeping. My heart was pumping as tears rolled down my cheeks. He has been a blessing to me. The only man who truly has ever loved me. I wanted to wake up and have all of this behind us. I could not watch him go through what I had gone through, and he did it with dignity and grace. I love him. I'm in love with who he is.

Three weeks flew by after my surgery. I was trying to learn to control the thoughts that bombarded my brain. The flashbacks were uncontrollable and created stress and insomnia. The surgery was not about the diagnosis of cancer. It was a window of opportunity to clean my mind of the past. Those awful events of my life had turned cancerous. They were eating me from the inside out. I believe God was trying to teach me to deal with my former life and come to a place in my new life where I could be free from the demons that constantly created the horrible flashbacks.

Dr. Magtibay had no idea how he helped me to trust and believe I was a warrior by overcoming some of the shadowy spooks that filled the nooks and crannies of my brain for years. The emotional healing process was slow but I was grateful to him for his compassion.

After my six-week post-op appointment with Dr. Magtibay, Eric and I decided to drive down to Mexico. For the first time in my life, I felt whole. Eric was gentle and kind with me. The scars of my past were gone, and the feeling of true love was overwhelming. Eric didn't see my scars. He took me in his arms and told me how beautiful I was.

Chapter 28

Angels and Autism

My life with cancer was sometimes overbearing. I spent so much time at Mayo Clinic. My sweet safe haven was Recker. I looked forward to every minute with him. He was my little buddy when his mama was working. When he was thirteen months old, he ran, ate everything we gave him, and loved to snuggle. He loved Toy Story, especially Buzz, Mickey Mouse, and playing outside. This little boy was the best distraction in my life. I never knew how much being a grandmother would affect my life in a positive way.

I was much better at being Bonbon than I was at being a mom. My face lit up when he came to our home. I loved when he would come running into my arms and hug me. On the days when Kayla kept him home, it made me sad not to see him.

Recker was fourteen months old when he was diagnosed with moderate to severe autism. For a few months, I had a feeling something was not right with him. When I had to fill out all the paperwork from Phoenix Children's Hospital, I knew. All of the symptoms I'd seen while he was in my care were down on paper. I know it must have been heartbreaking for Kayla and Jeremy. Where would we go from there?

I had no doubt in my mind that Heavenly Father had been preparing Kayla for this. She worked at an elementary school with special needs children, including several with autism. Being diagnosed so young was good since we could get him therapy quicker. I had faith and hope in Recker's future. I believed he was going to have an incredible life full of happiness and joy. The Lord has a special place in heaven for this little guy.

As I watched him playing innocently and enjoying life as he knows it, I realized how blessed we were to have the opportunity to be his grandparents. We spent so much time with him. Recker had been with me since he was born—at least a few hours a day for five days a week. While I was going through chemo, he saved me sometimes from wanting to be done with life in general. He brought so much joy to my life. Our entire family adores him, and we'd get so excited when Kayla and Jeremy came over with him.

On Sundays, the family comes for dinner. Sometimes we all just sat at the table and stared at him. We'd laugh at every move he made. He was incredibly sweet and innocent. When he'd fall asleep next to me, I couldn't help but shed a few tears. It was more for the unknown than anything else. He had no idea what was going on.

Our family didn't have a lot of knowledge about autism. My heart was aching for Kayla and Jeremy. I didn't know how to console them—just like no one could console me when I was diagnosed. I watched and read everything I could get my hands on about autism. There is nothing to prepare a family for this. We spent a lot of time as a family; one of my favorite trips was when we were all able to go to our condos in Mexico. I especially loved having Recker there with us. Our sweet little angel loves the outdoors. Eric and I let him wander down the beach while we walked close behind, counting as he picked up rocks and shells. I counted him pick up and throw the same shell back down 256 times. He was in his own little world as he jabbered. He ran, walked, and discovered new things along the shoreline. Every once in a while, he would make sure I was within his eyesight.

After the occasional grin or hug to acknowledge me, he would pick up sand and throw it back into the ocean. I wondered what his little brain was thinking. I wished there was something I could do to understand and help him. All parents want their children to be happy. I truly wanted happiness for Recker. I watched him play and decided he is a happy little boy who will never have to experience the pressure of life the way we do.

According to the Mayo Clinic journals, autism is a serious neurodevelopmental disorder that impairs a child's ability to communicate and interact with others. It includes restricted repetitive behaviors, interests, and activities. These issues cause significant impairment in social,   occupational, and other areas of functioning. Autism spectrum disorder (ASD) is now defined by the American Psychiatric Association's Diagnostic and Statistical Manual of Mental Disorders (DSM-5) as a single disorder that includes disorders that were previously considered separate: autism, Asperger's syndrome, childhood disintegrative disorder, and pervasive developmental disorder. The word spectrum was new to me, and I wanted to learn more. Autism spectrum disorder refers to the wide range of symptoms and their severity. Although Asperger's syndrome is no longer in the DSM, some people still use the term. It is generally thought to be at the mild end of autism spectrum disorder.

The number of children diagnosed with autism spectrum disorder is rising. It's not clear whether this is due to better detection and reporting, a real increase in the number of cases, or both. While there is no cure for autism, intensive, early treatment can make a big difference in the lives of many children. Hearing this was comforting since Kayla had Recker diagnosed at such an early age.

I could see so many symptoms Recker had manifested. As his grandmother, none of the statistics or facts mattered to me. Recker is perfect to us. I knew he was sent to our family to refine us and elevate us to a new level of communicating with our hearts. I was realistic enough to know I was confronting this trial on a totally different level than his parents. I can't speak for Jeremy and Kayla, but from my observation, his diagnosis has been traumatic and stressful. They needed our continued prayers for guidance and contentment as they journey through a difficult life trial.

Chapter 29

I Ran

For over a year, my right hip had been agonizingly painful at times. It was hard to stand for long periods, and my knees would give out on me. Sitting for too long also made it difficult to put one foot in front of the other without bringing tears to my eyes. I was sent for a bone scan since recurrence of breast cancer can show up in the hipbones. Cancer was ruled out, and I was referred to the pain center at the Mayo Clinic. Dr. Freeman is very knowledgeable, and we immediately bantered back and forth. Several times a year, he and I meet for cortisone shots.

I was finally given the okay to start my exercise program. This was great news. I was elated to find out I could get back to normal. Blake only had a few months left on his mission. If everything went as planned, my hair would be grown out enough to style. He never wanted to see me bald. With exercise back on the schedule, I would look healthy when he stepped off the airplane.

Brian and Kaitlyn invited me to come with them while they played tennis at Highland High. I put on my running shoes and decided I would try to walk a lap or two while they played. My hip might not allow me to walk far without too much pain. I ventured out with headphones. I felt a hair-raising flood of emotions as I stepped onto the track. I compared the moment to an artist with a clean canvas. I was not quite sure what the end result would be. It was just so important to take the first step, and I prayed it would be a success.

Four women were walking together and enjoying each other's company. They passed me. Oh, heck no. They are not going to pass me. I stepped up my pace. After the first lap, I cried like a baby. I did it. I walked an entire lap and had virtually no pain. Going into the second lap, I looked up into the stands and remembered sitting on the benches a year ago. I was bald as a cue ball, but I was proud as I watched my baby girl graduate from high school. It's amazing what I had learned about myself in a year. I would not change anything. My life was where I wanted it to be. When I thought about the times I had begged and pleaded with the Lord to let me have peace and let me accept whatever plan he had for me, tears filled my eyes.

As I was walking, all of these thoughts were going through my head. I finished four laps. On the fourth lap, tears were rolling down my cheeks—and I had the biggest smile on my face. With my thoughts all over the place, I had finished a mile—and not even realized it. I was not going to stop. It was the best therapy I could have given myself.

I watched a younger man doing sprints, and I was jealous. I love sprints. This made me think about cancer. My journey had not been a sprint; it had been a marathon. I hoped to finish it with dignity. I hoped I had taught my children something from what I had learned. Did they know how much I loved them? Did they understand that it is never okay to give up? There were times in my life when I felt like I was in a drought, feeling completely defeated. I just needed something or someone to fill my cup. I finished eight laps and thought, Are you kidding me right now?

The song All about Your Heart by Mindy Gledhill was playing on my iPod. It was perfect timing as she sang, You are brighter than the stars. Believe me when I say it's not about your scars.

It's all about your heart. I suddenly got a surge of energy and decided to run. My legs were actually picking up the pace, and I was running. The track made me feel at home. It felt right and comfortable. The track had always been a place where I could think clearly. I hadn't felt so free in so long. I was kicking cancer's butt, and it felt good. There was so much more to learn and so much more I wanted to accomplish in my life. I owed so much to God for seeing me through the toughest times of my life. It was time to give it back. It was time to move forward. I finally felt like I could be true to myself. Live an authentic life with all the baggage gone. I finished running the tenth lap. It was emotional when I finished twelve laps. I raised my hands in the air as if I was crossing the finish line in a great victory. The track was empty. I celebrated with tears of joy. I was sure my body was going to feel it in the morning, but for that moment, I was so happy.

I am an athlete and a competitor. Running was my passion, and that had not changed. I was so thankful for the time I had taken to be alone in my thoughts. I was happy for what I accomplished on the track and for realizing it's okay to shed a tear or two knowing where my life had been. I finally knew where I was going and life was good.

Eric and I spent more time in Mexico. I loved having alone time with him. We laughed a lot, and we cried sometimes. Life is good when I'm with him. I feel safe. I ran on the beach while the sun was just coming up. The cool ocean breeze was hitting my face. I had a poignant moment and thought about my journey. I saw some shoe prints in the sand and decided to follow them. When the water goes out, it leaves ripples in the sand. They are hard to run on because they are uneven. I always fear I am going to twist my ankle.

I followed the prints all the way to the wall, which was a couple miles. It made me think of the people in my life who have led the way for me. They have been examples to me, and they taught me the gospel. Stan Johnson was my seminary teacher. I learned how to pray to God for help and to listen for answers. He taught me how to read the scriptures and love them. He taught me life lessons I still use. I will forever be grateful to him.

As I ran, I thought about the young women leaders who paved the way for me. Their examples of faith taught me to have hope. On the run back, I searched for my shoe print so I could retrace my steps. To my surprise, there were no prints to follow. I realized I was on my own. I was trudging along through rough sand. Just like in my journey through abuse and cancer, I was sometimes on my own. My pace was slowing down, and I was really struggling to breathe. It wasn't long before I was back on track and following my prints.

I saw a print from a baby's feet. It immediately reminded me of my twenties. Having children and learning how to balance life with children, I sometimes got distracted and felt lonely. Without a mother to lean on, I looked to women in my life who had already raised their children. Maybe I could learn some things from them. I noticed I was running on some rocks or coral, which shook me out of those memories and into the present. I turned to look behind me. I've come a long way, but ahead I had so much further to go.

My feet were sinking into the sand, and I was struggling to keep up. I have been through times when I felt like I was sinking. Through a constant connection with Heavenly Father I've always been able to dig my way out of the sinking sand I sometimes thought would engulf me. It started to rain on my already difficult conditions. The waters were rough, the waves were strong, the sand was soaked, and the wind was blowing against my body. Just as my heart had been bombarded with problematic situations I have always been able to find shelter by listening to a still small voice guiding me back to safety. I felt the sun peek up and say hello. The warmth on my back put a smile on my face.

When I looked up I and saw my finish line for the day, tears came to my eyes. My life has been filled with distractions, disappointment, failure, and unbelievable pain. I have loved, felt love, found joy, and discovered I was never alone during all the rugged times. I was lonely at times, but I was never alone. I was finally running toward baggage instead of away from it. It was time to unpack the bags and put the past behind me. The finish line was in sight, and I was winning.

Since that run, I shattered an ankle and have not ran since. I now cycle 150–175 miles a week or walk for exercise. I also meditate and practice yoga.

Chapter 30

Where I Grew Up

As a child, our family moved several times. I decided to drive by the houses we called "home" in Phoenix. Floods of memories came back to me. The house I lived in during elementary school looked so small. In that house, my stepbrothers and sisters were taken from school. In this house my mom was pregnant with Lance and brought him home from the hospital.

One of the scariest things that ever happened to me happened there while my mother was cooking dinner and I was sitting at the kitchen table. I looked up, and a child was standing in the middle of our kitchen. She had red eyes, transparent pink skin, and extremely white hair in an Afro. She looked at Mom and asked if I could play with her. I found out she was an albino of African descent. We became friends, and then one day she was gone. I wonder where she is, who she became, and where she grew up. I realize as I drove away this house had memories, but it was not where I grew up.

I drove past our house on Fifty-First Avenue several times before I recognized it. I sat in my car for a long time in front of the house. We lived there during junior high. The Hulshoff family lived down the street. In the summer, we played kick the can and hide-and-seek with them every night. I had my first kiss on that street with a boy named Eric. I smiled at the irony of having my first kiss with a boy named Eric and giving my last kisses to a husband named Eric.

I'll never forget the day Elvis Presley died. Mom cried like a baby. I learned how to mow the lawn, pull weeds, and get grounded for lint balls being left behind on the carpet after vacuuming. This house was difficult to look at. It was the house where bad things happened. I was forced to choose between sparing Mom's feelings and my stepdad's desires. The tears were flowing as I stared at my bedroom window. So many times, I wanted to jump out that window, run away, and never look back. That house was filled with horrid memories, but it was not where I grew up.

Driving toward our house off of Seventy-Ninth Avenue, I was shaking. I did not know if I could do it. I wondered why I was doing this. I turned in, and Sara's house was on the left. I babysat for her sometimes. I was overwhelmed with emotions as I drove toward the house I lived in during high school and as a young adult. I imagined I could see my white 1965 Mustang parked out front. I smiled about my memories with friends in that car.

I took pictures on the front lawn in my cap and gown on graduation night from Alhambra High School in 1981. Little did I know that Lance would die in that house just a few years later. I will never forget that cold Veteran's Day morning. I wonder if the people living there now know what a special spirit lived in that house. I met Eric while I lived in that house. I fell in love with him while I lived in that house. I kneeled and prayed at my bedside for hours, begging the Lord to help me survive that house.

As I glared at the house, I couldn't help but remember so many awful memories. There was not a lot of love in that house. Verbal, physical, mental, and sexual abuse were a small chapter of my life. I knew good things were yet to come, but that was not where I grew up.

As I drove away, I looked in the rearview mirror. Good-bye and good riddance. I will never come back here again. The memories will never fade, but I believe dwelling on them will not heal me completely.

On my way home, I decided to drive by the homes Eric and I have lived in. I wanted to write down the memories I felt at each one of the homes. In Chandler, there is a house where Eric and I brought Kayla and Blake home from the hospital. In that home, we laughed, cried, and loved together. In that home, I worked hard to learn how to be a wife and mother. In that home, I learned to cook, clean, and be responsible for myself and for a family.

One night, a cricket was just outside our bedroom window. I was determined to get rid of it, Eric giggled at me trying to find it. I was so busy with being a mother that I failed to read my scriptures like I should. I compared myself to other mothers and wives. I let the world define motherhood. I struggled with self-esteem. I attended the Temple once a week with Eric's dad for more than a year so I could learn more. As I looked at this home and thought about the memories, I knew it was not where I grew up either.

I stopped at the Islands, a community we lived in when we welcomed Kaitlyn and Haleigh to our family. In that home, I continued on my quest to do everything right. In that home, Kayla broke her arm and had to have surgery. Blake broke his arm and several other bones jumping off everything he could climb on. Eric and I met Mike and Jenny Scow, and they have become forever friends. We celebrated my thirtieth birthday with the Scows while living in that home. In this home, I realized a dad should have respect and compassion for his children. I learned this by watching Eric with our children. In that home was the darkest time of my life. Through those front doors, I confronted the man who abused me. My mother walked away, leaving me with an empty heart. The guilt I felt for breaking up our "family" was so overwhelming that I went into a deep depression, but it was not the home where I grew up.

After the Islands, we moved into the home we are in now. I was broken, and my heart ached for my mom. I wanted that relationship to be mended. I tried so many times, and every time, I came away even more hurt than the time before. I once sat in a fetal position by the front door and cried until Eric got home.

David LeSueur was our church leader, and he laid his hands on my head and gave me a blessing that I will never forget. He blessed me to find peace in my heart. From that day on, I began to heal from my past. I finally realized none of what happened was my fault.

Haleigh was only eighteen months old when we moved there. All of my children were baptized on their eighth birthday while living in that home. In that home, I raised my voice way too much, trying to deal with being the mother of teens. I began looking to other woman for inspiration, advice, love, and recipes. I hated that I could not just get on the phone with my own mom for those things.

In that home, I watched our children face challenges. I spent hours on my knees and prayed individually for my children to understand the importance of obedience. I learned the importance of saying, "I'm sorry. I was wrong." We took pictures of each of our children going to prom. They all graduated from high school while we lived here.

Kayla, Jeremy, Kaitlyn, and Brian were married and had their receptions in our backyard. Eric and I gathered our children and son-in-law at the kitchen table to break the news that I had been diagnosed with breast cancer. Blake left on a journey of his own. I did not realize how much Eric loved me until I went through my cancer treatments. I realized I too had so much love to give and learned how to express it in this home.

Heavenly Father loved me and had been with me for every step of my life. I can see when he carried me and literally pulled me out of overwhelming situations. Still that house is not where I grew up.

During my forty-eight years on earth, I have learned that a house is just a structure built of wood or stone to create four walls and a roof. What truly makes a home is the love, compassion, respect, laughter, and joy felt there. A home is where a child should not be afraid to live. Every person in that home deserves to be listened to and hugged. Every member of that family needs to know they are loved, especially by their moms and dads. Every day, they should hear, "I love you." I wish I had lowered my voice and softened my heart when my teens were struggling. Knowing this makes me want to be a better mother, wife, and grandmother. No matter when we figure it all out, it's never too late. Heavenly Father loves us all that much.

I drove to the Mesa Temple and parked. I watched as people entered and exited. In his house, I searched my heart and soul and found answers to life's scariest questions. Who am I? What defines me as a woman? What and who are most important in my life? Have I done all I can do to be the kind of person the Lord would be proud of? What can I do to make life better for someone else? I learned that I am a daughter of God. He knows me by name and wants nothing but happiness for me. It is up to me to decide how I will obtain that happiness.

In the house of the Lord, I discovered my true identity. It had nothing to do with the size of our home, how much money my husband made, the style of clothes I wore, or the car I drove. I learned to listen to the spirit for answers and guidance. I learned how to truly forgive those who had offended me.

The answers came at different times in my life—when the Lord knew I was ready to hear the answers. When it was my season to learn what I needed to learn, I learned to let God work things out and put all my burdens in His hands. If I'm doing all I can do to be more like Him, it will all work out in this life or the next.

In the house of the Lord is where I grew up.

Chapter 31
Judge Not

I wish I could have bottled up the feeling of opening the e-mail with my son's itinerary. He was coming home on September 28 at 5:25 p.m. I did a little dance in my kitchen, smiled from ear to ear, and said, "Yes, he's finally coming home." I knew it was bittersweet for him, but it was all sweet to me. I missed him so much. I literally dreamed of that first hug, and nothing I can write will come close to explaining the feelings in my heart. So much had happened during those two years, but none of that mattered. I just wanted to have my family back together.

I had kept my promise to him. I never sent him any pictures of me. I e-mailed him every week, and I never talked about cancer. One of the letters Blake wrote to us really touched Eric and me. We were really impressed by how much he had sacrificed. It's hard to know some of the conditions he lived in. However, hearing him say he loved it melted my heart. He loves the Dominican people. Knowing he could see good in sometimes dreary conditions put my emotions on overload. He had grown from a boy to a man. I really never thought he was rough around the edges, but hearing him grow as much as he did made me realize how much refining and smoothing he had done.

Dear Mom and Dad

I've been thinking about the time I have left here in this country. It has really come to be part of me I mean I really consider myself one of them. I love these people, and I really honestly am going to miss them so much. Even the people that don't want to listen to us or the dogs that always chase and bark at us. I'll even miss the random drunk man who's always there to talk to. I've come to realize the things I don't like, are what I am going to miss the most.

Like when there is no light in the whole town for twenty-four hours, having to go to sleep drowning in your own sweat, being eaten alive by mosquitos. When there's no water to shower before you leave the house. No light to iron my shirt before church. Even when, no one is in their houses the whole day not even the members to give us some water or juice. Then it starts to pour down rain, these are the things I really am going to miss. I love this country, and I will always say it is my country … I am so grateful to be in the best mission in the whole world, with the best mission president in the whole world.

This week the things have been a little different after the hurricane. It took out a hotel right on the beach here and ruined the street. The place got pretty flooded. It's the first area I have been in where it kinda reminds me of home because there are cactus here. Ha-ha. It's not a place that normally gets a lot of rain.

This week has been pretty good. I think I gave my last talk in the mission. It was eight-thirty in the morning on Sunday we were preparing ourselves to leave and go pick up an investigator. President Diaz called and asked me to prepare a talk for church. I said, "Of course I'll do it." I thought at first it was for the next week. Then, fifteen minutes later, I realized he meant today, like now. He said to make sure it's a long talk because my mission president was going to be there. My talk went really well—considering I had little time to prepare. They told us the chapel is going to be remodeled and that we will be moving into a little house for five or six months. We are going to baptize this guy named Alvelino in a few weeks. He has been learning from different sets of missionaries for eight years, and his wife is a member. She's tried and tried to teach him, and so have the missionaries. We have been working hard with him, and we put a date for him so we will be baptizing him a week or so before I get home. I can't wait to see the look on his face and his wife's face when he gets baptized. This is one of the things I am going to miss the most. Seeing the lives of people change.

Con mucho amor,
Elder Blake Williams

So much changed in Arizona, and my son's life had been altered. He had sacrificed two years of his life to share the gospel with others. He had learned the importance of obedience and long-suffering. I watched how much he had changed through distant miles between us. He was organized, knew every minute of every day where and what he was supposed to be doing, and the Lord was ready to release him back to his mama. The excitement grew stronger as the days got closer to his arrival. The entire family was excited to see him.

September 27, 2011

I'll never forget the day we got home from taking Blake to the MTC. On September 23, 2009, I went in his room, sat on the bed, and cried. I have a lot of faith, but I wasn't sure what my future would be. I didn't know if I would have the opportunity to hold and hug my son again. I know it must have been so difficult for him to leave. I worried night and day about him. I wanted him to have a successful mission without worrying or stressing about me.

I understand why the Lord has order and precision; things are clearer than ever before. Timing is everything. Most boys leave on their missions when they turn nineteen. Blake was not ready, and it broke my heart at the time. I know the Lord is in full control. He understands more than we realize. Blake made the decision to leave when he was twenty-one. All of his friends who left at nineteen were just getting home from their missions.

Only six weeks before he left, I found out I had breast cancer. I thought it was is the worst timing ever. When I look back on that, I realize how much I needed to learn. Tears run down my cheeks as I think about what the Lord has blessed us with. My son is my hero. I love him so much. He endured two years with strength and reliance on the Lord to help him through some tough days and nights.

I'm sitting on his bed writing, and so many emotions are running through my head. He will sleep here tomorrow night. He will kneel and pray here in this room where I have knelt and prayed so many times. I've pleaded to the Lord on his behalf in this room. I see scriptures on his nightstand— the ones I have studied and pondered. Preach My Gospel is right next to my scriptures, and the pages are a bit tattered.

I read every scripture I could get my hands on about faith, hope, charity, love, virtue, knowledge, patience, humility, diligence, and obedience. I have a long way to go before I can say I have mastered even one of those attributes. It is time for Blake to come home, be with his family, and start his life. I know he must have some mixed emotions.

I have been dreaming of the hug I will get from him and praying that my health will be good enough to greet him at the airport without him being disappointed or discouraged. He made it through, and I made it through. We all pulled through two years. I wouldn't trade them for anything in the world.

The knowledge I have of our Savior's love for me and my family has been strengthened tenfold. I am so thankful to my friends, family, and the Lord for lifting me up when I thought tomorrow would never come.

When I pick up my scriptures and walk through his bedroom door, I will close it like a chapter in my life is over, but I am opening another door to walk toward a bright and beautiful future. Exactly two years ago tomorrow, I was having a bilateral mastectomy and being told my cancer had spread. Look at us now. Blake is coming home, and we are celebrating.

September 28, 2011

By the time I go to bed tonight, I'll be holding my son again. Blake became grounded and solid in his beliefs. He learned that some will listen and accept—and some will yell, scream, and slam a door in his face. No matter the outcome, he never gave up. Despite the naysayers, he accepts that not all people will understand why you do what you do. Some do not have what it takes to fundamentally change their lives. He was determined to be obedient, he did the same day-to-day practices for two years, literally wore the bottoms of his shoes out, ran from dogs, and lived in villages with no electricity or running water. He says those were the best two years of his life.

When Blake left, I felt so lost as a mother. I knew I could not be the one to answer his questions or comfort him when he needed it. I guess we both learned to do the best we could and turn the rest over to the Lord. I'm looking forward to hearing his remarkable experiences, the good, and the not so good. We both have learned that change is good.

We arrived at the airport hours before his plane landed. I bought him his favorite cookies from Paradise Bakery (ginger molasses). Our family made welcome home posters and paced the floor, waiting for a glimpse of him walking down the runway. He was the last one to arrive from his flight. My heart was racing, the girls were ecstatic, and Eric was crying.

When I watched the YouTube video his friends made of his homecoming, I was embarrassed. I jumped up and down, yelled for him to run, and ran into his arms. It was the best hug I've ever had. Having him home and making our family complete again was so sweet.

I could see a sadness in him. He was happy to be with his family, but he missed the Dominican people. He had a difficult time transitioning back into life. I was so touched by his testimony. He sobbed as he explained the journey he had been on. First on his list of things to do was eating at LoLo's Chicken and Waffles. The sound of that made me sick. I tried it, and it's not for me. Having a fresh juice and watching Blake interact with the family was all I needed at that moment.

When we arrived home, Blake was very emotional. He lay down on the carpet and moved his body as if to make a snow angel.

I asked, "What are you doing?"

He replied, "We have carpet! I have not seen or felt carpet in two years. I forgot or took for granted all the material things that make life easier." He slept on the floor for several weeks.

His eyes filled with tears. "Mom, I miss the Dominican Republic. Sleeping in a comfortable bed makes me feel guilty. Americans have so much and take it all for granted."

I hugged him, not completely understanding everything he had seen or been through but wanting to be strength for his return—like I had seen Viola do with Kurt.

For the next few months, Blake and I spent a lot of time together. I wanted to know every good, bad, and funny story. He didn't ask much about my journey, and I was totally fine with it. I asked him about seeing his family again.

"Well, your hair was shorter than I expected—and you lost weight. Dad looked happy as always, but he looked like he gained weight. Everyone else just looked a little older. Seeing Recker for the first time was interesting. Mom, can you tell me about autism? How did he 'get' it?"

"It's not something that is contagious. We don't know a lot about it. I just feel so blessed he was born into a family who will always love and accept him."

"He doesn't know me. He walks away when I try to talk to him. What can I do to help him?"

"Son, autism is very misunderstood. It will take him time to get to know you, but eventually, he will love you just like he loves the rest of the family. The more time you spend with him, the more he will become connected to you with his heart and through his eyes."

"Mom, what is your best motherly advice for your newly returned missionary son?"

"While you are dating, don't linger. If you are looking for a wife and don't like something, move on. When you find the one, you'll know—and don't waste time."

A friend printed this story and gave it to me. We all do some amount of judging in our lives. It's unfortunate, but it does happen. We just don't know what is going on in other people's lives. A doctor entered the hospital in a hurry after being called in for and an urgent surgery. He answered the call, changed his clothes, and went directly to surgery. He found the boy's father pacing the halls, waiting for the doctor to arrive.

The dad yelled, "Why did you take so long to get here? Don't you know that my son's life is in danger? Don't you have any sense of responsibility?"

The doctor smiled and said, "I am sorry. I wasn't in the hospital. I came as fast as I could after receiving the call. And now, I wish you'd calm down so that I can do my work."

"Calm down? What if your son was in that room right now? Would you calm down? If your own son died right now, what would you do?" said the father.

The doctor smiled again and replied, "I will say what Job said in the Holy Bible: 'From dust we came and to dust we return, blessed be the name of God.' Doctors cannot prolong lives. Go and intercede for your son. We will do our best by God's grace."

"Giving advice when we're not concerned is so easy."

The surgery took hours, and the doctor said, "Thank God! Your son is saved." And without waiting for the father's reply, he carried on his way running. "If you have any questions, ask the nurse."

"Why is he so arrogant? He couldn't wait a few minutes so I could ask about my son's state," the father said.

The nurse had tears coming down her face. "His son died yesterday in a road accident. He was at the burial when we called him for your son's surgery. And now that he saved your son's life, he ran to finish his son's burial."

When Blake returned from his mission, I could see so many changes in him. He now read his scriptures and had his personal prayer without being asked. He had a desire to be obedient. My son understands the power of forgiveness. He takes time to help the needy and goes out of his way to serve others less fortunate. To me, he is a perfect example of a peace giver. He knows the past of many friends, yet he still invites them into his circle with no judgment. Repentance and forgiveness have become near and dear to my heart. They are a vital part of my existence and living a truly happy life. Blake has taught me many lessons about repentance, forgiveness and judging other's.

In the movie For Love Of The Game with Kevin Costner and Kelly Preston, the lead actress said, "Wouldn't it be nice if everyone could wear a sign around their necks saying what kind of mood they're in or what was happening in their lives so we could just know and treat them different?"

Maybe we would be less critical of each other if we knew what people were going through in their private lives:

- "My husband just left me."
- "I just lost my job."
- "Someone in my family is dealing with addiction."
- "My marriage is struggling."
- "My child was just diagnosed with autism."
- "I lost my job."
- "I lost my home."
- "I'm being abused."
- "My child is rebelling."
- "I have cancer."

We all need to be a little kinder toward everyone we meet. I have had to stop myself many times and remember this story before I judge. I have been on the receiving side of the judgment, and it hurts.

When my girls were little, they danced competitively. A few times a year, we would have a competition that fell on a Sunday. In the LDS religion, we take the Tenth Commandment literally (Keep the Sabbath Day holy). We go to church and spend time with family on Sundays. It is all part of the LDS lifestyle. However, I supported my children and went to every recital and competition.

We sat as a family and watched. We brought our own snacks and did not purchase items on Sunday. I never felt I had anyone to answer to except God.

Once someone said, "Your daughters dance on Sundays? I would never allow that in my home."

I said, "Well, I'd rather have a child who dances on a Sunday than be the mother who gossips about them."

I felt judged when I chose to go the medicinal route for cancer treatments. I've been judged for my spiritual beliefs. The hardest judgment came when people found out about the alleged abuse by the stepdad. I wanted to defend myself, but I backed off. I wanted it to just go away. After all, only the Lord and I knew the truth—and that was all that really mattered to me. I realize that judging is a natural part of life, and we all do it to some degree. People sometimes don't know what they don't know. If they have never experienced the life of someone else, they just don't understand.

The pain in my legs, hip, and back were becoming increasingly worse. One of my doctors suggested a handicapped plate for my car. When I get out of my car, some people say, "Why do you need to park in a handicapped spot? You seem perfectly fine to me?" Others say, "You should be ashamed of yourself. Is that your grandmother's car?"

I bit my tongue the first time as the woman and her husband followed me into the store, gossiping and threatening to call the police. The second time it happened, I turned around and said, "I have cancer. The effects of it have left me barely able to walk. Back off."

I think God knew we would struggle with judging other people. Matthew 7:1–5 talks about judging. For the same way we judge others, we will be judged. There are opportunities in life where we will need to judge appropriately. During jury duty, we are expected to impartially judge individuals. Although judgment is a natural instinct, I try to catch myself before I speak or send a nasty reply in a text or e-mail. I'm trying harder to be mindful of where that person is coming from.

When someone disagrees with something we have to say, it usually has nothing to do with the subject at hand. It's typically about the pain or struggle they are experiencing. Give the person the benefit of the doubt and never underestimate the pain of a person. Every person in the world is struggling; some are just better at hiding it than others

When people do something I don't care for, I try to imagine them as solving the problem in a different way than I would. The Dalai Lama said, "People take different roads seeking fulfillment and happiness. Just because they're not on your road doesn't mean they've gotten lost."

Having a grandchild with autism has made me more aware of the criticism and lack of education people have. When people do things that annoy me, I try to remember that they might have hidden disabilities. Maybe they lack social skills because of the disability. It's not always about you or me. If someone is in your space, remember these words from Albert Einstein: "Everybody is a genius. But if you judge a fish by its ability to climb a tree, it will live its whole life believing that it is stupid."

We all need to feel good about ourselves. We need to be okay with our parenting, our bodies, our spiritual beliefs, and our inner selves. If we all focused on our own abilities instead the lack in others, we would never have the time or energy to judge anyone else. Counting other people's sins does not make you a saint in any way. Before you assume anything, learn the facts. Educate yourself. Before you judge anyone, understand the whys. Before you hurt others, try to feel what they feel. Before you speak, think about what you say. Is it worth it?

My own failures have taught me that judging others does not define who they are. It defines who I am. I decided to stop condemning other people. I made the decision to live in a way that I would not cause others to stumble and fall because of my inability to see past their imperfections. Dieter F. Uchtdorf said, "Don't judge me because I sin differently from you."

February 18, 2012

Blake had been home since September, and a few weeks later, he started to date Chloe.

Before I was leaving for work one morning, I could see his light was on.

He said, "Mom, can I talk to you?"

"Of course."

"Mom, last night Chloe and I talked for hours. I told her everything about myself, and she shared with me."

I raised my eyebrows and said, "And?"

"I'm going to marry her."

I hugged him and said, "I love you. Any girl who marries you will always laugh and be happy, but I'm really glad it's Chloe."

Let me tell you a little about this sweet girl. She danced with Haleigh and Kaitlyn. Her mother sadly lost her life to cancer just after I found out I had cancer. Chloe brings out the best qualities in Blake. They continually laugh, compliment each other, and are genuinely supportive of the goals they have made together and individually. I have never been nervous about who Blake would marry because we have always joked that whoever he decides to marry has to get the Williams' girls approval—and Chloe does. We love her and are happy for them to start their life together. We always knew Blake would marry a girl with dark hair and cocoa skin. Chloe is Peruvian. They will make some cute babies.

It was fun watching Blake prepare to ask her to marry him. He wanted his family involved, and we all packed up and went to Mexico. Blake and Brian planned the actual event so none of us really knew when it would happen or how. Chloe had no idea it was coming, which made it even that more sweet. To top it off it was on her birthday.

Brian gave the engagement ring to a young boy and asked him to walk up to our family and ask for Chloe. She was so cute. Looking surprised, she answered "Oh, me. I'm Chloe. How did you know that?" The cute little boy handed her the ring. Blake got down on one knee and asked her to be his wife. The entire family surrounded them as we celebrated with tears, laughter, and pure love.

The next few months were busy with wedding plans, doctor appointments, volunteering at a cancer center, and working at US Airways. They were married on May 25, 2012. We had their reception in our backyard; it was another beautiful night with friends and family. It was hard to believe three of our four children were married.

I watched Blake and Chloe drive off and wondered if he was feeling blessed. His life could have taken such a different road. Chloe was—and is—perfect for him. My heart was full of gratitude.

Chapter 32

The Ear

The months were flying by, and I was thinking about recurrence less and less every day. Every once in a while, I'd get a spark of fear, but for the most part, I was doing everything Dr. Northfelt asked me to do.

If cancer decided to ravage my body again, I had no regrets. In October, Eric and I decided to put another check mark next to one of the things on my list of things to do. We flew to Tahiti and enjoyed visiting each island. We were gone for two weeks. I love visiting places where I can listen to Frenchie speak French, and Tahiti was one of them. We stayed in beautiful bungalows on the sea.

When we were staying on Moorea, the sunset was absolutely beautiful. Frenchie and I sat on the beach, watched the sun fade into the night, smelled the fresh ocean breeze, and listened to the waves hitting the shore. I thought about Kurt serving his mission there. Every local we met greeted us with a smile, and they seemed to be so happy. I said, "I can see why Kurt had a hard time coming home from his mission. I'm going to call him right now."

"That's a great idea. Let me get my phone."

He walked toward me from the bungalow, and I sighed. I felt safe, loved, and relieved from the stresses of the world.

"Kurt, it's Monya. Eric and I wanted to call you. We are watching the sun go down in Moorea. It's so beautiful. The people have been so gracious and kind. Now I know why you loved your mission so much."

"Oh, where are you on the island?" I handed the phone to Frenchie so he could tell his little brother about our journey.

Eric and Kurt had a great talk. I could hear the excitement in Frenchie's voice as he explained the serenity we were feeling and the beauty we could see.

Eric said, "Okay. I love you, buddy. Talk to you soon."

I swam with dolphins, and we swam with sharks. I researched all there is to know about the different species of sharks. I've watched every "Shark Week" on TV, and I've always told my children I won't get eaten if I don't go in. Keep your friends close—and your enemy closer. Always know what is lurking around the corner. Sharks make me hyperventilate. I had no idea what our plans were each day, but Frenchie planned out everything. He said we were going on a boat ride to an island where they would prepare lunch for us. He "forgot" to tell me we were headed to shark-infested waters.

When the boat came to a stop, our guide said, "Okay. This is where we swim with the sharks."

I immediately looked at Frenchie. "Seriously? You have got to be kidding. You know I'm not getting out of this boat, right?"

"Come on. It'll be fun—and maybe it will get you over your ridiculous fear of sharks."

"Ridiculous? Oh no. Do you know how many people got eaten by sharks last year?"

"Of course I don't, but I'm sure you do."

"Yes. In the United States, fifty-three people were attacked. I'm not going in."

Frenchie dove into the bluest water I'd ever seen and began frolicking with the sharks. He looked so happy and waved me in. White tip sharks surrounded the boat, and I could see them for what seemed like miles. White tip sharks are not known for attacking humans, so I felt Frenchie was safe. I was scared to death as I inched my way to the edge of the boat.

Eric was coaxing me along slowly but surely. I jumped into the ocean of sharks, and I screamed a bit. When my body hit the water, I felt an instant pop in my right ear. I dismissed it because the sharks were more of a fear than the ear. I stayed in the water for approximately two minutes. From the water, it looks as though they are going to charge you. I swam as fast as I could to the boat. Our tour guide laughed really hard. He was following me with food for the sharks. This was an accomplishment for me. I still have no interest, but I can say I swam with sharks.

When I finally got back to safety, my right ear began to drain. I was sure it was just the water cleaning out my ears. However, from that time on, I found it difficult to hear. I resorted to my lip-reading talents until I could get home to see Dr. Barrs.

Frenchie and I still had a week left, and we wanted to make the most of it. When we arrived home, it would be time to talk about the ear problem.

Toward the end of our trip, I started having terrible migraines. My ear was draining black fluid mixed with a little blood. These new symptoms were nothing I could ignore. Since my ear had been an issue my entire life, I knew something wasn't right.

After we arrived to Arizona I was working out at the gym when something popped in my head. It felt like I was in a tunnel. I couldn't understand or process what people were saying. It was really strange and difficult to explain. My right ear began to drain and bleed.

I made an appointment at Mayo Clinic to see Dr. Barrs. His official title is Otolaryngology, Neurotology. He is in the ENT department and specializes in inner ear, and hearing loss.

I was sent for MRI, CT, and PT scans of my neck and head. The Mayo Clinic is always thorough in its testing. They do not want to make any mistakes. As much as I dislike tests, I appreciate knowing exactly what is happening to my body.

I needed to go to the audiology department for a series of hearing tests. I met Kelly Conroy, the audiologist, and she performed the tests. She was so kind and spoke so highly of Dr. Barrs. By the time she finished the testing, it was time to drive to the other Mayo campus and meet with Dr. Barrs.

He said, "So, I take it you came alone today?"

I nodded, and he sighed. That was not a good sign. He examined both ears and asked me to sit down so he could explain the significant hearing loss in my left ear. "Can you tell me the history of the hearing loss in your right ear?"

He listened intently, nodding every once in a while.

If there is a short version of my "history," that is what I gave him.

Dr. Barrs said, "The tests show you have significant hearing loss in your left ear."

"My left ear?"

"Yes, we tested both ears. Part of the reason for the left ear hearing loss is age. The other part is because you have overcompensated by using your left ear to hear."

I was so worried about losing hearing in the left ear. If my left ear were compromised, I would be deaf. Would I need to learn sign language? Over the years, I'd gotten very good at reading lips. I might need to sharpen those skills.

Dr. Barrs said, "There is a small tumor the size of a pencil eraser in your right inner ear canal. It is consistent with what a malignancy looks like. We need to remove it."

The pop and pain I felt in my ear was part of the settling of the tumor. There was also an implant in the canal that had become dislodged. This was news to me. I guess it was placed there during the surgery I had when I was twenty-nine. It was serving no purpose anymore, and Dr. Barrs suggested having it removed. I agreed.

He explained a procedure called a Baha implant. Basically the cochlear Baha reroutes and transfers sounds directly to my left ear. This makes it possible for me to perceive sounds from both sides. From what I understand, it is extremely effective for people with SSD (single-sided deafness). The device would not give me any hearing recovery in the right ear, but it would channel the sound from my deaf ear to my left inner ear, leaving my hearing ear undisturbed. It is implanted into the bone behind my right ear. It offers a more natural pathway to hearing for people who cannot hear with hearing aids and for children who might have middle or inner ear hearing problems.

Dr. Barrs was proposing implanting it at the same time he removed the tumor from the inner ear. He would take a skin graft from my upper arm to repair the eardrum. It was so much to process in one week. I was trying my hardest to be positive and happy, but I was not ready to put another surgery on the calendar yet.

I called Eric to tell him about the new discovery, and his instant silence was not surprising. I knew he deserved a break too. "Eric, are you there?"

"Yep, I'm here. I just don't know how to respond."

"Well, I'm not having the surgery … at least not now."

"Why? That sounds serious. We need to go forward with it. What did you tell Dr. Barrs?"

"Eric, I don't want to go back into surgery again. It'll be fine. Don't worry about it." What a dumb thing to say to the man who had seen me through so much. "Please don't say anything to anyone—not to church members and especially not to the kids. I just need time."

"Monya, you are taking chances I'm not willing to live with. You are my life, and this affects me too."

"I have to go now. I don't want to talk about it anymore—no worries." I knew he was upset, but I was not prepared to consider another surgery. Eric and I didn't talk about it any further.

He asked, "How are you feeling? How are you doing?"

I answered, "I'm doing great."

It wasn't that I didn't think about the consequences of not having the surgery. I thought about it every hour of every day. I just wanted some clarity, and I wanted it on my terms. I didn't want more doctors telling me what to do. I realized I was back to being arrogant, thinking I knew more than they did. After all, I had dealt with ear issues as a child and Mom never worried. Why should this be any different?

Near the end of the year, Eric and I arrived home after spending some time together. All of our children were waiting for us in the living room. They wanted to have a little intervention with me. There were some tears, and emotions were elevated. They told me their feelings about moving forward with surgeries. I had no idea they even knew I was struggling with it. I knew they didn't read my blog, and I was okay with that because as much as my blog posts helped me, they were difficult for my children to read. I'm not good at communicating. I didn't want them burdened more than they already had been.

My eyes immediately went to Eric. He was the only person I had told. He must have said something to someone. However, they were right. It was time for me to face Dr. Barrs and have the surgery on my ear.

Blake said, "Mom, you can't give up. You have to fight. Heavenly Father wants you to fight. We want you to fight."

I reassured them all that I was not dying, but I needed more time. I was now beginning to understand why Vi kept so much from Ray while she dealt with her breast cancer.

"Please do not do this to me. I'm tired. I don't want any more surgeries."

Kayla said, "Don't you want to be around for your grandchildren? Please, Mom, just say you'll think about it."

"I will think about it. I've been thinking about it. I'm just not ready—not now. Can we wait until after the holidays?"

We agreed to talk again after Christmas, but until then, they promised to let me figure it out on my own.

Chapter 33

Negotiations

December 2012

Are we allowed to negotiate with God? I'm a little fearful of this question, but I still want to know. I remember being fourteen years old and begging Heavenly Father to "get me out of the agony, and I would be a good person." He did.

When Blake left for his mission, I asked, "Please allow me to live long enough to see him come home." He did.

Once Blake got home, I asked again to please let me live long enough to see Blake find a worthy young woman who would respect and love him. He did. It'd been three years since my diagnosis and three years since my first cancer negotiations started. I had a feeling negotiations were going to come to an end. I promised my family I would make some decisions about moving forward with health issues after the holidays. My ear continued to drain blood and a black substance. I kept a cotton ball in the ear, changing it when it got soaked.

On Christmas Eve, we had all of our children and their spouses over for dinner. The only instructions I gave them was to be prepared to share a story of Christmas or one of their most memorable Christmases. I opened by reading "The Christmas

Train" by Thomas S. Monson. I shared a few of my favorite Christmas memories. When I was a child, my mother gave me a white Bible with my name written on the front. I thought I was never going to stop smiling. I still have that Bible. Another story I told was about when Eric and I were dating. His mom bought me a gift, but she could not find it. She searched and searched and felt so badly, thinking she had thrown it out with the garbage. I never cared about the gift, but I did like knowing she loved me. She always showed me love and genuine compassion. The gift of her love was worth more than anything she could buy. The last story I told was about the first Christmas that Blake was away on his mission. I was going through my chemo treatments. I missed him, and I didn't know if I would ever see him again. It made my heart hurt. Hearing his voice on Christmas was the best Christmas gift I have ever been given.

Haleigh got engaged a few days before Christmas to Scott. He told a story about his father. When Scott was only eight years old his father tragically died during the Christmas season. He said his dad always enjoyed giving gifts to Scott and his brothers. Recalling that year he said his family heard noises outside one night, they all ran to see what was going on. A family friend was hanging Christmas lights on their home. Scott said with a quivering lip he will never forget that act of kindness and generosity. As tears ran down Scott's face, I wondered if this family friend even knew what an impression he had made on this child.

Blake told stories from his mission. Tears filled his eyes when he talked about those two Christmases away from home. They were the best Christmases he had ever had, and it had nothing to do with gifts he received. It was about the service he was able to give to others.

My son-in-law Brian never cries. In four years, Kaitlyn said he only cried once when his grandmother passed away. I was impressed with his ability to see past all of the fun in Christmas.

He began to speak and the tears started. "My heart hurts tonight for all the mothers and fathers who will have a hard time going to sleep, not knowing how they will provide a memorable Christmas for their children."

I immediately put a blanket over my face. It was unbearable to watch him cry. He could hardly speak, and I was crying underneath my blanket. I said a silent prayer for all of those families. I thanked Heavenly Father for my family. We are truly blessed. I am blessed to have such wonderful sons-in-law and a beautiful daughter-in-law. They all shared stories and thoughts. By the end of the night, there was not a dry eye.

We made family goals for 2013. We got a five-gallon water jug and decided to drop our extra change in it. When it was full, we would give it to a family in need. I typed a quote from Les Miserables and taped it to the jug: "To love another person is to see the face of God."

We may not understand why some trials come into our lives. I sure don't, but I do know if I had not had those terrifying years, I would not be who I am today. I don't want to go back there, but the experience has softened my heart and helped me be more compassionate.

I often talked to the caregivers at a cancer clinic where I volunteered. The experience brought great joy to me. I interacted with patients who were agonizing over burned skin, bald heads, and medicines they couldn't even pronounce. They were trying to survive and enjoy the holiday season with the people who meant the most to them. I have tried to learn from the people who have entered and exited my life. Some survived, and some were not so blessed. The most important lesson I learned from these wonderful people was that life is precious. It is not meant to be taken lightly. Every person I met dealt with the journey differently. Some embraced it, and some had turned themselves into angry, bitter people. However, I loved those people and learned great lessons from them.

One commonality I noticed was that they felt helpless. They often felt sad and did not exactly know who to be furious with or why they were outraged. The emotions came flooding back to me. I had felt anxiety, depression, anger, and fear.

I received an e-mail from one of the patient's caregivers who wanted to know if it was "normal" to feel the anger she was feeling after the loss of her friend. She was desperate to know what she could have done to better serve her friend. There is no normal to life when you are diagnosed with cancer. While volunteering, I learned that people on this journey process it completely differently than their caregivers do. When I decided to volunteer, some people said, "Why would you want to be around that environment after all you've been through?" I always smiled and said, "Why wouldn't I? I'm learning more about myself and my sweet husband (as a caregiver) than I would have ever learned anywhere else."

I loved having opportunities to serve others. I learned to discern where and when to share my experiences with others. I met a woman who was diagnosed with stage IV pancreatic cancer. Her doctor gave her less than a month to live. Her doctor asked if I would mind sitting with her boys and talking with them while she got set up for radiation.

One of her two teenaged sons asked, "Is my mom going to die?"

I stood in shock and asked to excuse myself for a moment. I quickly went into the restroom and prayed. "Please help me know how to help these boys." When I returned, the boys were waiting for their mother. I asked them if they knew how to pray. Both boys said, "No. We have never prayed."

I asked, "Would it be okay if I show you how to pray?"

"Yes. We want to know how to do that."

The boys and I went to a private area. I said the prayer and said, "I don't know what will happen with your mother, but I do know you can be surrounded by the same spirit you just felt at any time. You can pray, and her spirit will always be with you."

The boys hugged me. Tears were running down our cheeks, and our eyes spoke what our mouths could not express. This was a heart-wrenching moment for all of us, and I will never forget it.

I met a couple in their eighties. They held hands and smiled at each other like no one else was in the room. I was drawn to their obvious compassion for one another. I had the privilege of spending some time with them. They had been married for more than sixty years. They never had any children and relied on one another for everything. She was going through radiation.

The man asked, "How did you endure your cancer challenges?"

I said, "I prayed every day in faith and hope that I would be relieved of pain and taught a lesson. I was intent on keeping a positive attitude. If I hadn't learned anything from this journey, it would have been wasted time."

He keenly listened and asked if I would pray for his wife.

I told him I would, and I asked if he prayed for her.

He said, "My wife and I have never prayed. We don't know how."

I asked if I could show them. They were receptive and excited. I showed them how to kneel together, hold hands, and pray. I asked them to do it every morning and night.

The next time I saw them, their relationship was enhanced. They hugged me harder than I had ever been hugged. They laughed and smiled. "Thank you for teaching us how to pray. We have not missed one morning or evening prayer. Wow, do you always feel a tingling in your arms when you pray?"

Tearfully, I responded, "Yes. That is the spirit talking to you." It is never too late to be teachable. At eighty plus years, they were willing to knock on the door of heaven. God opened it and allowed them to feel a special spirit to help them carry the burdens of life. The healing, strengthening power of heaven is available to all of us—no matter our age.

Negotiations? I learned that I can try as much as I want to negotiate with God, but in the end, He is in charge. If it is His will, I am not going to die until He is ready for me. There is still more for me to learn.

I know because my life has been spared so many times and I have been so blessed with knowledge it is my responsibility to share and care for other's who are not as fortunate.

Chapter 34

Ezra Joins Our Family

ric and I were overjoyed with our new little grandson. Ezra Ray Roussel arrived on February 23, 2013. He weighed in at nine pounds, eight ounces and was twenty-two inches long. I was blessed with the opportunity to be in the delivery room with Kayla and Jeremy again. There is nothing more miraculous than a baby being born. Ezra Ray was named after Eric's dad. We will have fun telling stories to Ezra about Ray. My children loved him so much. Ray was an amazing husband, father, and grandfather. I could not have asked for a better father-in-law. He often would call me and thank me for marrying Eric. I often reminded him I was the one blessed with an incredible family I loved and who I knew loved me.

Not long after Ezra was born, he was struck with severe respiratory syncytial virus or RSV. It is a common and highly contagious virus that infects the respiratory tracts of most children before their second birthdays. For most babies and young children, the infection causes nothing more than a cold. However, because Ezra was so little, the doctors were worried about him. They decided to keep him in the hospital until it cleared. Kayla stayed with him 24/7. Jeremy was there as much as he could be, but he also had to work. I had the privilege of taking care of Recker. He may be nonverbal, but he can make some noise. He had not been feeling well either. I took him to the doctor, and he had an ear infection, a sinus infection, and croup.

My love for Kayla had become more affectionate as I took care of Recker for a week. Seeing what she deals with on a daily basis became clear to me. Although Recker spends a lot of time at our house, it is a completely different story watching him nonstop for that long. It was quite a responsibility, and I took it very seriously. I loved every second of it.

At the doctor's office, he went through every drawer and cabinet he could get his hands on. He climbed under the desk, picked up the phone, played with the computer system, and twirled on the doctor's chair. It was all fun until the pediatrician came in to visit our little guy. He had a complete meltdown when the doctor looked in his ears. When he needed a steroid shot in the arm, I thought, Oh boy. He is not going to like this.

He screamed and threw his body around like a rag doll. Tears filled my eyes when he looked at me as if to say, "Why are you allowing her to do this to me?" I tried so hard to get him to settle down. I sang him a song, tried to rock him, and soothed him with calming words, but it just made it worse. I thought I should get him calmed before I walked back through the waiting area, but that idea was not going to happen. He continued to cry louder and louder until I knew I had to get him out of there. I made a dash for the door and out to the car, but he was out of control. I sat him down to open my car door, and he started to projectile vomit everywhere, including on me. It looked like an alien shooting out of his mouth. Oh my gosh. I felt so bad for him, but all I could do was hold him and love him. Kayla had told me about the meltdowns he had. I had not seen him work himself up so badly that he vomited. By the time I got his medicine from the pharmacy and made it home, he had calmed down and fallen asleep.

Kayla and Jeremy were missing him so badly. I felt sorry for them. Luckily they were able to come and see him at least once a day. I decided to take Recker to our condo in Mexico for a few days. Maybe if he were not in Arizona, it wouldn't be such a temptation for them to come visit him. I was pretty sure Recker had given whatever he had to Ezra. If Kayla and Jeremy were to transfer it back to Ezra, he would never get better. A few days away would be a good time for his antibiotics to work.

I had a great time with him in Mexico. He loves the outdoors, the ocean, the sand, the grassy areas, and the pool. From nine to six, he was running and playing outside. One day, he made a mad dash for the ocean. I was constantly running after him. I watched him play in the water for over an hour. I decided it was time to go to the pool. Recker thought I was picking him up to take him inside, and he started to scream. He tried to scratch his way out of my arms. Recker is extremely strong. I could barely hold him up. Everyone was staring. My swimsuit top was pulled down to my stomach. My breasts were fully exposed. I had to continue to the pool area or drop Recker. I chose to continue, thinking, No big deal. My breasts have been exposed to complete strangers before. I can handle this.

A Mexican vendor yelled, "Hey, lady, want to buy some sunglasses?"

I looked at him with a scowl and replied, "Are you serious?"

I finally made it to the pool area, and I'm quite sure I gave an eighty-year-old man a slight heart attack. I was so mortified. I wanted to look at him and say, "What? You've never seen a fifty-year-old woman's boobs exposed while carrying a screaming three-year-old boy who is scratching his way to freedom?"

Eric happened to be walking toward the pool. With his hands in the air, he yelled "What the heck are you doing?"

"I just wanted to see what it felt like to walk around with no swimsuit top on. Seriously?"

He ran over to help me, but it was a little too late. I calmly sat down on the chair, pulled up my swimsuit, and laughed. What else could I do? We both just laughed!

A friend of ours who is a plastic surgeon happened to be sitting at the pool with his wife. He glanced at me and said, "Wow, who did your reconstruction? They did a beautiful job."

His wife slapped his stomach and said, "Are you kidding me? Did you just say that out loud?"

He shrugged, but I told them it was no problem I knew he was observing the medical part of the reconstruction—and not necessarily the aesthetics. We talked about the nipple sparing Dr. Kreymerman had done. He told me I was being very well taken care of. I agreed and explained how much I loved Dr. Kreymerman and all the surgeons at the Mayo Clinic.

Parents of children with autism should be applauded. None of us understand what it is and why some children have it. I know that God knows and has a special place in heaven for the special little angels.

I am looking forward to more grandbabies. I'm moving into a new journey and phase of life. I'm a bit hesitant about living up to the task of being a grandmother who is worthy of these beautiful spirits He has entrusted us with. I'm a bit relieved to know my children will be so much better at parenting than I ever was.

Chapter 35

In This House

 cott asked Haleigh to marry him in December of 2012, and they were married in March of 2013. They only had three months for planning. Surgery would be on the back burner for now.

Haleigh could not have chosen a better man. We love Scott; it is so evident that he loves my baby girl with all his heart too. I think he might spoil her a little. We will be having our last backyard wedding reception. Scott comes from a large family, and they all live within miles of us. Haleigh looked beautiful, and Scott was so handsome as they made promises and vows to each other. My little girl is married, but I'm not ready for empty nesting. I knew this next chapter in my life was going to be really hard. I have been Eric's wife, Kayla's mom, Blake's mom, Kaitlyn's mom, and Haleigh's mom for so long. It was time to get acquainted with a new me. Redefining myself as an independent woman was going to be a challenge.

I have made many mistakes along the way. I raised my voice too many times. I wish I'd been more disciplined with them to practice on the beautiful piano Eric bought. I should have been more patient with everyday messes that truly didn't matter. Why did I worry so much about what others thought? I should have focused more on meaningful things. I had not always listened, but I felt I was the adult and knew more than they did. They have taught me to be a better person and a better grandmother. I learned from Blake that forcing a person is not of God. Forcing people comes from a dark place. Being inclusive and loving everyone is a much better way to live. It doesn't mean I have to agree with their ways of thinking or doing things, it just proves that we are all individuals with agency.

Many people asked me if I was sad about my last child leaving and getting married. I said, "No. I'm happy for them." However, not having my children around on a daily basis has been a hard transition. I am so blessed to have all of our children living within a few miles, I'm able to see them often and on Sunday's everyone comes over for dinner.

When my children were babies, I rushed things. When would nursing be over? When would they be potty trained? When they were sick at night, they always woke up Eric for comfort. I wanted kindergarten to start, yet I looked forward to summer vacations. I tried my best to teach them right from wrong. We read scriptures as a family. I taught them to pray morning and night. We gathered every Monday night for family night. Despite trying so hard to be obedient and do what I thought was best, it usually ended in frustration and tears on my part. I always believed it would pay off someday, and that someday was now coming to pass. Where did the time go? These children the Lord had trusted me with were now adults, and some were raising their own children. I wanted that time back—and maybe a do over. Knowing that was not going to happen, I chose to be a better grandmother. I believe I have been.

We had created so many precious memories as a family. I can enter any room in our home and recall a memory. Some are funny, some are spiritual, some are embarrassing, and some are bitter. In the kitchen, my children heard me say a very bad word one time, and when it happened, they scattered like mice. To this day, I wish it didn't happen upon their sweet ears to hear. We also gathered in that kitchen and learned to bake, cook meals, and share stories from our busy weeks while doing dishes and baking.

Our pantry is the length of our kitchen, and we have shelves upon shelves for food and large kitchen appliances, including a large freezer. We built our house around that huge pantry. When our children were little and into their teen years, every time a new friend came over, we got into the habit of measuring their heights on a wall in the pantry. There are hundreds of names on that wall. We even measured the cat; each measurement came with a name and a date. Every time I walk out of our pantry, I see those names. Sometimes I stop and recall those years with endearment. If Frenchie and I ever move from this house, we will take that piece of the home with us. That wall is famous with all who have entered our home.

Our "pretty room" was saved for special visits with friends, blessings before entering the hospital, and prayer. That is where the black baby grand piano still waits for someone to play it. The table we ate every meal on is now old, jagged, and ready to be replaced, but we have many memories of games played as a family. For every Sunday meal, we gathered around the table and listened as each child told us what they had learned in church that day. Recker had his own dance party on top of this table, and we all watched and encouraged him to be happy and have fun!

The family room is where our family held discussions and lessons about life were taught. Many tears and much laughter came out of that room. Eric gave all of our children father's blessings in that room, and we all gathered to listen to him on the night before school started every year. In the laundry room, there were many lessons on how to wash clothes, how to separate them, and how to work the washer and dryer. After a few white shirts came out pink, they each got it down. I remember locking the door to my office and having a dance party with my girls. We sang a Carrie Underwood song at the top of our lungs. Every bathroom in our home has been decorated and redecorated several times. I spent so much time getting sick in Blake's bathroom during chemo.

My favorite memory of all is the front door. Every day after school, it opened, and those little voices would yell, "Mom? Where are you?" They were ready to wrap their arms around my neck and show me their latest art projects or grades. Many acts of service have been delivered to my family through those doors. Hands have brought meals, and friends have come through that door to bless us with their love. Friends have come to pray with us on behalf of our children. Those sacred doors are open to anyone and everyone I meet. My home has become a refuge for many of my children's friends—and a few of my own. We have had a few friends struggling with their marriage, knock on that door with their young children in tow. We have welcomed them all with loving hearts and unconditional love.

What I would give to have those little footprints of mud dragged in from a puddle or sticky fingerprints on the windows, refrigerator, or freezer. I miss those days. Now they have their own families, hopefully bringing traditions and good from both sides of their families to create their own memories.

Chapter 36
Letting Go

After Haleigh's wedding, Eric and I planned a trip to Paris, Croatia, and Italy. Just before we left, I had a visit with Dr. Northfelt. He and I visited for a while. I had a lot of questions about the side effects I was having. He asked if I wanted to change the medicine I take every day to see if I would get fewer side effects.

I asked, "What does it do?"

"Blocks estrogen."

I replied, "What does the medicine I'm taking now do?"

"Blocks estrogen."

We looked at each other and laughed. He shrugged, looked at me with his big eyes, and smiled. "Half of my patients do really well, and the other half don't. All estrogen blockers have side effects."

I smiled and said, "Well, okay then, I'll stick with what I have."

I was moving forward in my life but still had some insecurities. I felt unattractive, undesirable, and ugly. Our world has put an emphasis on the beauty of breasts. Ever wonder why?

Someone said, "Just think—you'll get a boob job out of this."

That is probably something I would have said to someone before my diagnosis.

When Angelina Jolie chose to have her breast removed after finding out she carried the BRCA gene, I heard a news caster say "No big deal. She's Angelina Jolie. This will be easy for her. Give her a few days, and she'll be showing off her new set of breasts on the red carpet."

Why did the idea of reconstruction surgery by a plastic surgeon become a glorious event for a cancer patient? I don't care if you are Angelina Jolie or Monya Williams—most women are going to feel some level of anxiety.

Breast reconstruction should never be confused with breast augmentation. One is a choice, and the other is a consequence. Most women are sensitive, and society doesn't really talk much about the physical and psychological side effects of breast reconstruction. As much as I loved Dr. Kreymerman and his skillful work, he could have botched it up—and I would have still felt the same way.

Life after a mastectomy is a gut-wrenching psychological roller coaster for many women. Many women flaunt their augmentations, and why wouldn't they? They chose it, right? The difference is augmentation (store-bought) implants are placed under the fatty tissue to create a natural, more plump breast. The actual appearance is completely different than a mastectomy. When I had my bilateral mastectomy, all the breast tissue was removed down to the breastbone. There is no extra skin to slip an implant into. Expanders were placed in that area of my chest and pumped with water until the desired size was achieved. I wanted smaller breasts, but that was not an option. I had to go with the same size or larger. Going smaller would have left me with sagging skin around the implant. I went around and around with Dr. Kreymerman, but in the end, I knew he was right and was only doing what he knew was right for his patient.

The augmented woman has outpatient surgery. She goes home and resumes her life as usual with very little recovery and a new set of beautiful breasts. The reconstructed woman has her breasts removed, and if chosen (I chose this option), the expanders are placed. After a year of enduring extreme pain, the implants are placed. The scarring is different. Some women have no nipples and have them tattooed on later. It is a long, hard road to reconstruction, and recovery is not quite glorious. Losing my breasts forced me to be emotionally guarded.

Before cancer, I would say, "If I ever had to have my breast cut off, I'd be fine with it." In fact, I said that on a regular basis. I hated having large breasts after giving birth to four children. While I was volunteering, I overheard a husband saying, "Don't worry about your breasts. When this is all done, I'll buy you a brand-new set as big as you want." Oh, really? We are not talking about a new pair of shoes here. This is a part of our femininity—or what society has deemed to be part of our femininity. Somewhere along the way, it has really gotten jacked up in the interpretation of femininity. However, most of us buy into it. The last thing a woman needs to hear, especially from her husband, is his opinion about what her breasts should look like. This is usually not the focus for a breast cancer patient. It wasn't for me, and Eric never mentioned a word about it.

Knowing what I know now, if I could do it over again I would have my breasts removed and never touched again. (My only hesitation in saying that is how much I love Dr. Kreymerman, but let's leave him out of it for now.) If I hadn't met Dr. Kreymerman, and I knew what I know now I would have never put myself through that pain and misery. I do not have any feeling in them; they are for looks only. I've learned that breasts do not define a woman. Being feminine is not defined by my breast size, pant size, or length of my hair. I have been refined by going through this process, and I now have a voice. I've learned the power of discernment. I now radiate my light in a different manner. I look at all my scars and think, Scars are a roadmap to tell the a story of our journey in life. I have plenty of scars; physically and mentally, they tell a beautiful story of how I overcame and conquered fears.

Despite the strength I was trying to show, I still felt defenseless at times. The way I perceived myself before cancer was not at an optimal level, and it was probably about 5 percent physical and 95 percent psychological after the mastectomy. Protective walls of insecurities kept me from allowing Eric to see my breasts. It was a lonely, daunting time. It created an emotional rawness that took years to get over. When I finally did allow Eric to see my breasts for the first time, it was a sacred event. He assured me it would not change how he felt about me. I trusted in him, but I was still embarrassed when I exposed the scars. He was loving and gentle with his reaction and remarks.

I had no idea how susceptible and fragile I felt until we went on our trip through Italy, Croatia, and France. Eric and I were enjoying the beauty around us and inhaling the exquisite cuisine. When we arrived in Croatia, I could not get over the breathtaking elegance and charm of the country. We made no plans; it was a spontaneous, see-what-happens trip. Neither of us had any idea that the country was full of wealth and artistry. We looked at each other with disbelief; we always thought this quiet, never-talked-about-place was a third world country. It was as if we had just discovered a newfound secret land.

We rented a car and were ready for a mystical journey. Million-dollar yachts lined the crystal-clear ocean. The smell of lavender fields surrounded us. The homes were quaint and seemed to be taken from a fairy tale. We hiked mountains, explored caves, and saw bomb shelters. Croatians are very proud of their soccer players. Eric bought us Croatian jerseys, and we sat in the middle of the town square to watch a game on a big TV set up for everyone to watch. The first score was by Italy, and the crowd went crazy. I'm glad I don't know how to speak Croatian. I'm pretty sure the shouting was vulgar. It was like going to a Suns game and hearing the boos when the other team scored. I leaned over to Eric and said, "I wonder what is going to happen when Croatia scores. We have to stay."

When Croatia scored, huge roars echoed throughout the town center. Children waved Croatian flags, and grown men jumped for joy. It was so loud, and we could not have been happier for them. It was like being in a different world. There was so much pride for their country. We loved it and walked around with pride in our jerseys after the game. The game ended in a tie, but it was still so much fun.

In Hvar, we drove into a forest. Pine trees grew next to the ocean? The contrast was stunning. We drove for hours and never looked back. The spectacular view was nothing like anything I'd ever seen. Out in the middle of nowhere, there was a sign for a nudist camp. As we drove by, I had a sudden surge of courage. I asked, "Eric, will you turn around and go back?"

He wanted to know why.

I said, "Please just do it." I pointed to the camp and said, "Pull over … please."

As I opened the door and stepped out to walk toward the camp, Eric said, "What are you doing?"

I let his voice fade into the wind as I stepped closer to the entrance. The office was closed—or maybe they were out to lunch—but I dropped all my clothes at the entrance. Scared to death, I walked toward the ocean. I was completely naked and exposed.

I didn't look left or right, but I could tell there were people in the camp. They said hello, but I said nothing. I kept my eye on a huge boulder overlooking the brilliant Adriatic Sea. The walk was exhilarating, fast, and intentional. It was liberating. The closer I got to the sea, the stronger I felt. At that moment, I was the face of cancer. Physically, my body showed evidence with its scars. Emotionally, scars were hidden deep in my heart. I was about to release them all into that beautiful ocean, turn around, and not look back. I reached the boulder, closed my eyes, and—with outstretched arms and tears streaming down my cheeks—let it all go. It was if a hurricane of emotions pounded my head, heart, and soul at the same time. I felt an instant purification as the tears fell. I could feel my body purging every dark thought and feeling I'd ever had about myself. I know my happiness depends on me. I get to choose, but this moment clarified so many insecurities so I could move closer to that happiness.

I turned to walk away and saw Eric watching me. He had tears rolling down his cheeks. He knew exactly what I was doing. We walked out, holding hands, and looked forward to a new beginning. I scheduled my surgery with Dr. Barrs after a year of waiting. My ear had gotten progressively worse, and I had no more options. I finally had the surgery on the calendar. Dr. Barrs was pleased, and I agreed to have the Baha implant.

Chapter 37

I Forgive You

November 12, 2013, 8:15 p.m.

I've always wondered what this would feel like. My mom passed away today. A few months ago, her bishop called to ask if one of her daughters would be able to help. Since the step dad passed away members of her church took turns going over to mom's house everyday. She has always had severe rheumatoid arthritis. The older she got the more frail she became needing assistance to put her clothes on in the morning and off at night. She also couldn't drive and needed someone to take her to and from doctor appointments.

The task of helping her was weighing heavy on the congregational members. Sonya decided she would like to help and began driving mom to her doctor appointments, but driving a couple hours to take care of her in Phoenix was a little too much for Sonya. She made the decision to move Mom to an assisted living facility that was only a few miles from her home. Sonya only lives a mile from me in Gilbert Arizona, so that meant my mom was now living only a few miles from me too.

Mom was not in the assisted-living home for more than a couple of months before she was rushed to the hospital and passed away. Sonya and Kris were able to spend time with her before she passed. I chose not to. I had come too far mentally, and I had no regrets about that decision. While reading The Infinite Atonement by Tad R. Callister, I realized I needed to forgive my mother. I often asked myself how can you forgive the stepfather who abused you and not be able to forgive your own mother? These questions have haunted me. I've tried desperately to comprehend why a mother would walk away from her children and grandchildren. Why did she stay with a man who could do such heinous things to her very own flesh and blood?

For years, I have wanted to hear her say, "I'm sorry. This is not your fault, and I wish it had never happened." Even saying "I'm sorry" would have been sufficient. I was never granted those simple words or an "I love you."

For months I prayed asking Heavenly Father to please help me forgive her. After many sleepless nights I realized it was only hurting me to be unforgiving. I knew I would never hear those words I so badly wanted to hear but I smiled, knowing I had finally forgiven my mom. I changed the cycle of abuse by showing my children that kindness, service, gratitude, and forgiveness are essential if they want to live free and happy lives. I taught my children to own their mistakes and learn from them. I taught them the strength of saying, "I'm sorry." Mom did the best she could, and my children will do better than I did as a mother.

Since our trip to Croatia, I have let everything go. I felt so good about my life moving forward. One day, I had an overwhelming feeling I needed to let her know I had forgiven her. I was about to have another major surgery, and I decided to take care of one last thing. It was time to let her know. I was not expecting anything in return. My heart had finally been softened enough to acknowledge my weakness in not granting her the forgiveness I had in my heart for all the years of heartache and pain.

Two things happened. I sent a text to my friends Kathi Cluff and Marian Priday to see if they would help me. I wanted them to come with me to the assisted-living home while I spoke with her. I felt this was best and safest for me. I purposefully did not tell my family—not even Eric or Sonya— I was planning it for Friday November 15th 2013. Mom died on November 12th 2013.

The second thing I did was take my girls to a women's conference in downtown Phoenix called "Time Out for Women," there were more than 5,500 women in attendance. This is what I wrote in my notebook:

The spirit is so strong, my heart is pounding, and I cannot get Mom off of my mind. I'm letting go of willpower and relying on His power, I'm turning toward him—Yes, I can face my fears. I can face my mother. With a pure heart, I can say, I forgive you. I expect nothing in return. Heaven is not a prize for the perfect, but it is the future home of all who are willing to be perfected.

On Tuesday November 12th as I held my grandson, Sonya sent me a text: "Can you talk?" I did not respond, knowing Kayla was leaving soon. I just wanted a few more minutes with Ezra. As soon as Kayla left, I received a second text: "Mom is in the hospital. She is not going to live much longer. Can you come?"

I rushed over, and her hospital room smelled like sickness and death. I stood by her side and said, "Mom, it's Monya. I'm here, I forgive you."

Within a few deep breaths, she was gone. Sonya, Greg, and I were alone in a room with a woman who had caused so much pain in our lives. I felt the pains of devastation. Being abused can be fixed and forgiven. It's not like having cancer. Devastation was not about abuse, it was about our family being ripped apart. It was a daughter wanting so badly to have a relationship with her mother, call her for a recipe, talk about spiritual moments, and share heartaches. Our family was shred in half because of pride.

So many emotions went through me. Why couldn't Mom say I'm sorry? Why was I not given two more days to express my feelings to her? Was I being protected from more pain?

I knew Eric didn't care to be there when she passed but I called and let him know after she had passed; he left work and came to be with me. After everyone left, I asked if I could have a few minutes with Mom. Since Sonya and Kris had spent a lot of time with her over the past couple of months, they were ready to move on and go. When the door shut, I asked Eric to stay with me. I held Mom's hand, we talked about how small she was (eighty-eight pounds), and I kissed her on the forehead. Eric and I held her hand, and he offered one of the sweetest prayers I have ever heard. I did not expect that from him. He has always had such pain and anger toward my parents for what they put me through. That side of him was gone, and the spirit of healing began. I wept and could not control my emotions.

Now that Mom was gone, I hoped she could find some peace. Nothing that happened on this earth can be changed. I would never change any of it—even as hard as it has been. If I could talk to Mom today, I would say:

Mom, I want to be healed. I want you to know me. I want you to see the woman you helped create. Thank you for giving me life and for staying with me all those times I was in the hospital and didn't want to be alone in the dark as a little girl. Thank you for never saying anything bad about my birth father or his family. Thank you for teaching me how to sew—even if I didn't care for it. Thank you for teaching me to bake and love it. Thank you for not allowing me to drink soda and for giving me a choices between fruit or candy. Most of all, thank you for remaining true to your faith, taking me to church, and helping me anchor my testimony in Jesus Christ. I know you have been in pain for years, and I know leaving three daughters behind with no earthly resolve is bittersweet for you, but you are able to go into the arms of Lance, your only son. I know you did the best you knew how to do.

Today I went to the funeral home and watched as Kris fixed your hair. You were always so beautiful to me. I've heard it said,

"Time heals all wounds." I know time cannot stand still. Life goes on, and things get easier, but for some reason, I want you to know that not a day has gone by since Lance died that I haven't thought about him. Now as I think of him, I will always think of you with a perfect body and no more pain.

You are now able to go forward with this next journey, hopefully happy and able to look down on your middle daughter (Bonbon) and finally hear the words, "I love you, Mom." I have you to thank for the tears running down my cheeks, but it's time to wipe those away once and for all. There has been a hole in my heart for too many years, and it's time to release that pain and reclaim the parts of my life I have struggled with. I don't blame you. I forgive you. You are now home—no more sorrow or pain. The Lord will take over now and allow you and I both to heal.

November 19, 2013

Today, my sisters and I attended the funeral services for our mother. It's difficult to describe how I felt. Eric and I decided we wanted to position ourselves so that we could see and watch Stephen Phelps play the organ. I always feel peaceful when I listen to him play. He and his wife have been a tremendous example for me as we have tried to raise our children by their example.

I am grateful that my mother is peaceful with a complete healthy body, but I need some guidance. I believe there can be healing even in the deepest of graves. I need to humble myself; not all is calm in my heart right now. I feel lonely and weak, and I know no one on this earth can understand what I am feeling— not even Sonya. She said she felt a warm blanket of "comfort" around her during the funeral. Why didn't I feel that? For me, the healing started when I was able to be at Mom's bedside and say, "I forgive you." It was a tender moment, and I know she heard me.

Planning the funeral was pretty smooth going. Sonya knew exactly what to do and Kris and I followed her lead. We asked Susan to speak, she shared memories she and mom had and did a beautiful job. She loved my mom unconditionally. Mom's cousin shared memories from their childhood, I loved hearing about the fun lighthearted child mom once was. Sonya, Kris and I had close friends who supported us and came to the funeral. I was surprised I didn't recognize anyone in attendance from her neighborhood or church. If they were there none of them introduced themselves. Evidence to me she had lead a very lonely sad life in the end.

We drove to Phoenix for a graveside service. Mom was buried next to Lance exactly how it should be.

Chapter 38

Ear Surgery

*I*t was time to remove the dang tumor (mastoid) from my ear canal. I was sitting at work with my supervisor, and she interrupted me to tell me that blood was dripping onto my shirt. I grabbed a tissue and covered my ear. The blood looked black. I had to cover it constantly with tissue or it would drip out. When the tissue was not in my ear, it felt as though the wind was blowing in one ear and out the other. Maybe there really is nothing in between my ears.

Dr. Barrs will take off my ear and move it to the side of my head to see what is happening in the ear canal more clearly. My ear has been through so many surgeries that my ear canal is smaller than an infant's, which makes it hard to see how bad or good it is in there. Recovery will be long and hard.

Thursday December 5, 2013

Eric wanted to go with me to my last appointment with Dr. Barrs. He inserted a scope into my ear, and it showed up on a television screen. It was difficult to distinguish between the flesh and the infection. All I really saw was the infection.

In the past couple of weeks, it was swollen and tender. Since my mother's death, I had not really paid much attention other than to put new a cotton ball in when it started to drip. I have had more migraines than usual, and I was worried about my slurred speech.

Dr. Barrs took out his ear vacuum and started to suck out what he could. I was a little scared to see what he was doing. I thought it was going to hurt, but it didn't. It didn't suck anything out. He stuck a gadget down the ear canal to try to see what he could—and that hurt.

He asked me to take a seat next to Eric and said, "This is terrible." He showed us a large picture of the inner ear, which I had seen many times. He explained that he had not seen that type of infection come so far out of the ear canal. He asked if Eric would stay close during the surgery so he could get his permission, if needed to move forward.

He continued to clarify the seriousness of the infection. If it has gone into the bone, he would have to cut through the bone, which would leave a significant indentation in the side of my head. Since I was already deaf in that ear, it would not affect my hearing. If I had a normal ear, I would not have had any hearing after the surgery. He would take a graft of skin from my upper arm and place it where the eardrum was.

Monday December 9, 2013

Tomorrow, I will be rolled into another operating room at the Mayo Clinic. I've had anxiety all day. I told a friend that I was more nervous about this surgery than the bilateral mastectomy. Marian said it's because I know too much now. With the mastectomy, I had no idea what I was getting into except that I would go into surgery with breasts and come out without them. In most situations, I would say it's never okay to know too much. I wish I didn't know how hard it would be to recover—or about the process of fighting off depression after surgery.

My inner ear has been pounding. I can feel my heartbeat through my ear. I've been taking antibiotics, but they don't seem to be working. When I put the drops in my ear, it feels like they are hitting my skull. The pain is something that I have not felt since I was a little girl. The veins on my face and neck popped out, and I immediately turned red. My eyes teared up, and my nose started to run.

I've tried my best to have a good attitude, be positive, and smile my way through, but this hurts so bad it's hard to concentrate on anything but the pain.

I received a text from a good friend who was diagnosed with breast cancer about a year after me. Laurel had a single mastectomy and was diagnosed at stage 2b. Her text said: "The cancer is back at stage IV and has metastasized into several large organs."

I threw the phone when I read it. What happened? Why is this happening? She was diagnosed at stage 2? My mind went to a deep, dark place where I knew I shouldn't be. I sat on my bedroom floor and cried myself to sleep. In my sleep, I saw Eric's mom and dad. They looked so happy, and I wanted to stay with them. It felt comfortable and heavenly there. It almost felt like I was playing hide-and-seek, and I did not want anyone to find me. Vi held my hand and said, "You know you can't hide here, right?" With the snap of a finger, they were gone. I woke up, slammed my hand on the carpet, and yelled, "No! Please don't find me. Let me go back just a little bit longer."

A few weeks ago, during our family night, I asked everyone what would they do if they knew it was their last day to live. I had been thinking about it a lot since my mother died. My family wasn't quite sure how to answer. They were not prepared for this type of question.

If I knew it was my last day on earth, I would wake early enough to watch the sunrise and feel the warmth on my face. I'd go for a ride with Eric—no radio just the sound of our laughter. I'd turn off the phone and TV, gather all my family around me, and make sure each of them knew how much I love them. I'd hold my grandchildren. We would watch The Sound of Music and eat popcorn as a family. I'd take a picture with each of them and tell them why they are so important to me and why I love them so much. We'd go outside and watch the beautiful sunset, and then I'd have them sing me to sleep with my favorite songs.

Tuesday, December 10, 2013

Eric and I arrived at the hospital at 9:30 am. When I woke up in recovery around midnight, I asked if he got everything out.

The nurse said, "There are three boys waiting for you, and one of them wanted you to get a Turkey tattoo."

"That was probably my son Blake, or maybe it's Brian. He likes to hunt. Maybe he wants me to get a tattoo of a bow and arrow with a turkey."

They laughed and said, "Maybe. We'll check for you."

When they came back, I said, "Would it hurt your feelings if I don't get a tattoo? I think I would rather have Heather Lucas do it for me."

The male nurse said, "The PA for Dr. Kreymerman?"

I said, "Yes. Do you know her?"

"Of course. We all know them, but Dr. Kreymerman moved. He's not here anymore."

"I know, but I still don't want a tattoo."

The nurse laughed and said, "Don't worry, honey. We're not doing any tattoos tonight."

I realized it was just the medicine talking. I'm sure the recovery room nurses hear a lot of funny things.

When I arrived in my room, Eric and Jenny were there. My head was pounding. The nurse gave me a shot of morphine. She ended up doing it three times, but nothing would help. The pain was intense. Large doses of Percocet and morphine were not helping. I seriously thought my head was going to explode. The pain on the left side was dreadful and was moving around to the back of my head, this was unusual to me since the surgery was on the right side.

At around eight in the morning, the nurse called Dr. Barrs and gave me stronger pain medicine. This helped with the intense discomfort on the surgery site—but not the left side. Nothing could take that pain away. I didn't sleep at all.

When we were discharged the next day, I told Eric the pain on the left side was horrible. I thought I was going to vomit. I asked him to pull my hair back to see if there was anything visible. He turned the car around and took me right back to the hospital.

The knot on the upper left side of my head was as big as a tennis ball and bright red. I thought someone had dropped me on my head while I was in surgery.

Dr. Barrs explained that my head was supported by a blown-up pillow and in an awkward position for over nine hours. He didn't expect my surgery to be as long as it was, and with my head in that position, it caused a hematoma. He explained what he found during surgery. He was able to get the tumor out, but it was terribly infected. He got out all he could, but he was still concerned about an area of dead skin. He was going to watch it and might have to do another surgery.

When is it time to just say enough is enough? I was past ready to say I'm done!

I woke up one morning shortly after surgery feeling depressed and in tears. I looked at myself in the mirror—the same mirror I first stared at my flat-chested scarred breasts and the same mirror I had inspected every inch of baldness where I once had long, beautiful blond hair. While I examined myself, I wondered what was worse: being completely bald or partially bald? Dr. Barrs had to shave part of my head during surgery. I wondered if my prayers were being heard. I'm not sure I can face one more day of this.

If I learned anything over the past few years, it was desperation and fear. I knew I was walking a tightrope. I lit a fire log and stared at it for hours as the flames went to ashes. One day, my light will go out—and all that will be left is ashes. Will I have done enough?

I have been given so many blessings. I have come to learn that I am not in charge. I'm doubting myself and wondering if I'm really worth it. I don't want to have these feelings. I feel like I've done all I can do physically but I'm mentally drained and spiritually depleted.

Friday, January 3, 2014

I went to my postoperative appointment with Dr. Barrs, and the resident came in to ask all the usual questions. She poked around in my ear and said, "I'll be right back. I need to get Dr. Barrs."

He took a quick look and asked the resident to start on the next patient. Just before she left the room, he showed her something in my ear. He told her the black area in my ear was dead skin. In his thirty-one years of practicing, he had never seen skin die like that. He excused her, and I didn't see her again.

He used a scalpel to cut off all the black dead skin. There was a small area he couldn't get to without hurting me. He would deaden the area around it next time and take it out. He warned me "Hold tight. Things are going to get dizzy."

He began to vacuum my inner ear, and I couldn't keep my eyes open. I was so dizzy. The vacuuming was extremely painful. Dr. Barrs gave me a new regimen for cleaning my ear. He wanted to see if it would help the healing move along faster to swish out the big hole with vinegar and water. "It will sting a little. Make sure the water is at room temperature." He also explained the need to keep germs at a minimum, to stay out of public areas as much as possible, and wear a mask. I seriously cannot stand wearing that mask. He took the cap off of the Baha implant so it could heal. He would not be able to connect the Baha until March or April, depending on the healing process. I now have a visible screw going through the bone in the back of my head behind my right ear. The Baha was healing very well.

He helped me out of the chair and assisted me to a place where we could talk. "I can't get the ear cleaned out for long enough without it filling up with blood again. It's very unusual."

I asked, "Did the graft take?"

"Again, I can't get a clear view of the grafting area in order to see if it is healing correctly. Normally, I would not see you again for a few months to finish up with your implant but in your case I feel it's necessary for you to come every week until I see an improvement."

I asked if he could give me some hope that it was just taking longer than usual to heal.

He looked at me and said, "I have to be honest with you. I have never seen anything like this before. I don't feel comfortable giving a prognosis quite yet."

January 6, 2014

The day after I came home from the hospital, I asked Haleigh if she would mind coming over to wash my hair.

She said, "I'd love to do that for you, Mom."

As she washed, I could smell the blood.

Haleigh was careful not to get water in my ear, but it was a difficult task.

I reached up to move my hair over, and chunks of hair fell into my fingers. Tears immediately filled my eyes. I wrapped my hair in a towel, went upstairs, and tried to comb through it. Clumps were falling out.

Two days later, huge dollops of hair were still cascading off my head. I asked Dr. Barrs about it, and I was told that large amounts of anesthesia sometimes affects patients' hair. I have thought about Haleigh washing my hair so many times. It was such a small act of service, and knowing my daughter, she has probably not thought about it since. Those small acts of kindness mean the most to me. Haleigh's willingness to serve me was a touching moment. I tried to cover my tears while she washed out the bloody mess. When I think back to that day, I realize tears are a way of expressing an emotion. It's okay to cry or be overwhelmed by life's ups and downs. Buddha said, "If you light a lamp for someone else, it will also brighten your path."

There is a huge difference between serving and seeking validation. My daughter was serving her mother who was in need, but she never talked about it again. That's just who she is. The more I am able to feed positive input into my brain, the more I am able to give and share with others—and the more satisfaction I receive. Perhaps it took my youngest daughter to teach me that valuable life lesson.

We all need to avoid the pettiness that often comes with awareness of our own goodness when compared with the failings of others. Love one another in all circumstances. I don't think it was necessarily an easy task for Haleigh to come to my home and clean blood out of her mother's hair, but she did it with grace—and I was grateful she did it.

Chapter 39

Making New Friends

Our friends Shelli and Mark Richardson invited us to a car show. Barrett-Jackson started showing and auctioning exquisite automobiles in the 1970s. The car show comes to Arizona in January every year, and Shelli worked for them. I really didn't feel like going, but I remembered Eric's Mom saying, "If Eric ever wants to go for a car ride, you should drop everything and go. The dishes or whatever you think is so important can wait until tomorrow."

I was pretty sure my ear was going to be pounding no matter what. We made the drive to Scottsdale and met Shelli and Mark at the entrance. Shelli was managing a booth for Nerium International, an anti-aging company in the relationship-marketing field. I knew nothing about it.

There were people everywhere. My immune system was so compromised I knew I could not take the chance of getting sick, so I sat in the booth, observing behavior patterns with Shelli and her friends. Little did I know I'd join her business that night. Although I'd never heard of relationship marketing, I knew Shelli and the girls had something I needed: happiness. It was just the change I longed for—something to fill a void with my children gone. I couldn't remember the last time I went to lunch with a friend. There was no convincing or pulling of teeth; it just felt right. I handed over my credit card and said, "Sign me up. I want to be a brand partner." It was time to stop worrying about dying and start living.

The philosophy of the company was exactly what I had been trying to implement into my life for years. They believe that the best leaders are givers, not takers. They help each other succeed and provide selfless acts of service. At Nerium International, their mantra is real: getting real, being real, and creating real change. They also want to attract genuine people who can be themselves and have fun. They believe that no matter how successful or accomplished a person might be, there are always more improvements to be made. Daily self-development is essential in developing strong confident people, and I was told to read ten pages of a good book every day.

Nerium's blog says the product itself is rooted in science. Nerium's products are clinically proven, independently tested, and formulated with exclusive and patented age-defying ingredients. Nerium leads the way in anti-aging innovation. Proven formulas deliver real, visible results for the face, body, and mind. It's no secret that their formulas are based on ingredients that were originally developed in the biotechnology field and adapted for use in their age-defying products.

Within a week, my kit came. I opened it and called Shelli. "What do I do now?"

Shelli said, "You start sharing your bottles with people."

The idea was to find friends and family who would like to try the Nerium Night cream, take a before picture, show them how to use the cream, set up a time the next week to pick it up, and take an after picture to see how much their skin had changed. Simple enough. I could do that, and I did.

On Tuesday nights, I drove to training and started to learn more about the company and products. I felt like I was in a special club that required happiness, giving, loving, caring, and sharing.

These were all attributes I knew I needed to work on. How could I go wrong? I was delighted to work for a company whose tagline was "Making people better."

Danny and Liz were two of my trainers and mentors within the company, and they knew nothing about me. Shelli and Lori were also in my new club. I'd been friends with them for more than twenty years, and I trusted them. My friendship circle began to burst. I could not believe the caliber of people I was associating with, and I loved it. If people were unhappy, grumpy, or mean, they didn't last in our club. I liked those rules; they fit my new way of thinking.

I tried not to take my new club too serious this was supposed to be something new, stress free and fun. Learning new ways of connecting with people was exhilarating. Everyday I left the house with the thought who will I meet today?

During training I asked a lot of questions-I couldn't quite grasp how the system worked. I continued to share the product with people I knew and new friends I met. I soon found out 'Relationship Marketing' is just that.. building relationships and marketing a product I love.

Nerium does not pay for any advertisements so I was puzzled as to how they were becoming so successful in less than 2 and a half years in business. Liz said, "Monya, have you ever gone to a movie or restaurant, loved it, and recommended it to a friend?"

"Of course. Everyone does."

She said, "There's your answer. We don't advertise. It's only word of mouth."

"Okay. All I need to do is share this incredible anti-aging cream and get customers who like it too, and Nerium sends me free bottles every month—plus I get paid?"

"Yep. It's that easy. I earned my Lexus in ninety days, and Danny earned his Lexus and a $50,000 bonus in less than a year."

I have to admit I was curious and skeptical. I didn't really need the money or the car, but let's be honest who wouldn't like a new Lexus car $50,000 bonus just for sharing something they are passionate about? Seriously, I was more about the helping other people aspect of the business.

The CEO, Jeff Olson, taught us to take our time and be consistent. I began to read a book he wrote. The Slight Edge it is an eye opening book; he believed making slight changes in your life daily, done receptively over time would help mold a new generation of givers. Doing mundane things every day, like reading from a good book, would pay off eventually.

All the years of heartache and pain were going to finally diminish as I realized I had the power to be whatever or whoever I wanted to be. Although I was fifty, had raised four children, had two grandchildren (and one on the way), it was not too late to begin a new love for myself. I wanted to make a difference in the life of someone—anyone. I knew I could not be completely effective until I could look myself in the mirror and believe what I saw staring back at me. This new adventure fit me perfectly. I loved my new club.

I continued to read thirty minutes of scripture daily and then ten pages of The Slight Edge. I felt a shift in my thinking and a desire to wake up and be cheerful. I looked forward to Tuesday nights when I would meet with my new friends. Making smart daily choices and surrounding myself with contagiously happy, positive people would prove to be one of the best decisions of my life.

With my health issues, I may never be the top earner or even be able to monetarily succeed like so many have in the company but I've trained myself to be okay with that. I've always been a competitor and wanted to be the winner. It has been a humbling experience to let go of that part of my personality. Learning my own limitations has been an eye-opening process, but I've learned to not compare myself to anyone.

I'm living a life that is so different than any person I know who works with Nerium. I never know from day to day how I am going to feel or whether I will be thrown back into surgery. Every time I leave the house, I expect to meet people I can share this experience with. Because of this positive mental attitude, I have been richly blessed with opportunities I would never have had the pleasure of having. I show up and do what is expected of me. The business part of it will grow organically as I look forward to a full recovery. Eric has been so supportive and loves the positive impact Nerium has had on me.

Months after joining, I was invited to listen in on a conference call with a woman I admire. Mariel and Frank Filippone had never done network marketing, and I looked to them as an example. They had been with Nerium for just two years and were making a multiple six-figure income, yet their humility was what attracted me to them. I was ready to take notes, but I was not prepared for the emotion I would feel as I listened in.

So many people who have followed my story on my blog know I use the word hope a lot. I have studied it, pondered it, lived it, and tried to wrap myself up in the warmth of the promise it brings.

When Mariel began to speak with her team my line was muted. I began to blubber like a baby. There were approximately eight hundred people on the conference call, but I felt as if she was speaking directly to me. Gracefully and quietly, she spoke of hope. She talked about giving hope to others during times in their lives when they might need to know there are people in the world who care. Listening to her talk was another a-ha moment for me. I was directed down this path to be a light for others. It's interesting to be at the right place at the right time. I believe we are placed in those places, and nothing happens without a reason. Nerium, my new friends, and working on my self-development were all in alignment with what I needed at the time.

Jeff Olson went before the United Nations and presented March 20 as the International Day of Happiness. It was accepted, and every year on that date, huge orange happiness walls are erected all over the country. People can go and pledge what they will do to make the world a happier place to live. I loved this idea so much that I decided to try my own experiment I pledged to do 365 days of service for someone else and see if it changed me. Within a few weeks, I could tell the slight change I had made to my daily routine was working. I was helping others find happiness, and for the first time in my life, I was finding my own happiness.

It didn't take away my own needs and realities, but it has helped me become a better person. I've learned that I can be lifted up when I fall—and I am reminded of my potential. I've been prompted time after time as I'm guided to people daily that I have so much to work on. There is so much to learn, but by taking the hand of others like Mariel and Frank, I can be led and guided with thoughts of goodness and mercy. I can do it with humility and grace. I knew I still had a road ahead of me at Mayo Clinic, but most of that was behind me.

A ray of light was finally beginning to brighten my way.

Chapter 40
My Reality

Friday, March 6, 2014

I woke up with blood dripping from my Baha implant. I had an appointment with Dr. Barrs and got ready to go. The Mayo Clinic called to tell me Dr. Barrs would not be in today. I told them about the bleeding, and she told me I would be seeing the PA or a resident today.

I said, "No. I need to see an attending—this is serious"

The issues with my ear were getting worse. I wanted so badly to get past it.

When I arrived, they quickly took me back to an exam room. Dr. Barrs walked in. I was surprised but happy to see him. I asked if I had taken him away from something important. He told me he had recently visited a third world country to do some pro-bono work and thought he needed the day off to recoup. I explained how grateful I was to see him and thanked him for taking the time to come in the office to see me.

He took a look at the screw in the back of my head and turned my face toward the TV monitor. I could see everything on the big screen. He began to scrape the skin around the Baha. Watching it was disgusting. I had to close my eyes. When I don't watch what he is doing, it hurts less. He looked in my ear, and to my surprise, it didn't feel like it looked.

He tried to stick his vacuum down the ear canal and suck out what he could, but he didn't get too far. He went and got his nurse, and Kathleen took a look.

They agreed that I would be having more surgery. My ear canal was closed so tightly that he couldn't see into the eardrum. He knew it was not healing properly. The Baha was not connecting to the bone like it should, and more surgery was necessary.

They stepped out of the room, and I couldn't help but cry. I felt vulnerable and alone. I quickly wiped away the tears when I heard them coming back in. I put a smile on my face, bit my tongue, and listened to what they were telling me. I did not want to hear what they were saying. I let my mind wander off to a better place so that I could process it.

Dr. Barrs said, "Okay, so you understand, right?"

"Um, yeah. I think so. I come back next week, right?"

"Yes. Scheduling will call you."

So many thoughts were running through my head. I cannot take one more surgery. I don't want more surgery. Seriously? How do I go home and tell my family, friends, and coworkers? How much more of my ear can he take off? I felt a migraine coming on.

I drove down Scottsdale Road toward a hotel to meet up with Dr. Northfelt. Earlier in the week, he called and asked me for a favor. He was giving a lecture for general family practitioners throughout the valley about side effects of chemo and radiation. He asked me to speak about side effects I have had. When I drove up to the entrance, he was waiting for me. I tried to compose myself before getting out of the car. I needed to focus on what I was there for.

Dr. Northfelt hugged me and escorted me to a room filled with physicians. Someone introduced Dr. Northfelt, and he introduced me and another patient of his Lisa. He told the doctors about my diagnosis, and I was not prepared to hear what he was saying. I had an emotional moment as I listened to him explain my breast cancer diagnosis. I was listening to him talk about me, my life, my breasts, and everything medical that had happened over the past four years. I felt like I was in a tunnel, and every word of what he said penetrated my mind. Oh my goodness, this happened to me? It felt like I wasn't in the room or I was just listening in. The physicians were writing down notes and typing on their laptops my heart was pounding. My breast surgeon, Dr. Pockaj was siting on the front row and could see my anxiety, she gave me a quick smile and nod of her head. Just that simple act of kindness gave me reassurance and calmed me down.

When it was my turn, Dr. Northfelt began asking questions. My job was to answer them openly and honestly. I wasn't intimidated by the doctors and their knowledge of medicine. I just needed to share my journey. I wanted them to understand that I could be their mother, sister, aunt, grandmother, wife, or daughter. I am a real person; after all they were just people not defined by their credentials.

Lisa's diagnosis was stage one or two. For almost every question Dr. Northfelt asked about side effects she and I had opposite answers but our concerns were similar. I realized—no matter the stage of cancer—the emotions of hearing those words are the same for almost everyone.

We talked about neuropathy, bone pain, body image, insomnia, and sexual side effects.

When it was opened up for questions and answers one physician asked, "How has your quality of life changed?"

With a quiver on my lips and a tear in my eye, I said "Before the diagnosis, I thought I was happy. I was living a dream life, blessed with a husband who was financially blessed so I could stay home and raise our four children. We have a nice home, cars, no debt, and freedom to do just about anything I wanted to do. I seriously thought that was happiness. As I sit here with all of you, I can tell you without hesitation, that money, cars, and big homes do not bring happiness. Through my journey, I have learned who I am, how strong I am, who is important to me, and what is important to me. I can honestly say I'm the happiest I have ever been. I've learned that all the distractions I thought were so important were mere objects detouring me from real life and feelings of complete joy. All that really matters is my family and my doctors. I love them more deeply and purely than I ever thought I could. Life is a precious gift that so many take for granted. Dr. Northfelt promised me he would be with me through every step of my journey, and I believe him."

The lecture came to an end. Everyone stood and clapped. Several doctors came up to ask me questions. One asked if I had ever tried any natural paths. I thought, Who is this kid? He looked like he was sixteen. He represented the new generation of healthcare. He was very kind and I was impressed with his ability to connect, more physicians need to learn this art when communicating with their patients. I engaged in conversation for a few minutes until it was time to leave.

I'm not sure I said anything to help anyone in the room, but it did help me. I was more certain than I had ever been that the doctors and surgeons on Team Monya were with me because they cared about me as an individual.

Dr. Northfelt walked me out to my car and gave me a hug. I told him how much I love and appreciate all he had done for me. He thanked me for helping his lecture not be so boring.

I assured him he could never be boring.

As I drove off, I couldn't help but be emotional with everything Dr. Barr's had presented to me, and then sharing from my heart to a room full of physicians I'd never personally met, a few tears streaked my cheeks and landed on my shirt.

I am a modern day pioneer in my own right, paving the way for generations to come. Making some physical sacrifices and suffering with courage while trying to inspire others they can do hard things and still be happy.

I looked up and—without any rain in sight—saw a beautiful rainbow. What a sweet tender mercy. I smiled with peace in my heart.

Chapter 41
Never Give Up

April 14, 2014

Never give up. Those words have never resonated with my soul as they did on this day. I'd been dealing with the ear issue for more than a year. After my last surgery, I said, "No more. I'm done. I can't do it anymore." I wanted to give up!

On December 10, 2013, I went under the knife again. My life has been occupied with worry, stress and anxiety for more than four years. My wonderful family and friends have   supported, prayed, fasted, and served me—all with pure intent, good hearts, and no recognition.

So much of my time has been dedicated to the Mayo Clinic, doctors, surgeons, MRIs, CAT scans, bone scans, and blood tests. I've done everything they've asked me to do. .I love each and every one of the doctors and surgeons on my team, but I need a life outside of the Mayo Clinic. I made the decision to have no more surgery. I missed a few appointments the last couple of weeks, and quite honestly I don't care. I'm exhausted.

It was time for me to live. When Shelli asked me to be a brand partner with Nerium, I had no hesitation. I signed up, bought my ticket to a national conference in Saint Louis, and went home.

I had no idea what I'd just been handed. At the time, it was an impulse, but I felt good about it.

My ear was still infected and painful. I could not cover it up with a smile and say, "I'm doing great." Blood and blackness oozed from my ear and soaked up every cotton ball. I was constantly changing it and putting antibiotic drops into my ear.

With no resolution or answers at the moment, I went to Saint Louis with my friends for my first Nerium conference. I listened to a talk on Friday afternoon, took notes, and simply laughed with twelve thousand other people.

The speaker said three little words that popped me right back into reality: "Never give up." It was as if the spirit was whispering to my heart. I could feel the tears flowing down my cheeks. I made a mad dash to the women's restroom, hoping no one would notice my tears. I didn't want to bring my friends down off their adrenaline rush.

I sat in a bathroom stall with the door shut and the toilet seat down. Staring at the purple doors and counting the tiles on the dirty floor, I tried to compose myself. I did what I've done a million times. I prayed. When I least expect it, the tears flow in the most random places.

There is a difference between giving up and relinquishing to the inevitable. I've never been a quitter, I've always been a fighter and competitor. Those words from the eloquent speaker 'Never Give Up' were heart wrenching words to be confronted with. I was facing a long hard surgery, the potential of taking risks with my health were no longer an option. It was difficult to focus all my efforts on Nerium with so much riding on this surgery.

The noise of all the women sharing their happiness and spreading their joy with each other left while I spoke to God. I begged him to help me dry my eyes so no one would know. I needed an answer. Please tell me what I'm supposed to do. What am I supposed to be learning from these continuous diagnosis's?

I slowly began to hear the beautiful chatter of the women. I sat and cried a bit more. I stood up with my shoulders squared and my head held high. I needed a second or two to cry with no one watching. For a moment, I just needed to let those emotions out. I've been forced to face a deep pain—physically, spiritually, and mentally. I've been forced to face a villain, and there's nothing I can do besides get it out every once in a while. I know the pain is not going away anytime soon. I need private time to let it all out and not have anyone ask if I'm okay. Life for a cancer patient is just that way. I know all of this will be taken away someday; on the other side, I won't feel this pain. I've felt so much joy in my life, and these tears are not me surrendering to anything. It's something I need to do every now and then. I'm not as strong as I sometimes think I am.

He never said it would be easy. He said it would be worth it. I am reclaiming my life and spending more time with friends I have not seen for so long. Shelli was absolutely right when she told me Nerium was the way to get away from my cancer world. People have asked me why I'm involved with this "thing" called relationship marketing or any other business with all I have going on. They've asked why I would "waste" my time? My husband makes enough money for me to go and do whatever I want.

I want to answer that question The Lord has been tenderly watching over me, giving me his sweet grace and love all along the way. I know it must be hard for him to watch, knowing he can take my pain away. I am doing this 'thing' because I see it as an avenue to bring happiness to others who need to find hope in something better for their lives. For me, this is not about money or fame. It's simply about helping others.

None of the tragedies in my life are God's way of punishing me. Life happens. Other people made bad choices that affected my life. I've experienced every emotion there is to digest. Nerium came to me for a reason. It has been a great blessing and distraction for me. They are solid in their convictions of helping people. They stand on the beliefs of integrity, patience, and improving myself by reading from a good book everyday. Some of the most humble people I have ever met are in my Nerium club. Faith, charity, and acceptance of everyone are part of who they are. I've been given a gift, and I have a responsibility to learn, grow from it, and teach others to do the same.

After the conference, I knew why I had joined. My club was a happy place. Being with positive, happy people has taken me to a place where my heart can heal and my soul can soar while helping others reach their potential. Thank you to all who have supported me not only by becoming one of my dear customers but also those who have supported my decision.

While working at USAirways, I could feel my ear draining. Liquid was trickling down my neck. I quickly wiped it off with a tissue, hoping no one would see it. I was barely functioning, but I seemed to be getting things done.

As much as I tried, I could not wrap my head around saying yes to another surgery. I promised myself I was not going to do it again. I had come so far, but when Heavenly Father says, "You can do it," I just believe I can—and I do it.

The next day, I walked into US Airways and filled out medical leave forms and legal forms. I despise them. It's such a process, and writing out my estimated days away from work brought me to tears. I love my work at US Airways. I love my supervisors and managers. They have been patient, kind, and compassionate throughout my journey.

Just when I had gotten my trust back and was ready to move forward, I was slammed back into surgery once again. Sometimes the truth has been hard to hear.

April 30, 2014

Today, my ear decided to take a turn for the worse. Yesterday, I woke up with black on my pillow. I thought it might be dried blood, but it was fresh and black.

I felt really dizzy for most of the day. At church, I had problems concentrating. My ear was pounding in my head. When I bowed my head during prayer, I thought my head was going to explode. My equilibrium was way off.

When I stood up, I saw Stephen Phelps on the stand. I focused on the fact that I knew he was in pain too. It was my way of distracting myself. He is such an inspiration; not many know of his severe back pain, but he plays the organ so beautifully every week. His testimony through his music plays directly to my heart every time. I love music, any time I journal or blog I have my headphones on with classical or inspiring christian music playing.

I will be seeing Dr. Barr's in just a few days, he will know exactly what to do.

Chapter 42

A Serious Problem

May 8, 2014

I was in extreme pain today. I tried to blog, but it hurt to type.

I don't know what happened. I took a hot bath and felt fine. Eric came in to check on me and make sure I hadn't drowned. I went to sleep at 3:30 a.m. and felt massive pain in my ear. It went down into my jawline and throat and was difficult to bear.

I had some liquid in the left ear all week, which made it difficult to hear, but it only lasted three days. This pain was excruciating. I wished I could go to sleep and not wake up. I took the pain medicine to see if it would help. The pain was getting worse. My eyes were blurry. I recorded what was happening for Eric, just in case I didn't wake up I wanted him to know what happened.

After my bath, I brushed my teeth and changed the cotton ball because it was soaking through. I felt a pop in my right ear and then tremendous pain followed. I had no control over the shaking in my legs.

I went downstairs and screamed into a pillow on Blake's bed. I didn't want to wake Eric. I tried praying and concentrating on happy thoughts, but nothing seemed to help. I couldn't stop shaking, and my arms were shivering. Just before I knew Eric would be waking up to get ready for work, I crawled back next to him and pretended to be asleep. I didn't want to worry him, especially since I had a scheduled appointment with Dr. Barrs in a few hours.

Eric kissed me on the forehead and said, "Have a good day. I love you." As soon as I knew he was gone, I couldn't handle the pain any longer. I turned my head into the pillow and screamed as loud as I could once again. Screaming is a natural reaction to excruciating pain, but I'm not sure why I shoved my face into the pillow. No one else was home.

I turned over, looked at the clock, and sighed. I still had three hours. I got in the shower, thinking the water might make me feel better. Something was wrong. I could feel it. The pain in my inner ear was shooting down my jawline to the back of my skull, and the nerves in my upper ear were burning. The shooting pain wouldn't go away.

No tears were coming. I was more afraid than anything else. My friend came by the house to pick up some Nerium night cream for her daughter. Jori said, "Do you feel okay? You look like you have Bell's palsy?"

"I'm not feeling well, but I have an appointment with my doctor today. I'll know more later."

After saying good-bye to Jori, I went upstairs. The right side of my face was sagging. I had no control over the nerves or muscles. My lip was drooping to one side. I couldn't shut one eye, and there was no movement in my right eyebrow. I drove to Mayo Clinic, arriving early, and I was still unable to control the pain.

My body was shaking while I waited. It didn't take long. I was the first one they called. Dr. Barrs asked me to step onto the chair. He looked in my ear, cleaned out the debris, and helped me to the chair next to his desk. He asked, "How much pain are you in?"

I said, "My body is shivering. The pain is so bad. I feel like I have no control."

He excused himself, stepped out of the room, and came back with his nurse. With no explanation, they helped into a wheelchair.

Kathleen pushed me down to admitting. On the way, she said, "We are admitting you into the hospital. I'm sorry, but the only available rooms are on the fourth floor in cardiology. Are you okay with that?"

The pain was penetrating every cell in my body. All I could do was nod my head. I could care less about what floor I was on or the room I was in. I just wanted the pain to go away so I can go home.

I said good-bye to Kathleen and gave her a big hug.

In the waiting area, I could not control the shaking pain. The waiting seemed endless.

When they wheeled me to the fourth floor, the doctors in the elevator were cheerful and happy. They were excited about a surgery they were going to do. That was the last thing I wanted to hear about.

I called Sonya, and she said, "Did you drive yourself?"

"Yes. You know how I feel about people waiting around for me."

She sighed and said, "I'm on my way. I'll call Marian and Eric."

I said, "No. I won't be here long. I hate people having to drive all the way out here."

She asked if I thought she should tell my kids.

I said, "Yes, but tell them not to come."

Sonya did it anyway.

I spent the day with testing, pokes, blood drawing, scans, MRIs, and CT scans. As they began to get me ready, I understood it was not going to be an in-and-out day.

Blake was the first to arrive. He kissed my head and said, "I love you, Mommy."

Sonya, Kris, and Eric arrived too.

The pain was so intense that they decided an intravenous flow through my IV would be the quickest way to get rid of the pain. I was curled up in a ball of pure agony. My body was shaking uncontrollably.

I whispered, "Please put some medicine in my IV to put me to sleep. I don't want to wake up."

The sweet nurse knew I was speaking from a place of darkness and agony. "Sorry, sweetie. We can't do that."

"Eric, it hurts so bad. Please let this be the end, let me go now."

Eric was holding me and soothing me with his warm hands. My children and sisters were crying. The medicine was finally administered, but by the time it had entered my bloodstream, I was in pretty bad shape. It looked like I was having a seizure. I was curled up and shaking.

In the ICU, all my children had to witness it again. I felt so bad that they had to see their mother in such misery. I'm sure it was difficult to watch. I had never felt that type of pain, and my body reacted by curling up. I pounded the bed and wanted to be put to death. It's difficult to write, but it was my reality. Nerve pain is excruciating and difficult to explain.

Heather had worked with Dr. Kreymerman before he left, and she had become a dear friend. She came to check on me every day. She was a great resource for Eric and my medical questions. When I did not understand the lingo, she explained it to me in terms I could understand. Sometimes it was not easy to hear, but I like how straightforward she was.

I told Eric I'd seen everyone I cared about seeing besides my sweet little Recker. Just as they were wheeling me off to surgery, Kayla brought him in. He didn't like seeing me in that bed. I think he thought it was for him; unfortunately, he has been in hospital beds. I'm sure it was a reminder to him. It made me sad to hear him cry so hard. He was melting down. He brought me to tears.

I love him so much, and I wish I knew what to say or how to understand his emotions.

As they wheeled me into surgery, I had the pleasure of seeing Dr. Magtibay walking toward my bed.

He gave me a big hug and said, "I heard you were here. Dr. Barr's will take good care of you."

It was a happy moment for me; he has always been one of my favorite doctors. The mask was placed over my face, and I woke up in recovery. It didn't take long to wake up and return to my room. There were flowers everywhere. Dr. Magtibay even sent a beautiful bouquet with an uplifting note.

May 11, 2014

I was in the Mayo Hospital for Mother's day. The kids came to see me. I received a lot of text messages from family and close friends. Before the kids arrived, I decided I was going to be brave. I wanted them to feel better about what was going on. I was trying so hard. I even ate a cupcake.

The kids brought me a necklace from my friend Kara Kelly. With every surgery I have, she is always so generously giving of her talents. I started to tear up when I saw the necklace she made; it simply said: "Brave." How did she know I needed that today? I prayed for bravery. I was not feeling brave. I was trying though. I don't like my children to see me in that condition.

My body was not reacting the way I wanted it to. I hate hospitals. I hate pain medicine. I hate how my face looks.

Eric brought me the new Live Happy magazine. As soon as I saw it, I decided to put a half smile on my face and be grateful for being alive. My children are beautiful, my husband is incredibly supportive, and I have two angelic grandsons. I'm not sure what my future holds, but I am trying to be optimistic.

During that two-and-a-half-week stay at the Mayo Clinic, I had three surgeries. I was in and out of consciousness because of the pain medicine. Surgeons decided the infection killed the nerve that controls the right side of my face. It left me with partial facial paralysis.

Dr. Barrs said, "You are a lovely woman, and we care about you, but you have terrible genes." High doses of antibiotics couldn't even kill the infection.

During one of my surgeries, I opened my eyes—and I was in heaven. In front of me, Vi and Ray were wearing white. Vi was waving for me to come to her. I ran into her arms. As we embraced, a feeling of peace came over me.

I said, "Oh, I made it to heaven? I mean if you're here and Dad is here, I made it." Vi was beautiful; she and Ray were united, holding hands, and so happy. I just stared at her. I couldn't believe I was there.

Her piercing eyes penetrated my soul. She said, "You can't stay here, sweetheart."

I didn't feel anything but calmness and serenity. I asked, "Why? I don't want to go back. It's really hard."

With every bit of stillness and surety, she looked at me and said, "Heavenly Father sent me here to tell you what he wants you to do when you go back." She told me a list of things I was to do before it was time to go back to my heavenly home. I needed to share my story and try to give hope and faith to others who were struggling to hang on.

Ray looked at me and waved his arm to the left. There were children playing together. "Do you see those children? Those are your grandchildren." I started to walk toward them, but Ray stopped me and said, "You can't go over there. They can't see you." I stared at the angelic children. They were unbelievably joyful. I don't remember the sexes of any of them, but one had really white hair.

Ray looked at Vi and said, "It's time for us to get back to work." He pointed at me and said, "It's time for you to go back."

I woke up in the recovery room. I didn't want to be here—and I wasn't sure how I was going to fulfill what had been asked of me.

The knowledge of this, even if it was a dream, was overwhelming.

Kayla said, "Mom, what is wrong? You seem different."

I shook it off as moments of doubt and depression, but I was different. My world had come crashing down again, and I had to find a way to fight my way back to a life I could manage with the face I was left with.

Chapter 43

I Want My Wife Back

Saturday, May 17

Eric brought me home from the hospital, and as happy as I was to be home, I was still drugged up. I couldn't wait to get myself off of the pain medicine. The list of drugs I was "supposed" to be taking blew my mind. I knew they were doing it to control my pain.

At home, I slowly weaned myself off of them to make sure I was not in any pain. I knew I did not want to go through the torment I had originally felt. I took every precaution to make sure I was okay.

For the first couple of days, I slept hours upon hours. I tried to slowly wean myself off of the medicine. I eventually completely stopped taking all the pain medicine and went back to my regimen from before the episode.

A PICC line is a long, thin, hollow tube that a doctor or nurse puts into a vein above the bend of the elbow. It's gives a patient chemotherapy or other medicines. It can stay in place until treatment is done. I would be receiving my antibiotics from the PICC line. We arranged for a home nurse to come in and teach Eric how to administer my antibiotics. She would come back over the next couple of weeks to make sure everything was working correctly and to help with what I needed.

Every morning, Eric administered my medicine before he left for work. Twelve hours later, he did it again. Being left alone during the day was frightening to say the least. My usual pattern was to get myself off the drugs and then go into a depressive state of mind until I could get back to "normal." The process took me a few weeks. I was beginning to worry it was my 'normal' and that I would be too far gone to recover mentally.

One night, the home care nurse came by to take blood. She had a hard time accessing my PICC line. It was clogged up, and it took her more than an hour to pull out any blood. When she finally could, it felt as if blood was being pulled from my heart. I think she barely got what she needed.

Jori and her husband Dwight Udall came by to visit. I was happy to see them but embarrassed about my new look. Jori laid on my bed and visited while Dwight and Eric went downstairs and talked. I'm very blessed with compassionate good friends.

Wednesday, May 21

Eric and I woke up early. He had rearranged his work schedule so he could be there for my postoperative visit with Dr. Barrs. First, Eric had to access my PICC line. After fifteen or twenty minutes of putting all of his weight into it, he was finally able to push through. Once that was done, we headed to the Mayo Clinic. I looked at myself and said, "I don't think I have ever left my home looking like this. My shirt is wrinkled. I have no makeup on. There are bruises all over my face, arms, and hands from surgery. I'm a mess."

He said, "What? I think you are beautiful. What are you talking about?"

At Mayo Clinic, the smells hit me from every direction. People were looking at me as if I had a massive tumor growing out of the side of my face. I should have left my sunglasses on and worn a mask. I would look perfectly normal here.

Dr. Barrs came in with his resident. I felt foggy, but I remembered seeing Dr. Andy Coursin quite often at the hospital. It was nice to see a familiar friendly face. He's quiet, yet he seems to know he had made a connection with me. I liked this young man.

I told Dr. Barrs I had completely taken myself off of the pain medicine. I think he was surprised. He wanted me to be honest with him about whether I was feeling any pain or not. I reassured him and Eric that I was not in any pain. I was trying to clear my brain of all that junk.

Dr. Barrs said it was okay as long as the pain was gone. He looked inside my ear, and it was really corroded with dried blood. He asked me to take a seat next to Eric and told me exactly what happened during my stay at the Mayo Clinic. He took a piece of skin from my arm and covered the nerve with it. Within days, it developed gangrene. He showed Eric a picture; the flesh around it was healthy, but the nerve had died. It was completely black. It was being covered by packing in my ear.

"Okay. What is the next step?" Eric asked.

Dr. Barrs explained that he had a team of doctors available to help in surgery on June 3. There were some options. The minimum would be to go in and cover the nerve with a graft of muscle and wait. They could graft over the nerve and have another doctor reposition the nerves in my tongue over to the nerves that were not working in my face. I'm sure I got some of this wrong.

Eric said, "I want my wife back. I want her to be happy again."

Dr. Barrs said, "If you're asking if the right side of her face is ever going to be the same again, the answer is no. I'm sorry, but the nerve is dead. We cannot bring something back to life that is dead. You need to start loving the wife you have. Her face will never look the same again."

I could feel the tension.

Eric said, "I never said I didn't love my wife. I just want to see her happy again."

Dr. Barrs said, "She needs to learn to love the new Monya. I was fond of the Monya you and I used to know, but I also like the new Monya." I imagine it must have been difficult for Dr. Barr's to relay this fact to us knowing it was going to crush me. He told us to take a few minutes to discuss what we wanted to do next.

When he left the room for, Eric and I looked at each other. The questions were weighing heavy on our minds. What should we do next? Are we being hasty in our decision? We looked at each other and decided we were in agreement to get a second opinion. We were going to wait, pray as a family, and make a decision when we were ready. With nerves, there is a window of opportunity. We needed to make a choice, but not today.

I was trying, once again, to be courageous. I had finally gotten to the point where I was ready to ask, "Why?" I'd done all that I'd been asked to do—everything Dr. Kreymerman, Dr. Magtibay, Dr. Northfelt, and Dr. Barrs has asked. I was worthy of feeling joy. I was not surrendering, but I was tired. The pain was not going away, and it came from deep within me. It made me question everything I knew to be true—everything I had preached to my children to live by.

Life can throw us into unexpected storms. At those times, we can decide to push through and hope for strength to face our deepest pain or we can curl up in a ball and give in to it. Is the pain worth it? I know life gives us disappointments and hard experiences, but I had been forced into some of mine.

For my entire life, I'd had to stand up, be brave, put on my big-girl panties, and move on. I was not there. I just wanted to cry. I deserved to cry until every drop had left my body. Looking in the mirror, I was a different person. My face was partially paralyzed. I had no feeling on the right side, forehead, or ear. My speech was slurred. My eyebrow wouldn't lift, and I'd been told it was all permanent. My smile was completely crooked, my face drooped, and my right eye wouldn't close. We told Dr. Barr's thank you for setting up what he thought was going to be my next surgeries, but that we were not ready to make a decision without a second opinion. He explained the risks of waiting too long and we told him we understood.

We had one more appointment and quickly said our good-bye to Dr. Barr's. We left his office with our hearts broken and our brains wondering what to do next.

Eric took care of checking me in and getting our beeper. The seventh floor of the Mayo Clinic hospital was like the third floor at the Shea campus; for chemo administration. I could smell it as we stepped off the elevator. I sat in the chairs just in front of the elevator and in perfect view of the mountains, desert, and sunshine hoping it would help shake me out of the slight coma I was experiencing.

I kept thinking about Dr. Kreymerman and Heather. Most of the time, I looked forward to these visits. I sometimes had lunch with them in between appointments. Today Heather was assisting in a surgery. I was nauseous, and it was more than I could handle I had to run to the restroom several times while we waited. I think I was in shock hearing what Dr. Barr's had told us.

I couldn't help but wonder how many more times I would need to pick up the pieces and start over again. While we waited, I watched a nurse push a woman back in a wheelchair and ask if she was ready for her IVIG infusion. Sonya got those once a month. IVIG was used to treat various autoimmune, infectious, and idiopathic diseases. Sonya had an autoimmune disease, and was always so brave, she faced the storms with dignity. I love her and look up to her so much. For many years, she was a matriarch for me. Now, she could not even calm the storm raging inside of me.

The hurricane of emotions I was feeling was not just passing through; it was big. I can't handle it anymore. My body is giving in. I wish my tears could release my inner pain, but they don't. I'm constantly learning how to breathe again. This time it's more than tears; it's sobbing. I don't want to be left alone. I can't face it. The depression and despair are the villain with a different name.

People went in and out of the infusion unit. Some were bald, and some were carrying their chemo packs in backpacks. I was trying to have a pity party, and then someone would step off that elevator and give me a new perspective. A wife pushed a man with one leg in a wheelchair. Several people wore oxygen tanks, and another man was missing a hand.

As I inspected each of them, I was grateful for my own trials and triumphs. It took quite a while before we were called back.

A cute young PICC line nurse took us back into a room, but she could not access the line. She injected some medicine into the line and asked us to come back in an hour. I wanted some fresh air, and Eric decided to get food before meeting me outside.

The loudspeaker announced a code blue at the entrance. Can anything else happen today that will push me over the edge? I watched a woman take her last breath; the emergency team worked as hard as they could. I watched and wished it were me. What a hell of an exit. I'd love to drop down at the entrance of the Mayo Clinic on the way to my car. Take my last breath and be gone—done with the Mayo, done with pain, and done with medical decisions. I had no grace left, no patience, no remorse, no regrets, and no feelings. I was numb.

Eric was waiting for me, but none of the food looked good. Eric bought me a grilled cheese sandwich with tomatoes and a white chocolate Bundt cake. My body wanted to throw up every time I tried to eat. It mirrored so much of how I felt going through chemo. I would rather be sitting in front of Dr. Northfelt and having him say, "Your cancer is back." With cancer, although it is difficult to go through, I was given a chance to redeem myself and help others do the same.

I'd been told I have no options to change my face. I will never smile again. I'm not sure how to recover from this. I feel like I have a load so heavy I can hardly breathe. My strength is gone. I'm weak. I don't think I have ever felt as empty as I'm feeling now. We've asked friends and family once again to pray for me. They will ask the Lord to heal me or to give me strength to endure whatever is coming next. How many times do I need to do this? I know the answer before I even finish the sentence. I don't want to hear anyone saying, "Everything happens for a reason." I don't want to hear that. I'm sad, I'm scared, and I'm angry. What could possibly be the reason for this happening to me? I've been through enough!

After we finished up my PICC line on the seventh floor, we were given the green light to go home. I literally ran to the elevator. When it arrived on the first floor, I ran past the piano player and the area where the lady had just passed away. I glanced at the people in waiting room and said, "Eric, I wonder if that guy knows an angel got her wings today—less than an hour ago—exactly where he is sitting?" I ran as fast as I could to the car.

Eric said, "Sweetheart, you really need to keep your voice down while you're walking or running through the exit."

What an extremely difficult week. I don't want to look in the mirror. I want all the mirrors removed from my house. This diagnosis is much worse than when I looked at my breasts for the first time after my mastectomy. At least I could cover them up and have them fixed. The baldness was hard, but it never defined me. It grew back. Yes, this is much worse. How can I continue in this body, looking like this? If one person says, "But you're alive," I'm pretty sure I will kick them. Those words, although very true are not what I want to hear. They pierce my heart and my soul. I know they are trying to be inspiring and help me move forward, but I need time to clearly understand what I've been told today.

Wednesday, May 28, 2014

Life was going on outside of my bedroom. People were working and enjoying life. I want to do that. I have been lying in my bed very sick for months.

After some research, we decided there was a better option than what Dr. Barrs was suggesting. Heather wanted me to see a Dr. Lettieri, but he was out of the country. She was not sure when I could get in with him.

Eric and I were ready to be proactive. I called Dr. Kreymerman and asked him some suggestions. He knew some surgeons I could see. After sharing the information with Eric, he talked to another friend. Diana Lents had connections at a clinic in Cleveland. We were able to get an appointment with a specialist and would be flying to Cleveland in a week.

Diana would be going with me.

Thursday, May 29, 2014

This seems to be a never-ending uphill battle. I'm losing my thoughts to darkness. On days like today, I just need some answers. One came to me in a text message from Haleigh Brownlee:

Your kids deal with situations like this very differently. Everyone was a mess at the hospital. We were all crying. We all thought this was it. We thought we'd be planning a funeral, but your kids are all so very strong. They get that from you. They are very good at keeping face in tough situations like that. I think everyone just thinks that there is always going to be more time with you. That you'll keep fighting because you have for almost five years now!

We all love you so much; there are so many people rooting for you. There are still so many people who need to hear your story and feel inspired. You were given another chance a few weeks ago; instead of looking at it like another part of you missing or another surgery, think of it as another chance from Heavenly Father. You get to still be here on earth to see more grandkids, to see Mexico again, to watch your girls get pregnant, to see your sisters, to see more places with Eric, to sell more Nerium! I'm sure there were days four years ago going through chemo when you wanted to die. But can you imagine if your wish was granted then? You would have missed all of your kids' weddings, Ezra, and Paris! I'm sure there were days when you were a little girl that you wanted to die. When the pain of your family wasn't going away. But look at your life, Monya. Look at all the precious joys you've been given. Life sucks so bad, but with the bad, you get joy in tenfold. I love you. Put on your fighting pants and kick butt. I know how hard this is for you. You're handling it all so well. You can do it. There are so many people who support you and love you and will love you no matter what. You came very close to dying a few weeks ago. So right now, the only thing that's going to get you through this is focusing on why you were kept here and the things that keep you going. So many grandbabies you don't have yet. So many things with your kids' and adopted kids' (me) lives that you can't miss. My heart is so broken that you had to go through yet another trial. I want more than anyone for you to be relieved of the pain and misery. You're here for a reason; you're still fighting for a reason.

I love this sweet message of hope. She is educated well beyond her years and taught me a great lesson when I thought I couldn't go on.

Chapter 44

Cleveland Clinic

Monday June 2, 2014

I had a chance to get another opinion from a doctor at Cleveland Clinic. I took the opportunity with the attitude that I deserved it. I wanted to know if there were any other options for me.

I was worried when I told Dr. Barrs that we decided to get a second—and maybe a third—opinion. I would never want to hurt him. Dr. Barrs was unconditionally kind and understanding. This diagnosis had nothing to do with the skill of Dr.Barr's he will forever have a special place in my heart.

Another great friend who is a physician said, "You always say you want to live with no regrets. Do you believe this will be a regret if you don't take it?"

I knew my answer before he finished the sentence, "Yes, I would regret it." "Besides he said any doctor who is upset because you decide to get a second opinion—or a twentieth opinion— does not deserve to be your doctor."

I'm not sure if I agree with that last part. I have been so blessed to have the best team of doctors on my side, cheering for me all along the way. I love my doctors at the Mayo Clinic.

When I heard I needed to get used to the new me and that my face would never be the same, or that I would never smile and have facial expression again, I was devastated. All I could think of was my sweet grandchildren and the ones to come. I love to laugh and giggle with them. How can I show them my happiness without a smile? With all the modern technology, there has to be a doctor out there who can help. That doctor might not be at the Mayo Clinic—or even at another clinic—but I was willing to try.

Before leaving, I wanted my children and their spouses to know about the dream I had at the Mayo Clinic. I was nervous to tell them and did not know how they would receive my special experience. It had been a few weeks, and I was still trying to understand what I'd seen and been told. I interrupted the dream to them and clarified the feeling I had with Eric's mom and dad. I wanted them to understand the awareness I had of peace and serenity since nothing on earth was comparable to it. I told them I would take any pain, fear, or trial on earth if I could have that feeling back for eternity. There was not much conversation. I'm not quite sure how they felt about it.

Scott said, "How many children were there?"

I said, "I don't recall how many there were. All I remember was a white-headed child."

Brian and Kaitlyn were expecting their first baby at the time, but they had not told us yet. Looking back, I wonder if it was meaningful to them. Our third grandson, Phoenix, has white hair.

Tuesday, June 3, 2014

I boarded the flight at 5:25 a.m. to face either a storm or a tender mercy in Cleveland.

I pleaded with friends and family to unite in prayer for relief. We were hoping for the answers to come clearly and quickly. My right eye wouldn't close. I had chronic dry eye. To protect it, I was wearing a pirate patch. My right eye dripped nonstop. I had blurry vision and fell off curbs if I was not careful with my steps. It was so hard to stay strong, this was something I had not felt in a long time. Even when I was diagnosed with the villain, I felt more in control. This was a whole new level of fear. I was facing beasts I thought were buried and gone. Tears rose to the surface every time I looked at myself in the mirror. The stares of people affected me. I tried to look away and lower my head before they did. Diana was so sweet and reassuring for me. She guided my footsteps, and I could not have done it without her help.

Diana and I spent four hours with a specialty surgeon we were extremely impressed with Dr. Bernard. He possessed a kind bedside manner and came with incredible credentials.

His PA came in to discuss why I was there. She looked at me and said, "Can you give me the history of your ear issues?"

I began with the blow to the year as a child and ended with the current status-leaving out details as to make the history a shortened version. I felt like she was looking at me but not listening; she was typing everything I said yet She never made eye contact. I wasn't sure if she was just really focused or if I was being too sensitive. Probably the latter.

She stepped out to speak with the doctor, soon Dr. Bernard came back in with the reports from Mayo Clinic. He was very complimentary of all my doctors. He specifically mentioned Dr. Kreymerman and Heather Lucas. They were friends of his, and he admired them for their strengths in medical treatment. It was reassuring to have a doctor with a connection to some of my doctors at Mayo Clinic. Dr. Bernard agreed with Dr. Barrs about the window of opportunity to give the nerve damage a possibility of repairing. However, he did not necessarily agree with taking the muscle from my tongue.

He explained how the process at Cleveland Clinic worked moving forward. I needed to see an ENT and a doctor in neurology. Neurology needed to be involved because of my skull. When Dr. Bernard left the room, I sat in the window bench and looked out at the beautiful trees and lawns. My mind wandered. It was surreal. It took a lot of energy to keep my mind focused on the happiness I had in my life. I didn't want to be there. I watched a bird land in a tree and wondered if I would ever be that free. Will there be a day when I could spread my wings and fly?

The doctor did a quick assessment of my ear, some routine facial tests, and said, "Yeah there is nothing animated about the right side." I would need several surgeries to "fix" my face. He agreed that my face would never be the same. I looked at Diana and could see her taking notes, trying not to make eye contact with me; she was effected I could see it. I was and always will be grateful to her for being there with me, she knew just the right questions to ask.

I cried, I never cry in front of my doctors. I'm usually able to sucked it up until I get to my car, but this time was different; I was exhausted from the burden on my mind and shoulders.

The doctor explained how they would proceed with the nerve surgeries after the debris was cleaned out and the ear was healed. Instead of taking a muscle from my tongue, he would take a muscle from my inner thigh or a nerve from my ankle. He would also take the nerve from the left side of my face and pull it over to the right side, hoping to connect it to the good nerves on each side.

All of this information gave me a headache. I didn't understand a bit of what came out of their mouths. I didn't want to know, and I wanted him to shut up. I wanted to cover my ears and make it go away. Diana looked at me and said "It's ok sweetie, this is good we finally have some answers."

Within a few minutes, the PA came back in the room and told me she was able to make an appointment with a doctor who specializes in my "issues." She said she would try to get me as soon as possible. She also said neurology would also be on my itinerary.

I began to cry again. Diana teared up too. The PA had nothing to say, but she teared up too. I felt hopeless again. Diana felt very hopeful. She would help me through the tough days.

June 6, 2014

Dr. Haberkamp from the ENT department examined my ear, vacuumed it, and cleaned it up. He said the inner ear canal looked like it was healing properly. He also acknowledged that Dr. Barrs had done an incredible job on my ear. We both agreed that Dr. Barrs was a special man and I was blessed to have him as a doctor.

We made some decisions after talking to a few surgeons. The proposal Dr. Barrs gave me was reasonable, but three doctors told me that taking muscle from my tongue was a temporary fix. If I were an eighty-year-old woman, they might consider that option. The best approach for someone with a dead nerve was to take a nerve from my ankle. That nerve best replicates the nerve in my face. He would place it where the dead nerve was and hope the nerves on either side would grow back together. If this was successful it would take over a year of waiting to see if the nerve grew. This option could only be done if there was a good nerve to work with in my ear.

If there were no good nerves, they would take a muscle from my arm, connect it, close off the right ear completely with some tissue from my arm, and bring in two other surgeons to assist with this process. This surgery could be six months or more down the road. Dr. Haberkamp is an exceptional doctor, and I felt good about him.

June 9, 2014

For Diana and I the waiting was the hardest part. Everyday I called the doctor's office as soon as they opened. Day after day they were still working on booking the operating room. I learned really quickly blocking off twelve hours in an operating room is not as effortless as it sounds. Bringing three doctors in for the surgery is not an easy task either. Their schedules all had to coincide with the surgery time.

One day when I called I was informed that Dr. Bernard would not be taking on my case. He had been offered a job at another hospital. He explained to us that he didn't want to start something he could not finish. so he lined up a meeting with a different surgeon. He also advised us that the process they proposed would take a few more surgeries than they had originally anticipated. I was a little disappointed but completely understood why he needed to refer me. I just wanted to get it over with.

I was not prepared for the smells in the Cleveland clinic cancer center to do a number on me. I tried to keep from having anxiety. Emotions were racing through my body. I paced until they announced my name. It was time to meet my new surgeon.

His name was Dr. Barrish, aka Dr. Cocky Face. I didn't really care for him. He didn't communicate well with me, and he cared too much about his credentials. He was no Dr. Kreymerman or Dr. Bernard. Halfway through his explanation, he lost me with his bragging. He was trying to convince me he was a good surgeon. Sarcastically, I asked him to slow down and explain my procedure in "blonde" terminology.

When he noticed I was being seen at Mayo Clinic in Arizona, he said, "Oh, ha-ha. I don't recognize the Arizona Mayo Clinic as the Mayo Clinic."

Ok, now he was crossing a line with me "What are you talking about? Arizona, Florida, and Rochester are all Mayo Clinics." I was pretty frustrated. Who did he think he was talking to? If he were going to be my surgeon, it would be the first surgery where I didn't love and respect my doctor. He rushed me and never looked me in the face. He mentioned Dr. Kreymerman and said he might have seen his picture in the hall at the Cleveland hospital. He wanted to know if he was Jewish.

Confused I replied, "Yes, he is. Why?"

He replied, "Just wondering. He has a Jewish name, and I wondered if I knew him since I am Jewish." He leaned forward and pointed to the Yamaka on his head. Is this guy serious? What the heck does this have to do with me or my surgeries? What a presumption on his part. I could tell Diana was thinking the same thing. We both rolled our eyes in dis-belief.

Diana and I discussed it, not knowing if I should proceed with a surgeon I didn't feel comfortable with. We both concurred we were willing to let his arrogance go in one ear and out the other if his surgical skills were as good as he said they were. Most of what he was suggesting Dr. Bernard had already explained to me, and Dr. Kreymerman was just a phone call away to help me digest the rest.

My ear was a major emergency, but my eye was the most important issue. I was in jeopardy of losing my cornea and needing a transplant. Dr. Cocky Face was going to put a gold weight in the eyelid that would give me ability to blink when my brain told it to. There would be some training and rehab on my part.

He had significant concerns about the bone loss from the mastoid that had been removed. There would be some level of bone resection. All the surgeons agreed that if a good frontal nerve stump could be found, then a sural nerve graft was necessary. If there was a good nerve, they could use, they will do a nerve graft from the left side of my face to the right. It was best not to let it wait because of progressive osteomyelitic changes. Osteomyelitis is an infectious painful inflammatory disease of the bone, which Dr. Barrs had explained to me before I left the Mayo Clinic. If that was the case, they recommended a simpler reconstruction first. Most likely it could be done with a flap and skin graft. If it failed, I could get a radial artery free flap. He explained all the risks and benefits and was able to answer all my questions. He thought it would be possible in the next couple weeks. The symmetry of the mouth and eyelid would be later; the surgery and healing would take more than a year.

My speech was difficult to understand, and I slurred some pronunciations. I still do. My Ps and Bs require effort. I use my index finger to press on the right cheek, which seems to help. I was told I would learn to retrain my speech. With therapy, I would be reconditioning my brain to connect with my face. Even with all the surgeries and procedures I had ahead of me, I tried to remain positive. Diana and I made the best of a difficult situation. My life as I once knew it was over. My face would never be the same, and I knew it was going to take strength and patience to deal with the unwanted stares and opinions of others.

Even though I was having a hard time dealing with the looks from people. I understood why they stared. My face was an obvious distraction. A young child looked at me and said, "What's wrong with that lady's face?"

The sweet Mom said, "She's smiling at you with her eyes."

I cried a little and realized I smile with my eyes all the time with Recker. There have been so many times he stares at me with his eyes, and I know we are connecting. Learning to smile with my eyes and heart is how I would communicate with other people. I was touched by that young mother and thanked her for her thoughtfulness.

I was trying to accept the realities of my new life, and I knew there was no turning back time. I would no longer be spending six days a week at the gym, training for any marathons or smiling with my teeth showing. Some of those things I once enjoyed so much were also the things I took for granted.

God has a different plan for me. I'm still not sure what it is, but I get a little glimpse of it every day. Because my life has been spared so many times, it tells me I have more to learn.

June 19, 2014

I've been in Cleveland for two weeks, getting opinion after opinion. Dr. Kreymerman taught me to always ask a doctor how many times they have performed the procedure before committing to a surgeon. Dr. Cocky Face proudly announced when I asked him "I see at least forty patients before eleven o'clock every morning."

I wasn't sure that answered my question. This guy is unreal. So I said to him "At the Mayo Clinic, my surgeons actually know my name and take time to answer my questions. I'm glad none of them see forty patients in less than three hours. You didn't answer my question."

He turned around and said, "Oh, this is an easy surgery. I've done it hundreds of times."

I can be a little sassy when it comes to people talking badly about my family, surgeons, or the Mayo Clinic. Dr. Cocky Face was seriously getting on my nerves (no pun intended). I discussed the situation with Diana, and we decided Dr. Cocky Face definitely needed some practice with doctor-patient communication, but as much as we hated to admit it, he had great credentials. I could either walk away after weeks of waiting or go forward with him and put aside my personal feelings. I chose to move forward.

June 28, 2014

Surgery is finally scheduled for July 3.

I have so much to be grateful for. My life will go on—even though my circumstances have changed. I am determined to make the best of it—and not let this define me. I'm trying to practice what I preach by doing something kind every day for someone else—even if it was holding a door open for someone. The hospital had a very nice area to eat. I bought lunch for a woman in line behind me. She was so surprised and thrilled that she decided to pay it forward for the person behind her. That small act of kindness made me so happy. It was exactly what I needed. I desperately wanted to feel something—anything. Being limited at the hospital, I tried to give encouraging words and copies of Live Happy Magazine to everyone I could.

I missed my family and tried to FaceTime with Recker and Ezra every day. Kayla was so good about calling. Even if it was a few minutes, I relished that time. Dr. Kreymerman's mother, Evgenya came to visit me. She was gracious and lovely to talk with. I saw so much of her in Dr. Kreymerman, especially his gentle, compassionate side. I also had the opportunity to have dinner with Alex and Evgenya Kreymerman (Dr. Kreymerman's parents). Dr. Kreymerman looks so much like his dad, and I enjoyed hearing stories about him when he was younger.

I loved the time away from the worries and stress of the hospital and procedures. I will always cherish that time I spent with them in Cleveland.

July 2, 2014

It's the night before another major surgery, I hope and pray all will go well. Making decisions without Eric or the kids to help me is really hard. I feel isolated at times. I have always been independent, but in major matters with my health, Eric has always been my advocate and shoulder to lean on. He understands my fears and doubts and is virtually the only person who can calm me when the world gets too heavy.

The fear of living with a new face has been heavy on mind. The time I've spent here without family has given me time to really reach within and ask some gut-wrenching questions. Can I live a quality life with my face the way it is right now? Am I confident enough to live the rest of my life with people staring?

When children ask what is wrong with my face, I just tell them I have a boo-boo they understand what a boo boo is and are ok with that answer. Children are so innocent; it's the adults I have a hard time with. I understand most people do not intentionally try to offend but so many of us, me included need to think about what we say before the words shatter the heart of another.

During this seven weeks in Cleveland, I've found inner strength I never thought I had. I read my scriptures and The Slight Edge every day. I've had many spiritual experiences since my first surgery at the Mayo. I am trying to grow and move in a direction I feel comfortable with. Tonight I wrote letters to my children and Eric. There is always a risk going into surgery, and I want my family to truly know the happiness they have brought into my life.

A friend texted to say she had been thinking of me but didn't quite know the right words to say. "I hope you are able to get the answers you're looking for … if it is the Lord's will." When I read the last part, I couldn't get it off my mind. What is the Lord's will for me? I don't know the answer. That friend was the caregiver for two of her sons who struggled with health issues. She said she would gladly take their pain so they would not have to feel it. That resonated with me. I would not want any of my children or Frenchie to go through what I was feeling. Our Heavenly Father must feel this when he sees his children struggling. I know my circumstances at this moment are not going to change. I'm praying for a miracle—or to be strong enough to accept this new life and find a way to live happy.

I loved my sweet Haleigh's texts:

"Mom when are you coming home?"

"Good question. It all depends on how well the surgery goes. I'm praying it'll all go great so I can go home next weekend. I'm really scared."

"We miss you so much. I pray for you every morning and night. I have faith that the surgery will go well. Don't be scared, Heavenly Father is always looking over you—and Dad will be there."

"I'm looking forward to seeing Dad. This is the longest we've ever been away from each other. He's the only one who knows how to calm me when I get anxiety waiting for surgery. I never want to feel that extreme pain from the nerve again, like I did at Mayo."

"You are one the strongest women I know. I love you, Mom."

"I love you too. Thank you for being my daughter."

Preparing for this surgery, I feel alone—even though Eric will be here soon. The anxiety I'm experiencing about this surgery is different from what I've felt with other surgeries. I'm far away from home. It feels like the road is getting longer and longer, and it's harder and harder to maintain calmness. When all is said and done, I hope I will be a better version of myself—even with my face disfigured. I know who I am, and I know the kind of person I want to be, but the world can be so cruel.

Eric was a sight for sore eyes. After a month of talking, texting, and FaceTiming, we were finally able to embrace. I loved feeling his arms around me, and I wanted it to last. Staring into his eyes again was reassuring. Suddenly the world was okay. I knew everything was going to be okay.

July 3, 2014

We were taken to the waiting area at 5:30 a.m. Eric and Diana were with me. I paced the floor and did not want anyone to talk to me or touch me. I had jitters and prayed Heavenly Father would take it away. He did, and I was soon off to get ready for surgery.

Before Eric came back to see me, I said several quick prayers. I asked God to watch over the surgeon's hands—and if it be his will that he would allow me to heal from this odd, unexpected trial I was facing. I wanted to put my head under the pillow so I could scream, cry, and forge through this quickly.

Eric gave me a kiss on the forehead as they wheeled me into the operating room It was difficult to maintain my composure. Tears flowed onto my pillow. Wheeling through the hallways, I saw a wall that had many white coats on hooks. The coats belonged to doctors. Those doctors would arrive, take a white coat off the hook, and go to work. This was a sight I had never encountered at Mayo Clinic-I liked it.

The tears continued to flow as the nurses asked what they could do to help. I shook my head and watched them walk away, not knowing what to do. I was ready to move on with the surgery and put this chapter to rest.

I woke up in recovery, and I was in a lot of pain. While I was trying to process where the pain was coming from, the nurse said, "Mrs. Williams, it's time to wake up. Do you know where you are? How many fingers am I holding up?"

I touched my head to see what damage had been done. It was an eleven-hour surgery with what seemed to be a lot of anesthesia and blood. What's this? A neck brace? I'm confused.

Eric and Diana came into the recovery room. Eric told me I was beautiful. He was so sweet. I knew it wasn't true. How could I be beautiful? I had blood all over me, a swollen head, and staples across my bald skull. I asked, "Why do I have a neck brace on?"

The nurse said, "The neck brace is to keep you from moving your head."

I kept going in and out of consciousness. The driver wheeling me back to my room said, "Hey, darlin' What would you like me to sing to you while we stroll the halls?"

"Really? You are going to sing to me?"

"Sure. Why not?"

I said, "Okay. Do you know any Luther Vandross?"

"Girl, that is my specialty." He started singing a song entitled Here and Now.

I told him it was beautiful, but he should not quit his day job.

He put his index finger to his mouth to shush me.

I'm pretty sure serenading patients was frowned upon, but I enjoyed his sense of humor.

When Eric walked into my room, I was overwhelmed with love and peace. I didn't have to say a word, he knew what I was thinking. Tears were once again rolling down my face Eric asked me "What's wrong are you in pain?" I shook my head as if to say no. He and Diana looked tired. I think the waiting was long and difficult. I must have drifted off to sleep. When I woke up, they were gone. I was glad they could go back to the hotel to get some sleep.

The day after surgery was the Fourth of July. The doctors on my team sent their residents to visit me. The senior resident came in my room and introduced himself.

The junior resident asked, "How is your pain?"

I said, "On a scale from one to ten, about a five."

The senior resident interjected, "I see on your chart you will be given Dilaudid. That is a very strong pain medication. Is there a reason for that?"

"Morphine does not work for me any longer. It's what they've given me for the past couple surgeries, and it works for me."

"We have very few patients we administer intravenous Dilaudid to."

I wasn't sure if he was questioning me or trying to teach the junior residents something. When he walked out, he said, "Let the nurses know if your pain gets too bad."

Within half an hour, the pain was slowly rising. I beeped for the nurse and asked her for pain medicine. She said she would get it right away.

Within fifteen minutes, I beeped for the nurse again. "When will I get pain medicine? The spasms are getting worse."

She said, "I'm sorry it's taking so long. The resident did not put in any orders for pain medicine."

"Wait … what?" I was at a level eight—going on nine. I started to cry. "Can you please call my husband? He's down the street at the hotel. I want him here."

"Yes, we have his number. We will call him now and page the resident."

I heard them page the resident several times. I was in absolute agony. I tried to process happy thoughts, and happy moments. Sometimes it worked, and sometimes it didn't. I concentrated on the clock, waiting the arrival of medicine and Eric. I was crying so hard and trying to catch my breath.

The sweet nurses rubbed my arms and legs, and they were crying.

I tried to sing "Be Still My Soul" through the gulps of air. I sang "I Feel My Savior's love" and "I Am a Child of God." I was never able to finish any of those songs. The pain was excruciating.

I heard the nurses down the hall laughing and talking about their plans for the Fourth of July. Life was going on out there. I thought I was dying, and they were jubilantly enjoying each other. I should be with my family. What is happening to me?

My room was right in front of the nurses' desk so they could watch me and monitor my pain levels. I was staring at the clock and whimpering loudly. I was on my own. I felt deserted and alone. I was scared and crying the hardest I ever had in my life. I was yelling between breaths of air. Why have you ignored my pleas and prayers? Where was my divine intervention? Had the Lord forgotten me? I felt like it was going to be my last day on earth. I would not be able to say good-bye to Eric.

Through gasps of air, I asked one of the nurses if she had gotten in touch with him. She had not. I asked her to give him the letter in my bag in case I didn't make it.

In a sweet voice, she said, "Don't talk like that, honey. The doctor will be here soon."

The nurses paged him at least three times, but he never came. I knew as well as they did that he was not on his way. The pain and anxiety were going to kill me my heart rate was rising.

The other patients were complaining and telling the nurses to get my doctor or move them so they wouldn't have to hear me. I tried to stop crying, and the nurses were saying how sorry they were, but they couldn't do anything until they heard from the doctor. My desperate cries for help were falling on deaf ears.

After an hour and fifteen minutes, the resident came into my room. He walked up to me and arrogantly said, "Why are you crying? It can't hurt that bad."

I was covering my mouth because I knew my face was already distorted. Add crying to that scenario, and I'm sure I was extremely unnatural looking. I was embarrassed.

He said, "Why are you covering your mouth?"

I recognized that he was showing off for the junior residents but they actually seemed to be in shock too.

I screamed, "Please just help me."

Finally, the pain medicine surged through my veins with purpose and strength. My body was still shaking as I tried to compose myself.

As he walked out of the room, the nurse asked, "Where have you been for an hour and fifteen minutes? We have been paging you."

He looked at the nurse and said, "I don't have to answer to you."

I couldn't speak without trembling. I could not believe what had just happened. I had been weeping and thrashing from side to side for so long that it took every bit of energy I had. My heart was racing, but my blood pressure was low.

By the time Eric arrived, all was calm. He said, "Sweetheart, have you been crying?"

"Uh ... just a bit." I could see the hurt in his eyes as I told him what had happened.

"No one ever called me. I would have come." He kissed my forehead. "I'm so sorry that happened to you."

In retrospect, I realize it was probably better that he wasn't there. I'm pretty sure the young resident would have gotten an earful from Frenchie. I know he would have gone crazy from seeing me in that much pain.

I sent those beautiful nurses the Live Happy magazine and a note telling them how grateful I was for them during such a difficult time.

One of the junior residents came back to sit with me several times during my stay. He knew how to connect, and I was grateful to him.

July 10, 2014

Today I am happy. All my surgeons have seen me. They told me my ear looks great—and everything is healing perfectly. As for the nerve regeneration, it was a waiting game at this point.

My head was shaved, and I have staples from front to back and from one ear to the other. The entire inner ear was taken out, and a new ear was designed. I have no feeling in my right foot and ankle, which causes me to limp. (To this day, no feeling has returned.) I was in a lot of pain, but I was told I could be released.

During my final appointment, Dr. Cocky Face was admiring the staples and stitching he had done on my head. "Oh yeah. I did a great job. It looks fantastic." He looked into my eyes for the first time and said, "Do you think I need to lose some weight?"

I looked at him and shook my head in disbelief. With no response from either of us, he left the room. It was seriously a strange moment—one I had never experienced with a surgeon.

I will need to see Dr. Barrs once a week for the next few weeks after I get home. The doctors told me that major nerve surgery takes at least six months to see results. I didn't care. I just wanted to go home to Arizona, see Dr. Barrs, and move forward.

July 17, 2014

After being released from the hospital, I was not able to fly for a week. Diana's sister and husband were gracious enough to allow me to stay in their home. Angel and John treated me with great respect. I will always admire them for their Christlike service in taking a stranger into their home. I will miss them. Angel read me scriptures and a spiritual thought from the book Jesus Calling every day to help keep my hopes up and my testimony of Jesus Christ alive. Thank you, Angel. John is a true gentleman with unwavering love for his wife, children and grandchildren. He is a full-on Yankees lover, but I won't hold that against him. He kept his composure when I told him I didn't care for Derek Jeter.

At the airport in Arizona my family was there to greet me and take me home. Recker sat on my lap as Frenchie wheeled me to the car. I was so happy to be home with my them. Recker stared at my swollen, bandaged wrapped face with such empathy. He was saying, "I love you, Bonbon." and he was doing it with his eyes, we were connecting with no words.

Chapter 45

Change is Hard

August 19, 2014

oming home was refreshing—and just what I needed. Kaitlyn and Brian would be having our third grandson in February. The entire family was overjoyed. The transition back into life was more challenging than I imagined it would be. Making eye contact with family, friends, doctors, and even strangers was tough. My family loves me unconditionally, but I had changed. My confidence was being tested.

I tried to maintain some normalcy by continuing with my Nerium club. The first Market Party was absolutely terrifying. What I thought was going to be an intense night of anxiety ended up being a memorable evening. No one looked away. I was embraced with open arms, teary eyes, and huge smiles.

At times, I wanted to curl up and stay in the safety of my home. I was healing emotionally so much slower than I expected I would. I was trying so hard to break out of the four walls I'd built around myself. I wished I had someone to talk to; partial facial paralysis is not exactly something you see every day. Finding support groups or even one person I could confide in who could truly understand was impossible.

I lost my grasp and sometimes had a hard time being real. I hid how tearfully hard it was not to be able to smile. My frailties were being masked by a strong woman who had hard time admitting her weaknesses. My family was having a hard time with the change in my personality. I was frustrated because I couldn't make anyone understand how I felt.

I don't want to be changed, but I am. I feel like I am on display. I see how people look at me and quickly look away. I know because I have done it too. I don't believe people are vindictive or mean any harm. It's natural for a person to take a second look at something that is not what they are used to seeing. I just never imagined I would be the one on exhibit. I see them glance, look away, and whisper. The reality of this being a permanent part of life, my life, is incredibly overwhelming.

The only thing that really holds me together is knowing Heavenly Father sees the real me. He knows I'm struggling to understand the whys. I didn't ask for this experience, but I'm living it. I realize I may not be in charge of my trials, but I do have control over how I deal with them. I choose to take it slow. I proceed in faith and with the desire to continue to be the best I can be. I know this fear and pain I'm feeling needs to be turned over to the Lord, but for today, I'm frozen inside. I ache at times. I try so hard to hold back smiles or laughter for fear of what I look like to others.

I caught myself wanting to laugh when I heard Ezra's belly laugh—he is so cute—but I caught my reflection in the mirror of our entryway and cringed. Oh, gosh. This is what other people see? It immediately took me down so low.

I have so much happiness in my heart, and I want to show it, especially with my grandchildren. I am facing my biggest fear. To most people, a smile means happiness. Without a smile, the perception is she must be unhappy. How am I going to show others my happiness without being able to smile?

I definitely took my smile for granted. Naturally, I did not expect anyone else to understand how I felt. I was trying my hardest to be happy by going out and serving others. The act of service warms my heart and lightens my load, but it doesn't take away my realities.

I don't think a person can actually go through some of the things I have endured and be unchanged. People who feel discouraged and misunderstood should have faith, believe, and have hope for a better day. I wish I could say I am happy all the time, but that would not be true. I struggle with it daily. I know it is a choice, and it feels better than being depressed. You can wake up every day and decide to make the most of the life you have been given. It does not necessarily mean changing your world—but changing the way you look at it. It's a struggle, I am trying so hard.

Ezra was also diagnosed with autism when he was eighteen months old. Over the past few months, he started to regress. Kayla tried to prepare us, but I didn't want to believe it. After all, Ezra was doing everything differently—until he didn't. Little by little, he became distant. Kayla did everything differently with her pregnancy, thinking it could make a difference.

Ezra didn't get his immunizations like Recker did. His diagnosis was a shock for Eric and me. When I found out, I just wanted to scream, Why? I still do. I'm hurt, angry, sad, and blessed all at the same time. Mixed emotions rocked my little world, and it would take days, weeks, or months to get used to.

I want Kayla and Jeremy's dreams of having a typical child to come true. This does not mean they do not love their boys— they love them more than life—but all parents want to hear their children say "Mom" or "Dad." They need time to mourn. I guess we all do.

I don't believe these boys are doomed. Their futures are different, but not less than any of us. I know they can and will be such blessings to our family and to others. In their journeys, they will—against the odds—teach us. Through their sweet spirits, they will show us so much more about compassion and tolerance than we could ever learn in a book. Those sweet boys were sent to our family for a purpose. We may never know what that purpose is, but I've decided the reason does not matter as much as making the journey with them memorable and happy.

Autism is not fun. It is misunderstood. I know so little about why a child is diagnosed with autism. All I really know is that nothing changes for me. I love these boys unconditionally. I am their Bonbon, and through their eyes, I want them to feel my love.

I believe happiness and kindness should begin in our homes. I'm beginning to see the importance of teaching my grandchildren this simple principle. I want them to know that their strength and character will help them succeed in life. Autism does not hold them back from love of a family.

These boys are going to learn what safe relationships are and the importance of fairness, gratitude, courage, creativity, and grit. Unfortunately, they will also learn the harsh cruelty of some human beings. With help, we will teach them how to show up for challenges in a different way by being inclusive, compassionate, charitable, and non-combative. I see these boys for their potential—not for the behaviors they will have to learn to control. My purpose is to connect with them with my heart, share, serve, and grow with them on their journeys.

Chapter 46

The Price of Beauty

*A*t US Airways, I take reservations over the phone.

One day, a caller asked, "Are you okay?"

Not knowing exactly what he meant, I asked, "Yes, I'm okay. Did I offend you?"

"Oh, heavens no. Just the opposite. You are lovely to talk to, and I feel grateful it was you who answered the phone."

I thanked him and finished up his reservation. When I asked if there was anything else I could do to help him, he said, "Yes, you can."

I thought he was going to change the reservation, have me send him to rental cars, or add his dividend miles number.

He said, "Did you recently have a stroke? I don't mean to be nosy, but your voice sounds a little staggered."

For the first time, I was able to hear the truth from someone—a stranger. For the first time, a light went off in my head.

I replied, "No, sir. I didn't have a stroke, but I do have facial paralysis. Sometimes it's difficult to speak clearly. I'm sorry if you had a hard time understanding me today."

The gentleman said, "I want you to know that I understand your pain, but I want you to never underestimate who you are. Can you do that for me?"

I felt sweet peace come over me. I was healing from the inside out. It took a complete stranger to engage in an honest conversation with me. I wasn't imagining it. My speech was slurred. Many times, when I speak, I have to push my finger against my cheek to make it sound clear. Friends and family ask, "Why do you do that? We can understand you." It is just a natural reaction, and it makes things sound better in my head.

Facial paralysis has been the most challenging obstacle I have had to come to grips with. I've felt like I just can't do it anymore. I've begged for relief and for a complete physical healing. I have definitely felt broken, alone, and misunderstood.

To say, "I have partial facial paralysis" was a huge step forward. My physicians have been perfectly honest with me. Right now, there is not much hope for a full recovery—and there will be more surgeries. I like to hear the full truth and the bottom line, and then I can deal with it.

I was recently at a Nerium leadership training in Canada. As I religiously took notes, I was shocked when I heard the trainer make a comical statement about how much women pay for their beauty products. I heard laughing from the audience, but I was in another world. What is the price we pay for beauty? And I'm not talking about a monetary price.

Mark said, "Believe me, guys. There is a price for beauty."

Everyone laughed, including me. I pulled a quote from of my purse: "Physical beauty may be in the eye of the beholder, but inner beauty is something that shines from inside—and no one can deny it."

I always keep this anonymous quote in my purse to remind me of who I am and who I want to be. Mark was making light of how much women spend on beauty products to show the bargain of Nerium's prices when compared to retail stores. We all laughed at the reality he was presenting. My mind focused on the phrase: "There is a price for beauty." Has the world taken us too far away from a healthy relationship with our true selves? We all, men included, want to look good. Women want to be beautiful, but the question arises in my brain: What is beauty?

Through social media, billboards, commercials, and celebrity profiles, society has taught young girls that there is a standard to be met if they want to be defined as beautiful. There is nothing wrong with wanting style and beauty. Most women find satisfaction from a new haircut or color, a pedicure or manicure, a new pair of shoes, or a skin regime. Those are healthy, enjoyable choices, but they have nothing to do with beauty.

I sometimes hear people say, "But you're so beautiful." That hesitation with "but" has penetrated my heart too many times. I know there is not one person out there who has said those words to me and is comfortable saying it, but I've come to discern they love me and really just don't know what to say. I don't know what to say either. My soul is trying to heal, and it will take some time for me to be ready to accept this new life I have been offered. If I can finally accept that my beauty is always going to be defined by how I treat others, I will be okay. It's a process that will take some time.

I want to explain the differences between what I have been diagnosed with and a person who has had Bell's palsy or a stroke. Mine was brought on after the mastoid was removed from my ear canal and an acute infection followed close behind. Dr. Barr's exhausted every avenue in trying to get the infection under control. He told us he had never seen an infection like this before.

Bell's palsy and stroke victims can relate to the facial paralysis, but they cannot relate to being told it is permanent. Most people eventually regain movement and normal symmetry very few are ever diagnosed with permanent facial paralysis.

Birth can cause temporary facial paralysis in some babies and mothers. However, 90 percent of patients recover completely without treatment. There is a debate on the percentages of people who have permanent partial facial paralysis due to a nerve dying. I have read 1–4 percent, and a surgeon told me it was 2 percent. I never wanted to know percentages with breast cancer, and I don't regret that decision. Hearing percentages with the facial paralysis was a bitter moment I wish I'd avoided. However, knowledge is power. I'm more determined to find contentment in my life.

According to healthline.com, facial paralysis has a major impact on quality of life. Patients may lose confidence and feel embarrassed. In addition, facial paralysis can cause:

- facial pain
- headaches or dizziness
- earaches, ringing in one or both ears, and sensitivity to sound
- difficulty talking
- inability to express emotion
- difficulty eating or drinking
- drooling
- muscle twitching
- tearing of the eyes
- dryness of the eye and mouth

I experience all of the above. One of the hardest ones for me is eating in public. It is embarrassing for me. Eric and I enjoy going out to eat and being with friends, but I don't enjoy it anymore. When I decline, people always say "Why? I've never noticed anything different about you eating." That is simply not true. I've watched myself eat, and it is a distraction. My right eye squints and blinks with every bite. I have to drink with a straw if I don't want to drool all over myself. I appreciate my loving family and friends for being polite and kind, but this is another side effect many people don't understand. I will work through it.

I received another dose of reality one day walking into work. I have a hard time distinguishing between reality and rudeness these days. I am trying my hardest to be okay with living with how I look and know it is permanent. There are days I don't think about it. On the days when I do, it's usually because someone says, "Hey, Monya. I'm sorry to hear about your recent surgery."

"Thank you, but I am doing well. I'm glad to be back to work. Good to see you"

"I was just wondering. Do you think you could get plastic surgery done on your other eye to create some symmetrical lines?"

Seriously? Being put on the spot like that was about as uncomfortable as a call girl in church. I had no idea what to say. After a little hesitation, I said, "I haven't considered that option. Actually, I just endured the twenty-first surgery in five years. I've had six this year, I actually thought I would lose my life. I'm trying to accept what I look like and move forward." She said, "Well, you take good care of your skin. It looks good … except the right side is a little off centered from the rest."

"Ok, I have to stop you right here. I can't listen to this anymore. I am not trying to be rude. I'm quite sure you have great intentions and you're not meaning to insult me, but this has been one of the most difficult years of my life. I am alive. I'm working, and I'm trying my best to be okay with me—not the physical me but the whole self. The parts of my inner beauty I have never seen or known I could possess, this is a long ongoing process." Tears started to well up, which really ticked me off because I was trying so hard to be composed. "My skin looks good because of Nerium. The self-help I've gotten since my facial paralysis comes from reading good books and giving myself daily affirmations: I am good enough. I am pretty enough. I can hold my head high, knowing I am trying my hardest with all I have inside of me to face people and respect myself no matter what my physical appearance is."

She apologized for offending me. Why couldn't it just end at that?

When I started to walk off, she said, "I just thought you would want to know that there are plastic surgeons out there who can help you."

I acted as if I didn't hear her last comment. I wish I could say a huge shield of honor came up between us, but as much as I didn't want it to affect me, it did.

When I got off work, I went home, looked at my face in the mirror, and—like I do every day—I told my damn lips to smile. I worked on it for thirty minutes. It was pretty funny because my mouth didn't even try. I had to push my lip up with my finger over and over again. I did that and said, "Smile, dang it."

I can only smile with one side of my mouth. I can only lift one eyebrow. My right eye doesn't blink. However, I can listen with my heart—and I can smile with my eyes. Until my smile comes back, I will continue to work on true happiness in my life, surround myself with others who are compassionate and kind—people who genuinely give me space and appreciate that they cannot understand what I am going through—and truly believe I have a beautiful heart. I'm really trying.

The price I've paid for physical beauty is beyond what most people can imagine. When I look at people now, I see beauty with a different perspective. There truly is nothing more beautiful than men and women who can unapologetically be themselves. These people are rare and difficult to find. Loving my physical imperfections is uncomfortable at times, but I am learning to become purified from the inside out.

Once I get my inner strength back, my mind tells me I will understand and comprehend more about inner beauty.

Chapter 47

Magical Sounds

January 2015

My dear friend Sheldon passed away this week. I made a divine connection with him. Over these past five and a half years, we were able to connect on a different level than I could with other people. Sometimes all I needed to do was turn around during church to meet his eye. At that moment, we both knew. I could see in his face if he was having a good or bad week.

Sheldon was a quiet giant, and I never heard him complain. We shared moments, thoughts, and feelings about oncologists, medicine, chemo, and side effects. I attended his funeral with such mixed emotions. Watching his family enter the chapel was a surreal moment. My heart was full as I listened to them speak of Sheldon's courage, strong testimony, and faith in God. I still visit his graveside on Tuesdays. I know he is doing amazing things in a beautiful place. I miss him.

I kept my mind occupied the past couple of weeks by being involved with Nerium. Working on myself, sharing with other people, and simply stumbling through each day by keeping up with my 365 days of happy acts. Something amazing happened. I met with Kelly Conroy in the audiology department at the Mayo to have my Baha hearing device connected to my implant. I was not prepared for what would happen. I normally go to the Mayo Clinic with my itinerary in hand, going from one appointment to the next. With all that has transpired over the past few months, I had forgotten about the hearing device.

I met with Kelly for hearing tests and was fitted for my Baha, but it had literally been a year since my implant was placed. So much had happened, and the Baha had not been on my mind. I was blessed with a tender mercy that I really needed. I have a new person to love at the Mayo Clinic, and I will never forget that day.

Kelly was so compassionate and loving. She placed the device on my implant, made some adjustments on her computer, and customized the device to my hearing needs. What happened next was simply amazing. I wish I had it on video—or that Frenchie had been there to share it with me.

When she activated the device, I could hear everything so clearly and crisply. I smiled, and we talked for a while so she could make sure it was working well. We both cried as I explained some of the emotions I'd had that year. That spectacular moment was exactly what I needed.

We were in a small office, and the acoustics not optimal. The power of hearing began when I got to my car. I opened and closed the door several times to hear it like I'd never heard it before. When I started the car, the music was so loud. I quickly turned it down. I could not stop smiling. I backed up the car—and the sound of putting the car in reverse was something I had never heard.

As I drove down the Beeline Highway, I noticed a man walking. I pulled over and asked if he needed any help. He was out in the middle of nowhere, and I was worried about him. He assured me he had AAA on the way and thanked me. I wondered why he was talking so loud. I was overcome with emotion. I had to pull the car over a few miles away. I got out and walked through the wildflowers. I had never seen anything more beautiful. I looked at the brilliant blue sky and the fluffy white clouds and began to cry. I heard a bird chirp, and it was absolutely astonishing. For years, I thought I knew what it sounded like, but it was clearer than I had ever felt or heard it.

At that moment, I knew God was watching me. He really does love me, and he loves my birth father. I could feel the presence of both of them. I twirled in the Arizona desert with my arms high, thanking God for the gift of hearing. I knew my birth father was finally happy because his daughter could hear. No more guilt; that regret was over for him. I could feel him watching me. I knew he was finally able to move on with peace. I pulled myself together, got back in my car, called Eric, and could not believe how loud he was. Tears ran down my cheeks. He was so excited for me.

When I got home, the real magic happened. I opened the door and I heard the doorknob turn. When the door shut behind me, I screamed. It was so loud that it scared me. I did the same thing when my phone rang. I had "Happy" as my ringtone, and I almost jumped out of my own skin. Walking across my wood floors, I heard every step and began a happy dance, tapping my feet all over the wood. In the kitchen, I opened the microwave and shut it several times. I did the same thing with the refrigerator. I sat on my bedroom floor and wept. It was just the way it should be.

I could hear the carpet as I ran my hand across it. I said, "Thank you. Thank you so much for this unexpected miracle."

I pulled the string on my dental floss, and the sound was nothing I'd ever heard before. I did it over and over again until the container was empty. Turning the pages of my scriptures was amazing. I heard every crinkle of the thin pages. I sat on my bed in awe of what a wonderful day I'd been gifted at such a critical time in my life. I wanted to shout about how happy I was. Nothing is as beautiful as being able to hear everything.

I'd taken so much for grant-ed, especially the miraculous gift of sound, sight, and touch. I was elated and could not wait to explore more. I immediately turned my primary children's music on. One of my favorite songs has always been "My Heavenly Father Loves Me." I cry every time I hear it.

This is a few lines from a beautiful song I couldn't wait to hear.

He gave me my eyes that I might see the color of butterfly wings. He gave me my ears that I might might hear the magical sound of things. He gave me my life, my mind, my heart: I thank Him reverently, For all his creations, of which I'm a part.

Yes, I know Heavenly Father loves me.

The words meant more to me than ever before. I couldn't help but think Heavenly Father had been waiting for that day, preparing me, and refining me. He prepared my birth father beyond the grave as he suffered with guilt for so long. I was so happy for him too.

Receiving the ability to hear for the first time in forty-eight years was incredible. I heard things I'd never heard clearly before. What I wasn't prepared for was hearing things I didn't want to hear.

I was so excited to share my exciting news with colleagues. My overwhelming heart quickly turned to sadness. I gathered a few of them and told them about my experience. They were very excited and amazed, especially expressing how great it is that modern medicine had come so far.

While they walked away to their own desks, I heard them say:

- "I feel so sorry for her."

- "She is so strong."
- "Have you ever read her blog?"
- "I don't think her face is ever going to be the same."
- "She used to have such a beautiful smile."

None of these people would ever want to hurt me. I needed to be okay with me. I wasn't quite ready. I quickly wiped my tears so no one could see, and then an extraordinary thing happened. I lifted my head, looked out the window, and saw a spectacular rainbow between the trees. I felt Vi saying, "You've come so far. Enjoy this victorious moment."

Chapter 48

Dr. Lettieri

The past couple of months have been a mixture of emotions. I am so excited for our new grandbaby to arrive in February. Kaitlyn is so cute pregnant, and I love watching Brian transitioning from husband mode to the responsibility of becoming a father. They are going to be fantastic parents. Eric and I are eager for little Phoenix to be born.

I never heard back from the Cleveland Clinic after my last major surgery. The only interaction we had was between the insurance company and the billing department at the clinic. They are now charging me with "elective" plastic surgery to the face. I laughed out loud when I read this information from the hospital. I sent a picture of my face to the insurance company and explained that it was not elective.

They immediately replied, "Oh my. I'm so sorry."

My surgery was coded as elective, and the insurance company is still fighting with them. Neither Dr. Cocky Face nor anyone else from his office has ever contacted me. It was time to move forward with the nerve surgery and I was not going back to Cleveland.

After discussing my desire to find a local surgeon with Heather and Dr. Barrs, I decided to see Dr. Sal Lettieri. Heather recommended him when the facial paralysis first happened, but he was out of the country. He is employed by Rochester Mayo

Clinic, but he resides in Arizona. He works out of Maricopa County Hospital (MIHS) and Mayo Clinic in Arizona, specializing in head, neck and facial trauma.

I don't regret going to Cleveland Clinic, but I've learned I cannot force things in my life to happen. I can't manipulate God and his timing. He brings the right people into my life, so I can weed out the wrong ones. I know it sounds a bit strong, but there is always going to be good and bad. We cannot know the good without experiencing the bad. We cannot know the light unless we have experienced darkness. There will always be opposition to everything we do.

I will never forget meeting Dr. Lettieri. He has a great personality and his eyes gave me the confidence I needed to proceed. He didn't necessarily say, "All is well in Paralysis Land," but he did allow me to feel hope again. There were not a lot of options available.

I asked him, "What do you think is best, proceeding forward?"

Dr. Lettieri suggested a nerve cross-over surgery. He explained the importance of the cranial nerves five and seven, their functions and the risks involved. He told me he had performed this surgery on other patients and it proved to be successful. He also recommended replacing the gold plate in my eyelid with platinum, which he could precisely weigh and measure for my eye. He humorously said "You will be upgrading from gold to platinum." I laughed.

He would take the nerve from my right calf and weave it through the left side of my face. If it worked, the nerve should grow an inch per month, and then he would go back and find something viable to connect it to. The process would take more than a year.

I gained no comfort in knowing I needed to have more surgeries. I felt alone and disconnected from my family and friends. I shed some tears, knowing surgery was the only option, but I felt so amazingly protected by Dr. Lettieri. I had some serious decisions to make, and the unwanted opinions of people were stressful:

- "Why go through any more surgeries?"
- "You look great the way you are."
- "I would never have more surgery."
- "Your smile looks fine the way it is."

I am not a quitter. I am strong. I am willing to do whatever it takes to get my smile back. Vain? I don't think so. Some of their opinions made me feel as if I had a choice. It was not an optional matter. I was fighting against time with this nerve. I wanted no regrets. I was feeling confident with a surgeon who could truly understand the emotional roller coaster I was on—and he was willing to ride it with me. There is one suggestion I would give people who have not experienced someone else's trial: Don't assume you know how you would react if it were you going through it. You don't understand, and you have no idea how you would process it.

It's not difficult to explain why I love Dr. Lettieri. He is compassionate with a little bit of sass in his personality—kind of like me. I feel really comfortable and made a patient-doctor connection with him right away. He is very confident in what he does. There is a huge difference in doctors who are confident and those that are cocky.

At one of my appointments, Dr. Lettieri was explaining what he thought would be the best surgery for me. Instead of making the decision, he said, "I know some really smart surgeons. I'm going to call one of them and get his opinion." He pulled out his flip phone and called a colleague. He gave him my diagnosis and asked him what he would do. The other surgeon agreed with Dr. Lettieri's proposed procedure. He hung up and said, "In my job. I know some really, really smart people. I'm going to get one more opinion." He called another surgeon to make sure they all thought it was the proper protocol for my diagnosis. It was absolutely amazing.

I loved him at that moment; not many doctors would do that. In fact, no doctor I know has ever done that for me. Another time he texted me: "Call me when you can."

I was on a break at work and called him.

He said, "I've been thinking about your surgery." He told me about a change in the procedure of my surgery.

I interrupted him and said, "I trust you. I don't really understand everything. Just do what you know is best for me."

It felt really great to have a surgeon I could trust again. I have thought about his sincerity from a patient perspective; it is reassuring to know my surgeon is thinking about my procedures and wanting what is best for me. To have him call and text me is unheard of. I'm not sure about the connection he has with any other patients, but he is revered and loved at Maricopa Hospital.

I am always amused by his candor and wit; he's fun and easy to communicate with. He's Italian and loves his heritage. I enjoy hearing him talk fondly of his wife and children. He has a beam in his eye when he speaks of his daughter, and is so proud of his son but he gives all credit to his wife for raising two amazing children. I love that he has a passion for the profession and his wife. To be able to balance being a soccer dad, a husband, and a surgeon tells me a lot about his character. I feel extremely privileged and blessed that I was led to him. I call him my smile surgeon.

In December 2014, I entered the operating room twice with Dr. Lettieri. I surprisingly had no fear or anxiety. I'd come along way. When I had one of my postoperative appointments with Dr. Lettieri, Sonya was so sweet to take me. I wondered what she would think of Dr. Lettieri. I warned her that he would have a smart comeback about Monya and Sonya. I was right.

He looked puzzled and said, "Why? Are you twins?"

I said, "No it was the sixties."

He laughed and asked, "Do you have another sister named Tonya?"

I said, "Oh no, that would be too easy. Her name is Kris."

I went back to the operating room with Dr. Lettieri in February 2015, June 2015, and December 2015. Due to his confidence as a surgeon, I have gained more confidence in myself.

I believe Dr. Lettieri is among a dying breed of doctors who care more about their patients than about their impressive credentials or how much money they make. I simply adore him.

After one of my surgeries, a nurse in recovery asked, "How does it feel to be a patient of the famous Dr. Lettieri?"

I asked, "What do you mean?"

The two nurses at my bedside told me how Dr. Lettieri was the best and smartest trauma surgeon they'd ever known.

One nurse said, "If I am ever in an accident, burned, or need a surgeon, I've told my family not to take me to anyone but Dr. Lettieri."

A tear rolled down my cheek.

The nurse wiped it and said, "It's okay, sweetie. Cry if you need to. Dr. Lettieri will take the best care of you. You are in the hands of a rare surgeon. If he says he can do it, he will do it."

By the time this book is published, I will have had more than thirty-six surgeries in less than seven years—with a few more to go. I have had numerous surgeries with Dr. Lettieri at Maricopa County, and the rest were at the Mayo Clinic. I'd say I am pretty darn blessed.

Dr. Lettieri is a genius in his field. I will never regret the decision I made to see him. I know he likes things done perfectly. I believe he came into my life through divine intervention. I thank him every chance I get. I'm not sure he comprehends my sincerity in saying those words to him. Thank you is so underused, misunderstood, and used as a second thought instead of from a place of sincerity.

When I say thank you, especially to him, it warms my heart. I know he truly has brought light and joy back to my life.

As a trauma plastic surgeon, Dr. Lettieri has helped thousands of burn victims and patients with severely inconceivable diagnoses. One day, I was in his waiting room waiting to see him when my phone rang. Frenchie was checking on me. Two boys in their twenties were sitting across from me in the waiting room. I watched as they began to videotape me talking. I instantly covered my face with a magazine. They said, "F you, lady. We still got enough to post on Facebook." When my name was called, they were continuing to video, and then they laughed and flipped me off. Dr. Lettieri let me explain how it felt, and then he explained that the world can sometimes be cruel. He's seen it with other patients and reassured me that those boys don't know that I am much stronger than they think.

I have had some amazing doctors on my team, but during this chapter of my journey, I am most grateful to Dr. Lettieri for his empathy and understanding. He has seen tears dribble down my cheeks, but he always knows what to say to cheer me up and put things into perspective. I will always love and appreciate him for the concern he has shown me—and Eric—as we stumbled through this unbelievably difficult situation.

Chapter 49
The Mayo Moments

The Mayo Clinic has become a home away from home for me. I want to share some of the unforgettable moments I have experienced while pacing, wandering, and blogging in the halls of the place I have spent so much time. They are in no particular order. I always leave the house with a pen and notebook, ready to write down emotional feelings and funny things I witness. The Mayo Clinic is a people-watching buffet. The following excerpts were taken directly from my blog or my journal.

Never a Dull Moment

For those who have never been to the Mayo Clinic, it is quite an experience. It's like a little city. All the people who call it their second home have common interests, yet they are all in their own little worlds. This is what I experienced as I waited today.

I saw an older gentleman sleeping. His bobbing head reminded me of someone trying to stay awake in church. Then my eyes and ears were tuned to another man who was obviously from New York or New Jersey. He was very loud, and everyone in the waiting area knows his entire medical history. Every complaint was aired for all of us to hear. However, he was very polite and extremely entertaining.

I saw an elderly woman stroking her husband's head very lovingly. I found this interesting because she stroked his head as if she were running her fingers through his hair, but he was completely bald. She loved him, and I could tell they were in love by the way they looked at each other.

There were a lot of people texting today. One man with headphones was totally rocking out to the music—body movements and all. He was lovin' life.

Over the loudspeaker, they said, "Reverend Larry Johnson." All of a sudden, the New York funny man stood up, threw his hands in the air, and said, "Don't look at me, but God Bless Reverend Johnson." I had no idea what he was talking about but it was so funny.

A lady with an attitude walked by, looked right at me, and said, "This is a freakin' three-ring circus." I just smiled and thought, I love this three-ring circus.

I had an hour and a half before my next appointment. I decided to go to the cafeteria and watch the people, which was the funnest part of my day. There was so much going on around me. Where should I even start? I was talking on the phone.

Out of the corner of my eye, I saw Dr. Kreymerman walking by. He was talking on the phone with someone, probably his wife. He didn't see me, but I saw a woman in a pink breast cancer sweatshirt. I'm not sure why she caught my eye, but she stood up and took off her sweatshirt. Her undershirt came off with her sweatshirt, and she was standing in the middle of the cafeteria in her bra.

Are you kidding me right now?

Normally I would have felt really, really bad for her and would have tried to assist her, but she had no cares in the world.

The doctor at the table next to her tapped her as if to say, "Uh, you're half naked—in front of everyone."

She looked at him, shrugged, and took her time putting her undershirt back on. It was no big deal. That is a true Mayo patient. She has probably been so exposed to doctors, nurses, and students that she just said, "To hell with it. Who cares?" I know how that feels.

Born Again

Today at the Mayo Clinic, a man walked up and asked, "Have you been born again?"

It came out of the blue and took me by surprise. He and I were not engaged in conversation at all.

I answered, "Why yes. Yes, I have. Thank you for asking."

I thought about that question and wondered if I have been born again? I decided the man asked me that question for a reason. I was not sure what his reasoning was, but it sure made me think. In some religions, people are known to use the term born again to mean they have given their lives to the Lord. If that were my belief, I would say "Yes, I have been born again."

To me, being born again means every time we are faced with a life-altering challenge (sexual abuse, divorce, death of a spouse, or anything that causes your life to change), you ask, What can I learn from this? You don't turn it into a negative force that destroys everything in its path with anger, including your soul. You're able to step away, give it time, and ask the question. With that being said, I think I have been born again several times in my life.

I was born again when I finally forgave myself for so many things I had done to offend others. Reaching out to them and apologizing put me in a position to forgive myself. When I was diagnosed with cancer, I was not quite ready to accept this new life. I was given another opportunity to be born again when I faced it. I prayed and pleaded with the Lord to help me be a better person. I know He did.

Tests and Treatments

Today I have labs. I need to get the numbing cream on my port. I want to mentally prepare myself for stepping off of the elevator onto the third floor (the breast clinic and chemo lab). I'm not sure I can roll with the punches of the smells today. I don't want to see sick people waiting and I don't want to sit in those reclining chairs.

I look at my itinerary and see that they have scheduled me for labs on the lower level. I have never been there. Stepping off the elevator, there was no stench, lots of people, and no reclining chairs. They called me back quickly.

Why is the blood coming out of my arm instead of my port?

The lady had to stick me several times to get a good vein.

When I left, I felt as if I had been given a tender mercy. I didn't have to go to the third floor. My last appointment was on the concourse level. Yay—no anxiety and no smells. Can you see me dancing? I'm doing a happy dance right now with my arms in the air and a smile on my face.

***

When I entered the underground parking garage, it was so full. I decided to take my chances and try to find a parking space close to the elevators. I was blessed and found a space right next to the elevator. I hoped it would be an indication of how the rest of my day would go.

I was waiting in nuclear medicine for an injection. I had to fill out some paperwork, but it brought a smile to my face. The heading read "Pre-Pregnancy Assessment."

As I finished the assessment, a guy who reminded me of Jimmy Buffett sat down next to me. He had the hat, the shirt, and the laid-back attitude. I was hoping he would make us all laugh as we waited. Maybe he'd sing "Margaritaville" or "Come Monday." Instead, he sat there in his "One Love, One Ocean" shirt and board shorts, smiled ear to ear, and whistled. He made me smile for some reason. No matter what his prognosis is today, I think he is going to be happy.

My hip is really hurting. I think it's going to be a long day at the Mayo. I keep seeing people coming out of the room with a sign on the door that reads "Caution: Radioactive Materials." What is going on in there?

Well, there goes Jimmy Buffett.

I'm next to enter the room. Something about them saying, "We're going to inject you with nuclear medicine" just doesn't sound right to me. As the medicine goes in, I suddenly wonder if I was supposed to expect anything to happen. Were my eyelashes going to fall out or my organs burn from inside out?

Oh, Monya. Stop it. You've made it through worse than this. Pull it together.

I've become a professional at waiting. It's been two hours since my injection. I'm walking, talking, and still have all my eyelashes. When I'm called back for the bone scan, I was surprised that I was not asked to take any clothes off. I think this is a history-making day for me.

Rarely have I ever come here and not had them ask me to undress from the waist up or the waist down. My bone scans are done without taking anything off except for my necklace.

A bone scan consists of staying very still on a table that will slowly scan my entire body. It takes about twenty minutes. The doctor asked for more pictures of my hip, which took another twenty minutes. When the doctor was satisfied with all the pictures, she said Dr. Northfelt's office would call me when the results were in. I went back to waiting.

***

I went to the Mayo for some blood labs, and the girl taking my blood could not have been more than eighteen. She apologized before she stuck me. I guess that should have been my first clue that it was not going to go over very well for me. She stuck my arm, and it pinched and burned like no other.

I looked down, and there was no blood coming out into the vial.

She said, "Is that hurting you?"

I said, "Uh, yes. It hurts really bad. Take the needle out and start over please."

By that time, my rear end was up and out of the seat. I'm pretty sure she could tell by the look on my face that I was in some pain.

The cute little nurse said, "Oh no. I have a one-stick policy. I will get someone else to try."

Thank heavens for that. I was not willing to go through that ordeal again. I ended up with three sticks to the arms. I have a port sticking out of my chest so my veins don't collapse. I don't need to be stuck with so many needles—even if the needle is the size of a nail head. I would rather be accessed and stuck with that than be stuck three times.

I spent a few days at the Mayo Clinic to figure out what was going on with my hip and my back.

***

My new doctor walked in said, "Hello. It's nice to meet you." He had a darling German accent. He was all business after that. He never smiled or looked at me in the eyes. He had me doing all these different walks—on my toes, on my heels, walk there, walk here—and he never smiled or looked at my face. He will never be a Dr. Peter Kreymerman. He ordered more tests and sent me to the physical therapist. The entire time, he was looking at paperwork or his computer. So it was good-bye Dr. What's His Face.

While I was waiting to see the physical therapist the next day, Dr. What's His Face walked by and smiled at me. I don't think he even knew I was his patient. I was in the waiting room because he referred me there.

I love my physical therapist. Her name is Pauline Lucas. It's a good thing I like her since we will be spending some time together (six weeks of PT, two times per week). I will also be getting cortisone shots in my hip and back to help with the pain.

Dr. What's His Face diagnosed my hip with bursitis, and my back has arthritis from the chemo.

Pauline wants me to keep a log of the exercises I am doing every week. She was a little concerned when I told her how much I was running. She thought the cycling was a bit excessive too. I was advised that a woman "my age" should not be doing any excess exercise because it was damaging more than healing.

Too old? A woman my age? Seriously? What about the hundred-year-old man who finished a marathon a couple weeks ago? I have been told a few times by doctors that I should not be running the amount of miles I run every week. I want to run a marathon, and it's difficult for me to embrace the words, "You can't do it." I promised to cancel the half marathon I'd been training for, but I didn't promise not to do the 5K or 10K.

I refuse to crawl up in a rocking chair and die. For an athlete like myself, it is really hard to cut back on the things I love to do. I've always been driven to do better and go farther in each run. I wear my heart monitor to see how much faster I need to go to beat yesterday's numbers. I track my scores to improve my stride and endurance. I've learned that listening to my doctor's advice is probably the best way to go about accomplishing what I need or want for myself. Every time I think I know better, I end up right back at the beginning—with nothing accomplished. I get in the way of my own progress.

I am really sad not to be able to run the marathon next weekend. The doctors say, "You are one of the healthiest patients I have ever had, but you are also the most unhealthy patient I have ever had for a woman your age." Every side effect I could possibly get from chemo and radiation has happened to me. When I put it all in perspective, it could always be worse. I could be dead.

***

When I walked into the Mayo Hospital, I felt calm and at peace, until I stepped off the elevator onto the third floor. The chemo floor is where it all goes down. It reeked of chemo and made me sick to my stomach.

When I walked into the room, my eyes immediately went to a young girl who was having chemo treatments. She could not have been more than sixteen or seventeen. My heart started to race as I sat across from her and watched her being injected with the red dragon.

The nurse took my vitals and said I needed to calm down.

I thought, I wish I could. I really wish I knew a way to do that.

She accessed my port, took my blood, and I was outta there. When I got to my car, I had to take a deep breath and remember where I'd been, how far I'd come, and where I was going.

I knew today was going to be a very long day and made sure I had my laptop and notepad. I had lab work done and a brain scan. Since I had a couple hours before I'd see the doctor, I went to the cafeteria.

I looked up from my computer to see a man picking wax out of his ear. He smelled it, and then he ate it. With that same hand, he ate his French fries, picked his nose, stared at it, and ate it too. I was disgusted, but I could not keep my eyes off of him. He was so interesting to watch. Did he honestly think that was a well-balanced meal? This is a grown man—I can't make this stuff up—and it was sickening to watch.

The farmer's market was at Mayo today. They come once every six weeks. I just happen to spend enough time at the Mayo to be there many times when they come. I left nose picker to see if I could get something healthy for my nutrition and protein.

As I started to walk into the entrance, an older man dropped to the floor and died right in front of me. The loudspeaker announced, "Code blue to the dining area." His wife was hysterical as they tried to save his life.

Perspective is a word that came to mind as I got out of the way and found my way back to my favorite seat. I could feel all of my senses being touched. What I saw was both sacred and scary. The sound of his wife crying for help was excruciating.

I put my headphones on and listened to Hilary Weeks. I needed to drown out the heart-wrenching sounds. I could feel the anxiety starting to fester. I had no medicine with me, but I closed my eyes and went to my happy place.

A sudden whiff of sickness filled the air. I had nowhere to go. I was stuck. The doors were blocked off until they could remove the man's body.

I've come along way with training my brain to block out negative energy, but it was too much. I texted my friend Liz and told her what I saw. Her exact words were: "I wish you didn't have to spend so much time there." Boy, oh, boy—me too.

***

The resident starts asking the usual questions. With his handy little pen, he is writing notes. Just about as cute as he could be, he pulled out his own notes.

He said, "Bend over and touch your toes. Lean back, walk forward, turn around."

I asked if he was new.

He responded, "Yes, but I know what I'm doing."

Whoa there, tiger. I'm just wondering—not accusing.

Dr. Cutie Pie seemed nervous. He looked at me, smiled, and said, "They won't let me abbreviate anything here at the Mayo."

I smiled and said, "You mean like LOL?"

We both laughed, which lightened up the room a little. He left the room, and Dr. Freeman came in.

When I was getting my cortisone injection, Dr. Freeman was gentle. This time, it hurt more than I remembered. I've never cried while getting an injection, but I did this time. It didn't help that I could see everything he was doing through the mirror in front of me. I watched him take the long, nasty needle and stick it in my hip. He gave it a little push and shoved it this way and that way to make sure the entire area was covered.

I was embarrassed when I cried. Just when I thought it was over and the tears were gone, I had to turn over and get my lower back injected. I almost came off the table. I was really shaking in pain.

Dr. Freeman turned to the PA and asked, "Did you see how I did that?"

Really? I'm right here. I can hear you.

Then he said "Pull up your britches, and we can get you into the recovery room."

My grandmother used to say that when she wanted us to be brave, wipe off our knees, and move forward.

***

I woke up this morning with a puddle of blood on my pillow. It was all over the side of my face, neck, and ear. How did I sleep through that?

I went to the Mayo to have it checked out. By the time I got there, I had to change out the bloody cotton balls four times because they were saturated. It wasn't painful, but it was messy.

When I arrived at the Mayo, I had to wait a bit because I did not have a scheduled appointment. I looked around at the people, but there was no one I knew. I watched a woman in a wheelchair, and she intrigued me for some reason. I could hear her talking with her partner about different things, but I was more interested in why both of her legs were amputated and one arm was gone.

I kept to myself until her partner asked if I would pass her a magazine.

I said, "Sure. Which one do you want?"

The three of us began a conversation, and I was able to ask about her medical issues. She was in a horrible car accident. She was rushed to the hospital, and when she woke up, her legs were gone.

I asked how that made her feel.

She said, "At first, I didn't know they were gone. I was just happy to be alive, but when I was told about the loss of limbs, I was very depressed—almost to the point of suicide."

"Understandably so," I said. "How are you dealing with it now? It's been a while—and you have had to get out into the world and live again?"

She said, "I'm alive. That is a blessing in itself, but I had no idea how kind people could be. I normally considered people to be judgmental and rude. There are those who stare, but for the most part, people care."

I believe that inside every person is a caring heart. It is a natural instinct for people to look at a person who is bald with cancer or a woman who has lost limbs, but most of the time, we just pass them by and forget to give them a smile or two.

When my name was called, I said good-bye. I knew I would probably never see that woman again. I wanted her to know she had left an impression on my heart I would never forget. I asked the nurse to wait a moment, went back, and told the woman what a saint she was. I hugged her, and we exchanged e-mail addresses.

With tears in her eyes, she said, "Thank you."

Do Something Good

I woke up and knew I was going to spend the day at the Mayo Clinic. I have this love-hate relationship with that place. I love it for obvious reasons, and I hate it for more obvious reasons. The drive to the Mayo was much shorter than I expected. My thoughts were roaming, which is kind of scary for anyone else driving down the Beeline Highway. I was thinking about how the mountains are beautiful, the desert is dry, and who I will meet today.

The third floor always smells of sickness and chemo. The odor is difficult for me to stomach. I've been so nauseated anyway. In the waiting area, I see sick people. Some look really, really sick, and I wish I could hug them and tell them everything will be okay. I know as well as they do that there are no guarantees with cancer. I'm not there for long before I walked to the infusion lab. It was loaded with people, which made my heart sad for each of them.

My nurse today is Allison, and she is pregnant. Seriously? Can she smell what I smell? "Do these smells bother you?"

"What smells?"

Whoa. What just happened? It's hard to believe she can't smell what I do.

Last night, Kaitlyn and Haleigh Brownlee helped me put some treat bags together for all the patients in chemo. After Allison accessed my port and took all the vials of blood she needed, I walked through the chemo lab and visited with patients who wanted to talk. I gave them a snack bag and was inspired by each and every one of them.

My favorite part of coming to the Mayo is how the people who are facing life-threatening diseases smile and are so positive about life. Perspectives change—and I loved all the perspectives today.

I met one of Dr. Kreymerman's patients, and we high-fived each other and talked a little about him. Everyone loves him.

The cancer patients I met were gracious enough to let me take pictures with them. What an honor. I loved sitting and talking with them. A common thread bound them all together: happiness, smiles, and peace.

When I arrived at the Mayo Clinic Scottsdale Campus, I realized it had been a few months since I have been there. Anne Monte, an elderly woman, was playing the piano. It reminded me of a year ago. Tamy and I were at the Mayo for a chemo appointment, and Anne was playing the piano. She began to play a familiar tune. Tamy and I walked up and said hi to her—and Tamy sang along with the music.

I watched her play the piano so beautifully as I waited for the nurse to call my name. I saw an amazing thing happen. Someone came and lifted Anne her into a wheelchair. She smiled and said hi to me as she passed. What a cute woman—and how wonderful that she volunteers to cheer people up with her music. She's another one of those earthly angels!

***

On the elevator from the parking garage, I was surrounded by sick people. I quickly put on a mask. A couple was trying to decide what floor they needed to get off on. They obviously had not been here much.

I said, "When you come to this campus, remember that you always have to get off on the concourse level. Push the big C button. I can direct you where to go next if you'd like."

With a sweet smile, the wife said, "Oh please. We are not familiar with this building yet, and we would love some help." The only word I heard from that sentence was yet. I took a look at their itinerary and noticed they were going to the same floor I was. I walked with them to the second elevator and showed them the way.

She was pushing him in a wheelchair, and it was obvious that he was in some pain. After getting them in the line they were supposed to be in, I smiled and told them it was a pleasure to walk with them.

When I checked in, I had a bunch of paperwork to fill out. They just wanted to make sure I was not pregnant. Seriously? I once again found myself laughing out loud in the waiting area. There was no waiting this time. The receptionist took me straight to the nuclear medicine department.

Funny Things Happen

When I went to the Mayo Clinic on Monday I had to remove my clothes and put on the ugly robe. When I was finished with my tests, I stepped behind the curtain and pulled it shut. I was kind of waiting for the technician to leave, but she never did. I hurriedly got dressed. I kept thinking she was going to pull back the curtain or try to take a little peek.

I said good-bye to her and drove home. I kept thinking about how I loved the sports bra I had just picked up. It is so comfortable. It almost feels like I didn't have one on. It turns out I didn't have one on. When I changed into my nightgown that night, I realized I had forgotten my bra at the Mayo and had not been wearing one all day. I am a true blonde. I must have had a little brain fart or had chemo brain—or maybe it was my subconscious saying Ditch the bra already, girl.

***

When I was in Cleveland, I only brought one suitcase with one pair of jeans and a couple shirts? I thought I would only be there a couple days.

While I was standing at Macy's, I heard something behind me hit the wall. I turned to look, and there was a significant splatter of blood. My ear was gushing bright red blood down my neck. I felt a puddle forming in my undergarments, but I was afraid to look. I grabbed my ear, but it was not stopping. There was blood everywhere. Diana and her sister Angel were amazed at all the blood.

The sales associate took me to the bathroom and sat me on a chair. The blood was still gushing out and saturating the towel. I could feel the blood going down my throat when I put my head back. Angel was on her knees and doing the traditional Catholic crossing-her-head-to-chest, shoulder-to-shoulder, Father-Son-and Holy Ghost-prayer. Diana was embarrassed and asked her to stop, but I appreciated it. Looking back on that part, it is comical.

Macy's called 911. I asked them not to because I didn't want to pay for an ambulance when I could just drive to the clinic. However, it was their policy.

As soon as the EMTs saw inside my ear, I was lifted into an ambulance and had to repeat the history of my ear issues.

When I arrived at the clinic, they rolled me into the emergency area and was told to put me in room thirteen. Oh no. I am very superstitious. "No. I will not go in room thirteen. Please don't take me in that room. I'll wait in the hallway. Do not take me in there."

The EMT asked why I didn't want to be in that room.

I said, "It's not a good number. It's bad, and I need all the blessings I can get right now."

He laughed at me and rolled me into room thirteen.

Yikes.

Diana and Angel waited with me until a doctor could come.

An ENT cleaned me up and called Dr. Haberkamp, but he was deep into a surgery and would not be able to come. We waited for one of his residents. He finally opened the curtain and said, "Hello."

I said, "Did you have to be so dang cute?"

He laughed, and when he walked closer, I saw a hickey on his neck. "Um, you know I can see that hickey. You're not fooling anyone."

He laughed and said, "I'll have to talk to my wife about that."

The nursing staff, residents, surrounding doctors, Diana, and I got a great laugh out of it. Thank goodness for a sense of humor. He took it so well.

Special Moments

I arrived at the Mayo Clinic really early, and the underground parking lot was empty. No one was playing the piano, and there was no greeter to say, "Welcome to the Mayo." No one else was in the elevator. The gift shop was not even open yet. The halls were empty and unusually quiet.

I love the cute Russian lady who always checked me in. She always said, "Good morning, Monya." She even told me my hair looked so cute.

After I checked in and got registered for my procedures, I sat down in the waiting area for the chemo lab. I heard a man talking to his wife about her faith. He was not buying the idea of "faith as a mustard seed" and having faith will cause you to be healed. "We have shown our faith, we have prayed day and night with pure heart, and we have asked the Lord to help us. We read from the Bible every day, but we are at the Mayo Clinic, getting ready for you to go in to chemo treatment. You are dying. Jesus Christ had faith, and he still died. His Daddy could have saved him, but he didn't. He let him die." The man was of African American heritage, and I loved his Southern accent.

Is he trying to give a pep talk to his wife? Because it's not quite coming out that way.

He turned to her and gave her a hug. "I just love you so much, and I hate to see you going through this. I'm frustrated because we have done all that we have been told to do by the doctors and the good Lord. I feel as though we are not getting any answers here."

Wow. I cannot believe what I am hearing. Of all days to have an appointment. I chose today when it's all quiet except for one man who could be heard from across the room? Maybe I need to hear what he is saying. Did I have enough faith?

Three bald women came into the waiting room for chemo treatments. They all looked really ill, and a sudden attack came over me. Seeing where they were in their treatments, the reality of what I had been through flooded my brain like a tsunami.

How do I do that? They look so sick. Did I look that sick? I just want to get out of there—seeing it all brought back some horrible memories.

I couldn't breathe. My chest felt like a weight was on top of it. I stood up and began to pace. I knew people were looking at me. I could hear them saying, "Is she okay?" I just wanted them to get away.

When they called my name, I was able to snap out of it long enough to walk over to the nurse. I wanted to get it over with. We walked into the chemo lab, and I was still a little dazed. I faked my way through it.

Accessing the port was really painful. When she flushed it, an immediate medicinal taste hit my taste buds. She asked if I was okay.

I said, "Yeah, I just never get used to that taste." She took six vials of blood, put a Band-Aid over my port, and scooted me out to my next appointment.

*****

At the Mayo Clinic, I met an extraordinary person who I will never forget. This special man was sharing his death experience with me. I'm not sure why we were led down this conversational path, but I am so happy we did. I learned that many people are so afraid of dying that they forget to live, including me.

He taught me a great lesson about death. He said he had a heart attack and actually died. In a humble way, he explained his experience to me. The doctors pronounced him dead. One doctor continued to shock his heart until he came back to life. While he was dead, he had every emotion run through his body. For every time he had been mean or had hurt someone while he was alive, he felt what that person felt when he had hurt them.

He told me he felt the sins all over again—the ones he had never taken care of or apologized for while he was alive. The feelings remained with him for short minutes, and some felt like months. This led me to believe we all have a purpose in this life. We all have a meaning for being here. Life is not an accident. The people we encounter are not mere coincidences. His life was fundamentally changed after that experience. He values life—and how he treats others.

It was a casual conversation, but I will not soon forget it.

Birthdays at the Mayo

At the Mayo Clinic, every patient has to give his or her full name and birth date before every appointment. If you have five appointments in one day, you say it five times. My first appointment was for lab work. Latisha was drawing my blood, and she called me Montoya a few times even after me repeating my full name and birthday. I didn't have the heart to correct her, but after her fifth poke, no vein was working. I wanted to yell, "My name is Monya. It's my birthday. Don't make me cry. Just find the dang vein." Six pokes later, she found it and sucked out as many vials she needed. I was on my way to appointment number two.

In the waiting area, so many sick people were coughing. I decided it would be a good time to put on my mask.

A lady said, "Today is my ninetieth birthday."

I hope I live to be ninety. She was so cute and proud of the brown scarf her daughter had gotten her. Looking around the room, I realized I was the youngest patient in the room. The grandpa sitting in front me had the largest ears I had ever seen. I wondered if they keep growing with age. If it is, he looks ninety. If he makes it to one hundred, his ears will outgrow his head.

My brain was wandering. I snapped back to reality when they announced my name. You know you're a frequent flyer at the Mayo when the person announcing your name remembers you from previous appointments. He even pronounced my name correctly. He said, "Happy birthday. And you're fifty today." He said it as though it was amazing I'd made it to this great and powerful number. Well, what did I expect from a twenty-year-old guy?

All the people in the waiting area were staring at me, and I realized I was young in comparison. It could be worse. Good to know!

"Undress from the waist up." I wish I had a nickel for every time I've been given that line over the past couple years. The cute girl doing my ultrasound was super quiet. I tried to crack a few of my silly jokes, but I could not get a smile or even a grin out of her. She was all business.

After the ultrasound, I waited for the biopsy. As I was writing in my journal, my cell phone rang, which is definitely a no-no at the Mayo. I scrambled to answer it as fast as I could. I felt the stares and breathing down my neck from other patients and staff members. It felt like I was sitting in a sacred chapel. They view cell phone use in the waiting area as a complete and utter lack of courtesy.

By the time I could get to my phone, the caller ID told me the Mayo Clinic calling. I wanted to laugh out loud. They were calling to tell me my white blood cell counts were really low. The doctor was canceling my biopsy for the day. I wasn't sure if I should be happy or sad. I really didn't want to have a biopsy on my birthday. I knew I would squirm until they finally called me back for the inevitable biopsy.

I was told to keep a mask on in crowded places or where I felt vulnerable to bacteria. Are you kidding me? That pretty much describes everywhere I go and every person I come in contact with.

Chapter 50

In the End

As the time got closer for me to speak at the SAP Center in San Jose, knowing my face would be on huge jumbo screens gave me tremendous anxiety. The only person I told was Eric, and all he knew was to watch the live stream on the last day of the convention. My heart was weak, and I was struggling to be brave and strong.

What was I thinking when I agreed to expose myself to strangers? I didn't have a connection to these people, and they did not understand the full story of my life.

It was easy for me to disclose my life on my blog; it didn't require looking into the eyes of the readers or hearing the reactions from the crowd.

I met with Renee a few times to go over what I would say. She was elegant and graceful. I had an instant connection with her. She coached me on my timing and listened intently as I shared portions of my story. I wrote some notes, but nothing seemed important or relevant. I prayed for the right words to say. I know we all feel broken in some way or another at times, but not giving up is the secret power we all have inside of us. If I could just relay that feeling to the audience, then I felt I had done what I came there to do.

A peace came over me before I went out onto the stage. I couldn't read my notes through teary eyes. I resisted putting on my glasses. Renee said, "I want them to see your eyes." I wanted it to come from my heart. I had to condense five and a half years into ten minutes. I knew there was no way I could convey all the emotions we'd lived through in that amount of time.

I shared bits and pieces that were relevant to what I was being asked to do and how Nerium contributed to my attitude of never giving up. I was amazed by the love I felt as I spilled out my life since the facial paralysis. It was badge of courage and bravery to uncover myself to such a large group of people. I traced the steps of where I'd been, and it was overwhelming to process my own journey.

I have wrestled with shame and discouragement. I've felt like I have let people down. I've wondered if my own children were disappointed in me. The life-changing alteration of my face brought me to my knees and eventually helped me understand my journey. I intend to end it better than it started. My perspective on life has changed. Seeing the world through different eyes has lightened my heart and soul. I can't say I have fully conquered my fears. I still doubt myself in so many ways.

Trusting myself to fight through the past few years has been empowering. It was been worth the sorrow and pain. Giving up my pride to understand that this is the life I was intended to live was hard. I'm slowly beginning to believe I can move mountains. I've felt the changes inside of me. I'm beginning to understand that I'm me because of where I've been and the experiences I've enjoyed and withstood. Once I had taken all the information I needed from my personal journals, I made the decision to take them all—with the exception of the first journal my mom gave me—to the desert and burn them. It was a cleansing, emotional experience. I did it because the truth is written here in this book; my children now have my life story.

After reading The Slight Edge several times, I decided to look in the mirror every day and tell myself I was beautiful. I told my mouth to smile. After a year of this repetitive action, I looked in my bathroom mirror during my daily affirmations when something incredible happened. My smile appeared. It was awkward and uneven, but I was elated. I still work on my smile every day. With the help of Dr. Lettieri and daily practice, I will prevail.

When Sheldon died, I wanted to give in and give up. I realized the Lord was waiting for me to do my part and fulfill a promise. At the Mayo, I had a dream. I had no idea how I was going to give faith and hope to thousands of people. I'm still not sure I can or have, but I know things always turn out how they are supposed to.

Shortly after returning from Cleveland, this book was picked up for publishing. I was asked to speak to eighteen thousand people, and other speaking engagements followed. This is my marathon. I am living my destiny, and I'm finally beginning to understand that I don't need all the answers right now. It's never too late to start all over on a path that will move you forward. Step up to the starting line and run as fast as you can. Tomorrow might not come. This is the time to love others, share a kind word, and be true to yourself. You will find the strength to pull yourself out of any situation.

There are days when I have to remind myself about who I am. I have to convince myself that I have the power within me to be happy. True happiness cannot be given to you. It cannot be bought, and it certainly cannot be faked. When you are completely happy, you live with no regrets. When you are at peace with who you are, your spirit illuminates and becomes contagiously beautiful.

Frenchie and I went to see the new version of the animated Disney movie Cinderella. As I watched, I was engulfed in the story. There were so many parallels to my own life. Cinderella said, "Have courage and be kind for where there is kindness there is goodness, and where there is goodness there is magic." It gave me a clear and precise picture of the unparalleled beauty of courage and kindness in the face of humiliation, suffering, and shame.

Cinderella looked stunning, but it was not her glass slipper or beautiful ball gown that first caught the Prince's eye. Her inner beauty captured his attention—her courage and her kindness. In the end, kindness isn't weakness. It's strength. Submission isn't pitiful. It's beautiful and courageous.

We all have the power within us to make our lives happy. It is a choice. I walked out of that movie with a renewed conviction. No matter what happens in my life, I will be happy. My circumstances do not dictate my happiness in life. I know I have to live with a strange diagnosis, but I will not let it define who I am. I am embracing who I am and who I can become by the service I give to others and the calmness I feel in my heart. I am finally fulfilling the promise I gave to Heavenly Father by living the life I was meant to live.

Chapter 51

What I've learned

We do not heal the past by dwelling there; we
heal the past by living fully in the present.
—Marianne Williamson

*H*ealing from the past is my responsibility. I need to own my life, own my failures and successes. No one else can determine my happiness. Going through the storms of life, letting the earth move beneath me as I walk toward the rainbow, and remaining steadfast and grounded will allow my fears to diminish. I can't feel completely whole until I learn to love myself. Waiting on someone to love me will never give me satisfaction if I don't respect and honor myself first.

Ultimately, I've learned to be present in every moment of my life and not waste time worrying about the future or what other people think about my decisions.

***

Be careful with your words, once they are said,
they can only be forgiven, not forgotten.
—Unknown

The power of words, what we say and how we talk to each other, and body language can tear us down or build us up. Words hurt as much as the bruises of physical or sexual abuse. It was easier to forget the physical abuse than to overcome the words uttered, especially when delivered in anger, and humiliation. For me, the hurtful words were like going through a Chinese water torture.

Slowly, over time, I stopped recognizing it as persecution. It became a gradual erosion. Hearing the same negative verbiage day after day and year after year penetrated my brain. Permanent scars can be left on the heart when harsh words are shattered across the soul.

When we say words in love, they never go away. Words live on—even when we're gone. I'd rather leave an impression of kindness and love than scars of fury and animosity. The capability to say "I'm sorry" is essential to learn at a young age.

***

What you are, speaks so loudly. I can't see who you are.
—Ralph Waldo Emerson

It's honorable to authentically be yourself. When I decided to mount my feet in complete wisdom and breathe in the moments of life that were—and are—worthy of remembering, I found happiness. I've learned that my heart will convey the beauty I have within me. When I take interest in another person's life—instead of dwelling on my own—it shows I have emotions. I sincerely care for people and their feelings. I want to make a difference in the world. I believe it comes from showing kindness and sincerity in my actions toward others. I will always be true to myself. I am a beautiful daughter of God. I know it, and I know God loves me just the way I am. Living in the real world—with real-life experiences—has pressed me forward and not held me back.

***

If you talk to a man in a language he understands, it
goes to his head. If you talk to him in his language,
it connects with his heart. -Nelson Mandela

There is a difference between communicating and connecting with people. I communicated with my birth father very little, but I had an endearing connection with him as my biological father. During the few times I saw him, I felt a connection. As a child, I looked into his fiercely blue eyes and held his huge hands—and it made me desperately want to hold on to him. Mom communicated with me in a language I never quite understood. Because of the confusion, we never connected as a mother and daughter should have.

***

From every wound there is a scar, and every scar
tells a story. That story says you survived.
-Unknown

The physical scars from my surgeries tell part of my story. The emotional scars have been difficult to embrace. I recognize I am a human learning from unusual circumstances. It's okay to feel the pain, learn from it, and then teach others. My scars do not define me. My heart has been purified because of those scars. I have done more than survive. I am thriving in spite of all the scars. I've chosen to look beyond my physical imperfections and concentrate on evolving from the inside out. This process takes time, but it is worth the effort.

***

> If you judge nothing, you will be happy. If you
> forgive everything, you will be happier. If you
> love everyone, you will be happiest.
> —Unknown

Blaming others for my lack of happiness is ignorant. People can hurt and disappoint me, but I choose how I handle it. Living an intentional life requires discipline.

Retraining my brain to think positive thoughts has been an evolutionary process and has brought me great joy. Serving others with a loving heart brings me satisfaction. Judging people does not serve any good purpose. I realize it is difficult for some people to forgive, but I know it is crucial for moving forward. I chose to forgive even though my offender was not apologetic or sorry. Forgiveness does not excuse the perpetrator's behavior. Forgiveness prevents the behavior from destroying my heart and soul, and it allows me to live free and be happy!

***

> Beauty is how you feel inside, and it reflects in
> your eyes. It is not something physical.
> —Sophia Loren

I know beauty is not about my looks, makeup, or clothes. True beauty comes from being myself, and the more I show who I really am, the prettier I will be. I've learned that inner beauty is unlike physical beauty, which takes the spotlight for itself. Inner beauty shines on everyone. It catches people and holds them in its embrace, making them more beautiful too.

The Lord does not look at the things man looks at. Man looks at the outward appearance, but the Lord looks at the heart.

Once I learned to see myself through the eyes of God, I found a completely different woman staring back at me in the mirror.

***

There are no perfect parents or perfect
children, but there should always be perfect
moments along the journey. --Unknown

Love should never hurt. We all know that physical and sexual abuse are unacceptable. It is much more effective to recognize a hurtful word or action, apologize sincerely, and try to make it right. Wanting to be the "perfect" parent is impossible and can be downright annoying to children. They don't expect us to be perfect. My parental imperfections have helped my children, grow, learn, and develop into compassionate, caring adults. Most importantly, I've learned to forgive myself.

***

The poorest man is the one whose only wealth is money
--Unknown

There are a lot of things money cannot buy: integrity, manners, love, morals, character, respect, kindness, joy, patience, humility, faith, charity, common sense, hope, virtue, knowledge, diligence, trust, and happiness. People cannot be wealthy until they possess attributes money cannot buy. It's good to have money to provide for your needs and indulge in some wants, but it's also good to check yourself every once in a while to make sure you haven't lost the things that money cannot buy.

***

You only live once, but if you do it right, once is enough.
—Mae West

Every time I thought I was being rejected, it was actually redirecting me to something far more important. Most of my hardships taught me important lessons. By weathering the storms, I could finally see the rainbow behind each one of the trials. No matter what—whatever decisions I make or life makes for me—the one thing I have control over is my happiness. No one can steal that from me.

Epilogue

*T*here has to be an ending to every book, right? I'm happy to say the ending to this book is a happily ever after. I love knowing the Lord has created a way for me to be close to him—no matter where I am. When I feel sad, lonely, happy, overwhelmed, pained, or joyous, I know I can pray anywhere and anytime—and God will be there. I practice this as a solemn, sacred privilege. I often close my eyes, breathe in, and quietly ask for strength or say thank you!

Eric and I recently spent some time in Mexico. The peace and serenity being next to the ocean was exactly what I needed. Eric is amazing, and I feel so blessed to be his wife. I don't enjoy driving, and my eyesight has gotten so bad since my facial paralysis. I usually sleep on the way to and from Mexico. Eric listens to the love channel (one of the silly things I love about him), but we talked the entire way. It felt like we were at the condo faster than usual. I loved spending those two days with him—away from the real world in Arizona. We laughed, watched movies, went to eat, held hands, and did not think about what was going on at home. We had no phone calls and never connected to the Internet. It was just the two of us, and it reminded me of the olden days.

On our way home, we talked about our children and how blessed we are to be parents of children who are not perfect but have true testimonies of Christ. They understand how to be good people and make good choices, and they understood why they should do those things. We reminisced about when we dated. I talked openly about my feelings of growing up in a home like I had, and he just listened.

I said, "Did you really love me—really, really love me—when you married me?"

Eric said, "I did, but I never knew how much more I could love you until now."

"I love you too. I love that we can talk about stuff and that you understand me."

"I'm sorry I couldn't protect you … and that I wasn't there for you."

"It's okay. You didn't know me—"

"I know, but I would have protected you. I want to protect you now. I never want you to feel that pain in your life again."

I look forward to our relationship growing even more. With each treasure and trial we go through together, I know our love will grow stronger and become unbreakable. I'm uncertain about my future, but I know Frenchie is the one I want to share every bit of it with. Falling in love with Eric was easy, but allowing that love to take root has been extremely rewarding. I want to grow old with him because I know the best is yet to come.

I believe there are angels among us. Some touch our lives with their examples of strength, compassion, and faith. Some have already passed on and frequent our lives with their spirits every once in a while. Vi and Ray Williams are my angels who have crossed over into heaven. I have felt them with me when I needed strength or endurance. They rescued me from a darkened world I believed I was doomed to live in forever. I miss them and think of them often.

My sisters are my constant angels. I think about them all the time. I was not as open and forthright with them during my treatments, but I don't regret it. I hope I was able to keep them from unnecessary worry and grief. They both have suffered through their own health and personal issues. I wanted to do what I thought was best for me and keep as much positive information flowing into their brains as possible. I knew they were praying for me; what else could they do? There was nothing else to be said or done. I love these angel sisters of mine.

Tamy was an angel who took me to every one of my chemo appointments and then back the next day for my shot of Neulasta. I will eternally be grateful for her compassion and service. There are angels who brought dinner to my family for months and months, and they will never know how much that meant to me. Those angels are still helping us out. The silent angels who serve are the ones who amaze me. How can our lives be blessed by those who choose to be invisible? I want my children to understand that feeling of service. I have angels who leave me messages of hope with cards, letters, and comments on my blog.

I can't help but think that the angels that touched my life are not random. The Lord placed them in my path for a reason. It's my job to recognize them and be in tune enough to feel it. It makes me wonder how many times I've been out of tune. How many times have I been caught up in too many worldly things and not acknowledged the many other angels who have tried to embrace me? Have I ignored chances to help others?

Some angels have been strangers, including the lady who smiled at me on a day when I really needed it. I've never personally met some of the most influential angels in my life, but I know the connection is eternal.

Opening my circle of comfort and allowing others to bless my life with what they know has not been as difficult as I thought it would be. My life is abundantly blessed. I hope I can give back and be an angel to someone in need. We are all divinely entwined and connected.

If we were to take a huge ball of yarn and have the first man or woman who walked the earth hold it and then pass it on to the next generation, repeating over and over again, I think we would be surprised by how we are all linked in some way. Across the world, those strings would go. There would be no borders, no colors, no races, and no religions. If we could imagine it or see it from above, we would be impressed, awestruck, and a little humbled.

I heard a church leader Kent Richards say, "The Savior is not a silent observer. He himself knows personally and infinitely the pain that we face."

As I face the next hurdle, those words will stay in my heart and mind. I feel peace and comfort. Whatever the Lord has in store for me, it is his plan. With his help, I Can-cer Vive. He will silence all my fears, calm my troubled heart, and lead me with his gentle hands back home to live with him again one day.

Heaven is real. I've been there. I've felt the peace and serenity and been enveloped in perfect unconditional love while there. I will never deny that he knows me. He knows my pain and my fears. He's felt every disappointment and every triumphant, joyful moment I have felt. I have felt him taking me by the hand and leading me to a light brighter than any light imaginable—and that is where I want to be.

I want God to look at me and be proud of what I have accomplished in this life. I'm not ready to leave this earthly life yet, but when I do, I want to stand before the Lord and hear him say, "Well done, thou good and faithful servant. You truly are my daughter. Come unto me and dwell in peace."

Acknowledgments

My love for the physicians and medical staff at both Mayo Clinic and MIHS (Maricopa Integrated Health System) runs deep. I've witnessed dedicated men and women devote their time and passion to patient care; it's more than impressive it's made my journey endurable.

I have been blessed with friends near and far who have prayed for me, cried with me and laughed alongside me. Without their support my journey would have been unbearable. Many have encouraged me with their gifts of service, and I would be remiss not to mention some of them: Mark Christensen, Mysti and Timmy Brown, Tamy and Tom Scheurn, Taz and Kathy Evans, Joe Pottle, Jenny Ruttinger, Diana and Terry Lents, Lori and Jeff Blandford. The congregation of the Gilbert Sixth Ward, and the members of the LDS church who reside in Highland West and East Stakes have given endless hours of service on behalf of my family; it is with a humble heart I say thank you!

This book would not have been possible without the devotion of the editorial committee at Archway Publishing. Simon Schuster/ Archway Publishing saw a noteworthy story and encouraged me to put it to paper—with special regard to Peter Lee, who always greeted me with a smile and gave me professional advice.

The only writing I had done was on my blog and personal journals. I have to admit I'm not a writer. My grammar is horrendous. With their help, I was able to turn my journals and blog posts into a story of my life that is easier to read.

Kayla Stobaugh from Simon Schuster served as my concierge-her patience and kindness were much needed and appreciated.

I also want to acknowledge all the faithful followers of my blog. When I was approached I thought of so many of you who also encouraged me to write a book. As you know writing a book was on my 'things to do' list but realistically I knew it would be difficult; every time I wanted to give up I was reminded of your faith in me to finish.

Listening to inspirational music has always been a calming experience for me. Thank you to my good friend Hilary Weeks. I know I can always count on her words and music to uplift me and help me get through the hurdles in my life.

Stephen Phelps, another inspirational friend, plays the organ every Sunday for our congregation. Many times, I have felt his testimony of Christ being relayed through his heart-pounding music. He is amazing, and I love him.

I often listen to Josh Menden and Clyde Bawden when I journal and blog. I don't personally know Mindy Gledhill, but her music has helped me understand my worth as a woman, especially her song "All About Your Heart." Music has been a vital part of my healing.

Each one of my children Kayla, Blake, Kaitlyn, Haleigh and their spouses-I love you more than you will ever comprehend-thank you for your patience during this journey.

My grandchildren Recker, Ezra, Phoenix, Weslie, Theo, Archer and those still to come-Bonbon loves you-always be kind to everyone-and choose happiness over anger.

Finally, I want to tell Frenchie how much I appreciate him for allowing me to take so much time away from him to finish this book. He has seen the tears and time I've put into writing. He often woke up in the middle of the night to remind me that I needed my sleep and said, "Tomorrow will be a new day."

References

The Bible (King James Version)

The Book of Mormon

The Doctrine and Covenants

The Anti Cancer by David Servan-Schreiber, MD, PhD

The Slight Edge by Jeff Olson

Live Happy by Deborah Heisz (http://www.livehappy.com)

The Infinite Atonement by Tad R. Callister

Preach My Gospel (lds.org, search under manuals)

Hillary Weeks: http://hilaryweeks.com

Mindy Gledhill: http://www.mindygledhill.com/light-shines/

The Mayo Clinic's Journal on Autism

National Breast Cancer Foundation (http://www. nationalbreastcancer.org)

Health Line (http://www.healthline.com)

World Cancer Research Fund, Food, Nutrition and American Institute for Research on the Prevention of Cancer

Connect with Me

So much has happened since I CAN-CER VIVE was published, keep up to date with me at: www.monyawilliams.com